BRINGING MORE LOVE INTO YOUR LIFE: THE CHOICE IS YOURS

This personal awareness course

- Can be both very gentle and powerful

- Helps you to increase your self-understanding, self-acceptance and self-mastery

- Asks you to examine objectively your own experience

- Presents a variety of questions and exercises for you to complete as an essential part of your learning

Other books by the authors

Opening Doors Within
Eileen Caddy (edited and compiled by David Earl Platts)

By Eileen Caddy

The Dawn of Change
Flight Into Freedom — Eileen Caddy's Autobiography
Footprints on the Path
Foundations of a Spiritual Community
God Spoke to Me
The Living Word

Video tape

Opening Doors Within

BRINGING MORE LOVE INTO YOUR LIFE: THE CHOICE IS YOURS

A Step-By-Step Guide from the Findhorn Foundation
Using Psychosynthesis Principles and Techniques

Eileen Caddy

David Earl Platts, Ph.D.

Findhorn Press

Set in Garamond on Macintosh SE and Classic
Cover painting © Hannah Albrecht
Layout and design by Ronald Morton, Bay Area Graphics
Authors' photo by Chris Lowe
Printed and bound by BPCC Wheatons, Exeter
Published by Findhorn Press, The Park, Findhorn, Forres IV36 0TZ, Scotland

Printed on an environmentally-friendly paper

CONTENTS

BRINGING MORE LOVE INTO YOUR LIFE IS . . .

LIST OF COURSE EXERCISES AND TECHNIQUES

ACKNOWLEDGEMENTS

Publishing a book is always a group effort, and so we have many people to thank.

First, we express our deep gratitude to Sandra Kramer for the original inspiration and encouragement to create a book based upon our workshop. What a wonderful editor she is, too! No editor could ever be more kind, patient and supportive than she has been.

A manuscript is only a stack of pages (or, in our case, computer disks) until the designer goes to work on it. We have Ronald Morton to credit for turning our words into a serviceable book.

Vibrant colour has been added from the brush of Hannah Albrecht who created an original watercolour for our cover. An inspired contribution, all the more special from a dear friend.

We especially appreciate the loyal and loving support of Lorna Richardson throughout the eighteen months the writing of this book has taken. She deserves a gold medal for the invaluable assistance she has given from start to finish, not only for thoroughly reading and checking each new draft of the manuscript, but also for just 'being there', bringing more love into our life.

For commenting upon early drafts of the manuscript, we wish to thank Volker Buddrus, Judi Buttner, Judith Firman, Nina Menrath, Caroline Myss, Eva Marie Rüegg, Patricia Sankey and the Manchester group, Floyd and Kay Tift and Diana Whitmore. Their helpful suggestions have truly enriched this book beyond measure.

We are also indebted to the participants in our workshops at the Findhorn Foundation and around the world who have helped us develop and refine our approach to the topic of learning to love. We appreciate all they have given us throughout the years.

We also pay special thanks to the Findhorn Foundation Education Branch staff and the other community members who have supported our workshop at Cluny Hill College over the years.

To Roberto Assagioli and to the staff of the Psychosynthesis and Education Trust in London which follows with great integrity and respect in his tradition, we express our heartfelt gratitude for the principles, methods and strategies — and the inspiration — they have contributed to this book.

Many of the exercises we present have evolved from within the international Psychosynthesis community of writers, group trainers and individual guides. We have credited the original source when it was known. If unintentionally we have overlooked other people, we would be grateful if they would come forward to be acknowledged in subsequent editions.

Finally we commend you, the reader, for choosing to bring more love into your life, and so into the world.

WHAT IS THE FINDHORN FOUNDATION?

The Findhorn Foundation is an international spiritual community, education centre and charitable trust located in northeast Scotland. Founded in 1962 by Eileen and Peter Caddy and Dorothy Maclean, it comprises a central core of members who live and work together, as well as a wider community of people who share its values and vision.

While it has no formal doctrine or creed, the Findhorn Foundation holds that an evolutionary expansion of consciousness is now taking place in the world, and that its divine source, centred within each human being, is accessible directly through prayer, meditation and other spiritual disciplines.

The Findhorn Foundation encourages the taking of individual initiative and responsibility while drawing upon the support and synergy of group living. It holds that work is love in action, and fosters service and synthesis on both personal and planetary levels. It celebrates the intelligence, interconnectedness, love, sacredness, unity and wholeness of all life. Community members seek to embody and express these principles in their daily life. They offer a regular programme of short courses and conferences reflecting their ideals to the thousands of guests who visit throughout the year to participate in the life of the community.

For more information, refer to the reading list in the *References* section, and request a current Guest Programme from the Accommodations Secretary, Findhorn Foundation, Cluny Hill College, Forres IV36 0RD, Scotland.

WHAT IS PSYCHOSYNTHESIS?

Psychosynthesis is a holistic educational and psychospiritual approach to human growth and development. It was introduced by the Italian psychiatrist Roberto Assagioli, M.D. (1888-1974), who formulated four steps towards achieving a harmonious inner integration, true self-realisation and right relationships:

- Gaining understanding of our personality and its behaviour patterns
- Achieving control of its various elements, such as body/feelings/intellect
- Realising our true self: discovering a unifying centre deep within
- Achieving psychosynthesis: forming our personality around this centre.

The unique contributions of Psychosynthesis are its recognition of the essential transpersonal or spiritual nature of the human being; the high value it places upon intuition, creative insight and inspiration; and its development of the Will as a psychological function, resulting in personal empowerment and a greater capacity to make and implement life-enhancing choices. Psychosynthesis creates a safe, gentle, positive atmosphere for self-exploration: one of its guiding principles is to accept and include patterns of behaviour, rather than to judge or negate them.

Psychosynthesis helps us to understand and master our problems, improve our relationships, realise our inherent creative potential, contribute within a wider social and planetary context and explore life's meaning and purpose. It holds that to love well calls for all that is demanded by the practice of any human activity, namely an adequate measure of discipline, patience and persistence.

Psychosynthesis integrates its own principles and self-help techniques with approaches drawn from relevant classical and contemporary psychologies. Versatile, eclectic and creative, it can be applied to a wide range of personal, interpersonal and professional activities and concerns. Refer to the reading list in the *References* section for more information.

FOREWORD

Tell me how you love and I'll tell you who you are. We each have our unique way of loving which sometimes fulfils us and often betrays us. We may love freely or we may love possessively; we may love passively or we may love aggressively. The way we love tells much about who we are and how we function in the world. It can be seen as a microcosm of our existential situation.

Many teachings, both eastern and western, tell us that the purpose of life is to learn about love. Of all the possible experiences known to human beings, love is the force which can unify what we are. It is a cure for depression, loneliness and anxiety, a remedy for rage and isolation. It unleashes and liberates our creative powers, and brings us freedom and peace of mind. It is amazing that so little is written about love in most psychology books, when it is the most central and important experience of all — the ultimate health- and strength-giving force.

When do we learn most about how to love? Where it begins, of course, is in the first days and months of life in the primal relationship with our mother. But as adults we can be just as open to learning about love. In moments of disappointment and pain — when we have been betrayed or betrayed ourself or when we have experienced loss or injustice — we are more vulnerable, our psyche less firmly organised, and this perhaps creates an opening where love can come in. On the other hand, we can also learn about love when we are creative and present, open to ourself. If we are using our creative resources and expressing ourself in life, then we are open to love.

In our society today we are too embarrassed to confront love fully. It is not cool. It is twee and too soft. Others will laugh. We are loath to admit what amateurs we are in an age so advanced. It's hard to admit we don't know much about it. And yet in quiet moments of solitude, who, I ask myself, would not *long* to bring more love into their life? Wouldn't we all make this choice if we had the courage?

I remember the innumerable times in my life when I have made this resolve, and the equally innumerable times when I have failed. I always build my hopes up that this time it will be different. This time I *will* do it — love more freely; transform my limited perceptions; find that place in me which loves without judgement or condemnation; relinquish control of my loved ones, trusting that the universe is basically benevolent. Alas, I never quite make it. This book renews my optimism.

As a teacher and psychotherapist I am constantly touched by this longing in human beings to bring more love into their lives, and equally by their torment at not achieving their goal. I have never met a client who didn't in some way reach deeply into him- or herself for what was good, worthy and authentic. No matter how many layers of aggression, hatred or pain we have to uncover, at some point we reach a deep, poignant moment of recognition — that what makes life worthwhile is to love and be loved; that without first loving ourself, there is nothing to give to others; and that the source of love and wisdom lies within.

Few authors have the courage to present in such systematic detail the arduous work necessary to evolve our way of loving from an amateurish, haphazard experience to a consciously-created one. This book is not for the faint-hearted. To embark on the work of this course requires steadfastness and commitment.

Basic assumptions *Bringing More Love Into Your Life: The Choice Is Yours* makes are that a primary lesson in life is learning to love fully, and that, as spiritual beings, we are pure love. Such ideas, although beautiful and noble, need to be verified by the reader and his or her experience. This book clearly creates the means by which to address our obstacles to these assumptions. For that which blocks us from loving is the very pathway to it. Only by embracing our shadow and unlovingness can we find the fortitude to choose to bring more love into our life.

10

Step by step Eileen Caddy and David Earl Platts take us through the universe of love, and evoke our will and motivation to choose to take matters into hand and heart. Knowing them both for many years, I feel sure they have tested their principles and techniques thoroughly in their own lives before presenting them to you, the reader. This book is born out of their experience with many, many people whom they have encouraged in their workshops to take the risk of learning to love.

Choosing to bring more love into our life is not about trying to be more nice and loving — it is about using our will to explore feelings and emotions, attitudes and beliefs and previous life experiences which shape our consciousness and inhibit our capacity to love. Through probing deeper into ourself and embracing our obstacles, we are led to the opportunity to choose to trust, to be honest and open, to be aware, to accept, to act, to forgive and to be free.

The final choice is always ours. It is not an easy path, and yet, with the tools and techniques of this book, the authors provide resources for the journey. If systematically applied, these resources will, I feel sure, bear fruit and achieve results of which we can be proud.

DIANA WHITMORE
Psychosynthesis and Education Trust
London
31 January 1992

INTRODUCTION

This course guides you gently through a carefully sequenced journey of self-exploration. By the time you reach the final pages, you will have traversed both your inner and outer landscapes, will have a compass and a map to help you chart new directions for yourself and a record of your travels into the universe of love.

Both this course and the workshop it is based upon follow these principles:

1. While love takes many different forms, a useful working definition of love is *compassionate acceptance and respect for ourself and others*.

2. As human beings we are born with the full capacity to love. It is our God-given heritage, a divine spark existing within everyone, a spark which can be found and fanned into a brightly burning flame.

3. As spiritual beings we are pure love, with a need to express our basic nature: to love, to serve, to feel wholeness and oneness with all life.

4. As a self-defence in response to painful experiences we have had, we have erected protective barriers within ourself which also prevent love from flowing freely in and out. We have developed fears, resistances, beliefs and patterns of behaviour which keep these barriers firmly in place.

5. The primary lesson in life is to learn to love. It is why we are here on earth, and thus it holds the highest priority on our time and attention. No other lesson is as important or as necessary for us to learn.

6. We cannot love others until we first love ourself, and many of us do not love ourself or others very freely, fully and fearlessly.

7. A basic reason many of us do not love ourself is because of doubts we have about our own sense of worth, having formed very early in life a negative belief about ourself such as 'I am not good enough', 'I am a failure', 'I can't do anything right' or 'I do not deserve love'.

8. We can *choose* to accept and respect ourself and others. We can *choose* to change our beliefs and behaviour. We can *choose* to take down our barriers and experience love's natural flow within us.

9. Bringing more love into our life is the result of learning how to make these choices and how to put them into effective action. Choosing requires an intention to change and a willingness to take action. Personal empowerment and a greater sense of freedom come from making choices.

10. Helping us to make and implement these choices is a loving, pure, permanent centre deep within us which is unaffected by our mind's chatter or bodily conditions, and which animates, integrates and directs our life.

11. We are always standing at a crossroads where we have the choice to bring more love into our life. It is a choice which often has to be made over and over again, day by day, moment by moment.

12. Our choice to be more loving may be facilitated by learning and applying relevant principles and techniques presented in a step-by-step programme of personal awareness exercises, many having their origin in Psychosynthesis, a transpersonal, humanistic psychology which holds that self-mastery begins with self-knowledge and self-understanding.

This course invites you to make a free and informed choice — one which will nourish and nurture you — and then helps you take steps to put it into action in a clear and confident way.

BEFORE YOU BEGIN

When you commit yourself to this course and its theme, you begin a process of exploration, discovery and development, one which may continue long after you come to the final page. Consider your time spent here as a seed-planting, aware that whatever you harvest later depends upon how well you cultivate and nourish the crop as you go along.

Consequently we suggest that you take at least one full week or longer to move through each of the ten sessions, and that you limit your study to an hour at a time to allow for assimilation before continuing. In this way you are more likely to experience the course as a step-by-step process as it unfolds slowly within you, the way it does for participants in our workshop.

Offering Education, Not Therapy

We are teachers, not psychologists or psychotherapists, and this course is intended as *education* rather than *therapy*. It is designed to increase *awareness* of your attitudes and behaviour towards love (especially the ones which limit you), and to offer alternatives to help you bring more love into your life.

While the topics, methods, exercises and techniques of the course can be quite revealing, powerful and healing for people, the authors accept no responsibility for individual reactions to the course and its materials.

We do note with satisfaction as we present our workshops that many people report they find our educational approach to have great and long-lasting therapeutic value for them as well.

Using Discernment

We have no absolute answers for you, no definitive solutions, no easy recipes, no short cuts, no quick fixes, no magic wands.

We do have our experience as human beings and as teachers which we share willingly and openly with you, but we do not expect you to accept wholeheartedly or unreservedly everything we say or invite you to do. Rather, approach this course in a spirit of discerning adventure, eager and curious to explore whatever may be of value to you, and finding ways to use it creatively in your own life.

Exploring Three Stages

This course consists of three stages. The initiatory or ground-laying stage began when something inside you said 'Yes' to doing the course. The seed-planting and cultivation stage begins now as you address in earnest the topics within these pages. The integration or harvesting stage begins when you carry into your daily life all you have learned.

Focusing Upon Sessions

All ten sessions are divided into six parts:

PART 1. MAKING CONNECTIONS. We notice that taking part in the exercises tends to prompt between sessions a variety of memories, ideas, feelings, insights, dreams, 'unfinished business', interactions and other relevant events in your inner and outer life. We regard all these occurrences as an important part of your ongoing exploration, and therefore we reserve space at the beginning of each session for you to use as a personal journal. Updating your unfolding process and making connections with the theme, issues and exercises of this course helps you to recognise, accept and utilise these relevant happenings in your daily life more effectively, and also makes this book a more complete record for you. Be alert between sessions to capture such inner and outer happenings. You may wish to write them down as soon as you become aware of them, rather than waiting until you begin the next session to remember and write about them all.

PART 2. TAKING STOCK. We explore your experience of the topic in question, how you feel and think about it and your typical patterns of behaviour with it, before launching a deeper investigation later in the session. In so doing, we follow the scientific method of going from the known to the unknown, and noting what is familiar to you before introducing new, direct experiences.

PART 3. EXPLORING PERSPECTIVES. Then we share our own personal viewpoints. Remember, however, these are *our* perspectives. Yours may be different. If something we say helps you, accept it with our blessings. Otherwise let it be.

PART 4. GAINING AWARENESS. We follow with exercises designed to provide you with increased awareness of your personal behaviour, for *with awareness comes the freedom and power of choice*. We all have blind spots, that is, attitudes, habits and other behaviour of which we are not aware. Blind to our own blind spots, we have no control, power or choice over their effect upon our life. But as we become aware of such patterns of behaviour, we *do* have a choice — to continue them in the same habitual way (which may or may not serve us) or to change them for something else which may offer us much more, such as greater freedom, empowerment or fulfilment.

PART 5. DEVELOPING POTENTIAL. Up to this point in each session you are becoming more aware of your own experience, that which *has been* or *is now* in your life. This part invites you to build upon your present awareness and to go beyond it by offering you opportunities for creating new direct experiences, gaining new perspectives and taking new steps forward towards that which *can be*.

PART 6. APPLYING IT. Simply increasing your awareness is not enough to ensure your bringing more love into your life, or for that matter to do anything else. The final necessary step is to *use* what you are learning, to *do* something with it, to integrate it, embody it and anchor it in your everyday life so that it becomes a natural part of you. We help you to begin this process in the final part of each session. In the later sessions we present several optional exercises which help you to apply the course principles. Do these optional ones only when you can choose freely to do them, rather than taking them on as an obligation with their own added pressure. Pace yourself. Take your time. The course is a process to unfold, not a race to be won.

Forming a Support Group

This course is designed for you to do all of the exercises completely by yourself. However, if you wish to derive increased benefit, we suggest that you form a small group (3-6 people) to meet regularly each week to share with one another your experience of the material. Meeting as a group allows you to learn from each other and to give and receive encouragement and support. Refer to the final section, *Suggestions for Using the Course in Small Groups*.

Finding a Support Person

We also recommend that you ask someone to serve as a support person for you. It should be a close friend, mentor or confidant, someone you can talk to freely, someone who is willing and available to be with you periodically (face to face and by telephone), someone who is a good listener (without having personal needs to offer you advice, judge or 'do' something) — in short, someone who supports you and your development with love and wisdom.

We feel it is important for you to be able to discuss with someone your feelings and thoughts as a way of grounding the experience and integrating your learning from the course. At the end of each session we ask you to discuss your experience of the session with your support person before you begin the next session.

ABOUT THE EXERCISES

There is no right or wrong way to do any of the exercises. The only wrong way is *not* to do them at all, skipping over them and promising yourself to go back to them later, after you have read through the entire course. The exercises, more than 125 of them, *are* the course.

As you are doing this course only for your own benefit, try to be as honest and open as you can with your responses to questions and with your full participation in the exercises. Make an agreement with yourself to express anything and everything, and not to hold anything back. Realise that the more open you are, the freer you are.

Repeating Our Instructions

As you move through the course, you will find that we use identically-worded instructions in many exercises. We use this repetition purposely as a means to reinforce and deepen your experience of the course; therefore do not skip over the instructions because they are familiar to you. Rather, go through them methodically, allowing the repetition to strengthen your developmental process.

Writing Directly in the Book

Most of the exercises ask you to write down responses to questions to help anchor, clarify and expedite your unfolding process. Writing also serves as both a catalyst and a catharsis, and stimulates different creative and introspective juices to flow. Rather than your having to keep a separate notebook, we provide space for you to write directly in the book. As children many of us were told to respect books and never to write in them, but this book is completely different. Do write and draw *everything* directly in this book so that it becomes a living journal, a complete and ready reference for you. If you ever need more space than is provided, simply clip, staple or tape in an extra page.

Drawing Freely

Some exercises ask you to do one or more free drawings directly in the book. They are intended to bypass your conscious mind and elicit valuable material more directly from your unconscious mind. Therefore we encourage you to be as free and spontaneous as possible in your drawings, allowing your hand to pick up a crayon and move intuitively and creatively across the page, perhaps to express a quality, feeling or tone in an abstract way rather than to reproduce a faithful photocopy of an image.

If you have the 'I have never been able to draw' syndrome, acknowledge the feeling and then *choose deliberately* to go ahead and do it anyway. You are doing this course only for your own benefit, so why cheat yourself by not experiencing all of the exercises! Refer to 'Dealing with Your Resistance' below.

The only supplies you need for this course are a pen or pencil and, if you prefer, a set of coloured drawing pens, pencils or crayons.

Getting the Most from Visualisation

We include in each session at least one creative visualisation exercise in which we ask you to *imagine* something, that is, to picture an image, symbol or entire scene in your mind's eye. Many people find their imagination functions more easily when they close their eyes, as it helps to focus their attention inward, and so we begin these exercises with the instruction to close your eyes. Other people find their imagination functions more easily if they keep their eyes open. Follow whichever method works better for you. Do not be discouraged if at first you do not get vivid images — the imagination is a function to be developed. While most people are able to see images in this way, others may hear, feel, know or sense images more readily than they see them.

Treat whatever comes to you in the silence the same way as in processing dreams, that is, symbolically, not literally. No symbol has a uniform or consistent interpretation or even a general meaning. Therefore *always* explore the image to discover the *quality* or tone it conveys *to you*, its essence rather than its surface or literal meaning. For example say the image of a dog comes to you in an exercise. What quality might it have *for you?* The identical symbol might represent any number of different qualities, including:

The Quality Of	As Suggested In
Aggression	Dog fight
Animal Passion, Instinct	Dogs playing and mating
Dependability, Reliability	Dog tricks and habits
Deterioration	'Going to the dogs'
Determination	'Dogged'
Dominance, Domination	'Top dog'
Energy, Vitality, Endurance	Sledge dogs
Laziness, Ease	'A dog's life'
Loyalty	'Man's best friend'
Luck, Good or Bad	Chinese astrology
Obedience	Hunting and sheep dogs
Protection	Guard dogs
Service	Guide dogs for the blind
Submission, Subservience	'Underdog'
Territoriality	Marking, claiming space
Unconditional Love	Dogs responding unstintingly
Work	Bloodhounds, drug-sniffer dogs

Which one of these universal qualities (or still others) may apply in a given instance depends principally *upon you.* The same symbol might mean something entirely different to another person doing the same exercise, or to you doing a different exercise or doing the same exercise again at a later time. It also means there are no 'good' symbols or 'bad' symbols, and no need to be embarrassed, ashamed, frightened or put off by a symbol simply because of its outer or literal appearance.

Rather, *explore* the symbol first, allowing its primary quality for you to emerge in the same spontaneous way as the symbol itself, before using your intellect to consider, analyse or interpret the symbol for possible meanings or connections.

Some guided imagery exercises call for you to imagine yourself being or doing something. In such cases assume the perspective of being *in* the scene as an active participant, experiencing it with all of your senses, rather than the perspective of a passive, detached observer, one step removed from the scene, watching yourself as you might watch a video replay of yourself. It is the difference between 'imagine *being* a dog lying in the sun' and 'imagine *watching* a dog lying in the sun'.

Pre-Recording Exercises

Record onto an audio cassette the exercises which ask you to close your eyes and then visualise or meditate. Pre-recording allows you to participate in the exercises freely without the interruption of having to refer to the course instructions during the exercise.

When you record, read the text quite slowly and include ample pauses in which to take the action suggested. Leave a pause on the tape of 10-30 seconds, or whatever time seems comfortable and appropriate, at every set of dots (. . .) to allow you to experience each part fully.

Staying with Your Feelings and Thoughts

Some exercises may cause memories of certain events, people, feelings and thoughts to come to you. They may be happy ones, sad ones, angry ones, tender ones. We see this process as a healthy sign. Give yourself full permission to think the thoughts, feel the feelings and re-experience the events as a way of accepting, transforming and integrating them more fully into your life. Remember also to talk regularly with your support person as a help to you in this process.

It is quite natural for feelings of impatience, frustration, doubt or discouragement to surface occasionally in a course of this kind. If you experience such feelings, recognise them, acknowledge them, accept them, but give them no room to grow. (As the saying goes, while these so-called 'negative' feelings may knock upon your front door, you do not have to invite them in for dinner!) At such times simply take one session, part, exercise, page, paragraph, sentence or word at a time and then proceed to the next one. Otherwise you may allow your own reactions to hinder or stop your progress unnecessarily.

Lay aside all blame, criticism and judgement of yourself. *Accept that nothing is or was ever wrong with you.* If a lesson can be learned from something which has happened, learn the lesson and then move onward. Do not allow yourself to stand still. To sit on the fence. To wait indefinitely. Rather, choose deliberately to take action. To move on. To grow. To become more whole.

Dealing with Your Resistance

We vary the exercises in each session to give you different experiences. It will be worth noting in the space provided for your response which of them you find easy and fun to do and which seem to be more challenging, perhaps even prompting some resistance to doing them.

For example you may become restless or bored with the repetition of our exercise formats. If you do, then you might be focusing your attention more upon *our structure* than upon *your process of personal development.*

How can you tell when you are resisting? One way is when you give yourself a reason to avoid doing an exercise or to avoid beginning or continuing a session or perhaps even to avoid doing the entire course. Such reasons might include, 'This is too: easy/difficult, silly/intense, shallow/deep, mental/emotional, elementary/advanced or time-consuming/time-wasting.' Or 'Now I have to: take a break, make a telephone call, go to the toilet, have a cigarette or drink a cup of coffee or tea.' Obviously it is natural and necessary to take such breaks, but notice if you use them to *avoid* doing an exercise or proceeding through the course.

If you do feel any resistance, first acknowledge it without judging either it or yourself and then *choose deliberately* to go ahead and do the exercise anyway, *despite* your resistance. Often such resistance fades away if given scant attention. If it does not go, it may prove quite insightful for you to examine directly the nature of your resistance, how it limits you and how it serves you.

We take the view that if this course has found its way to you, it is because it has something to offer you.

Re-Doing Exercises

For many people, the barriers they have erected within themselves against giving and receiving love fully have a long history and are firmly entrenched, reinforced by years of repeating patterns of behaviour. Therefore we suggest that you re-do any exercise as often as you wish to gain additional insight or to reinforce and develop a personal process.

You may be surprised with the results you achieve by doing the same exercise daily for a week or even for a month. A Psychosynthesis trainer we know says that doing these exercises only once to learn more about yourself is like hitting a tennis ball over the net only once to learn more about your tennis game! Systematic, repetitive practice is the key to success with the exercises in the course.

Giving Us Your Feedback

Finally we welcome your comments about your experience with the course. Address all correspondence to the authors care of Findhorn Press, The Park, Findhorn, Forres IV36 0TZ, Scotland.

CHOOSING TO ALLOW

PART 1. MAKING CONNECTIONS

Welcome to *Bringing More Love Into Your Life: The Choice Is Yours*.

We designed this course originally as an intensive workshop presented each summer in seven very full days for a group of 24 people in a residential setting at the Findhorn Foundation.

Here you will be on your own, although we hope you feel our loving support, and you can take as much time as you wish to move through the course. Give yourself a full week or longer for each session, and do no more than one or two parts at a time, nor proceed for more than an hour, to allow you to begin to digest and apply the insights you gain.

First, if you skipped over the section Before You Begin *(p. 13), go back and read it carefully before continuing*. Do it now. When you have read it, write below the name of the friend who has agreed to serve as your support person during the course.

_____

Purpose

The purpose of Session One is to find out how you feel about love and what it means to you, provide an orientation to love and explore ways of bringing more love into your life.

In this part of each session we normally invite you to review the preceding session and then, using these pages as a personal journal, to record the feelings, thoughts, dreams, interactions and other inner and outer happenings which have been prompted by it, making connections with the theme, topics and exercises of this course.

In this first session, however, we begin by asking you to consider what you would like to achieve from the course. A clear statement of purpose guides you through your studies and keeps you focused upon what you want.

Perhaps you already have a clear sense of purpose. If not, to discover or to clarify your purpose, write in the space below, *'MY PRIMARY PURPOSE IN DOING THIS COURSE IS . . .'* and complete the sentence with whatever thought comes to you.

_____

_____

_____

_____

You now have a general purpose, but what about your specific objectives? As this course is about bringing more love into your life, *what precisely do you want?* For example is it something you wish to be, to do or to have in your life?

_____

_____

_____

_____

Would either or both of the above responses foster a change of some kind in your life? If so, *are you willing for your life to change?* It means that *something* in your life will have to be *different*. We ask because we find that many people *say* they want to change, *and* they also want everything to remain the same! Affirm below, *'I AM COMPLETELY WILLING FOR MY LIFE TO CHANGE AND TO BE DIFFERENT.'* Then record any feelings and thoughts which writing your affirmation may prompt.

_____

_____

_____

_____

The course is based upon the principle that self-mastery begins with self-understanding. It asks you to examine your own experience as objectively as you can. Consequently, the more honest and open you are in applying yourself to the questions and exercises in the course, the more you benefit. Affirm below, *'I AM WILLING TO BE COMPLETELY HONEST AND OPEN WITH MYSELF DURING THIS COURSE.'* Then record any feelings and thoughts which writing your affirmation may prompt.

_____

_____

_____

_____

Sometimes we are our own worst enemies. In many different ways, we sabotage or defeat our best efforts to get whatever we want. We adopt patterns of behaviour which enable us to resist or avoid having to confront certain things. Bringing these ways out into the light from the beginning helps us to watch for them throughout the course. So, consider for a moment how might you sabotage or prevent yourself from achieving the purpose and objectives you have listed above?

_____

_____

_____

_____

It is important that you *choose* to bring more love into your life from the very beginning of this course. It is important that it becomes your deliberate intention from this page forward. Affirm below, *'I CHOOSE NOW TO BRING MORE LOVE INTO MY LIFE, AND I AM BRINGING MORE LOVE INTO MY LIFE DAY BY DAY.'* Then record any feelings and thoughts which writing your affirmation may prompt.

_____

_____

_____

_____

Next in Part 2 we find out what love means to you and how you feel about it.

PART 2. TAKING STOCK

In this part of each session, we survey your past and present feelings, thoughts, beliefs and typical behaviour patterns relating to the topic of the session.

Defining Love

The word love means different things to different people. It is sacred to some people and meaningless to others. Yet all people have an inner response to love in one way or another.

Some people use love to refer to sexual desire. Others use it to describe feelings of affection and romance. Some people use it to reflect appreciation and caring. Still others say it is the universal principle of attraction and union.

How do you feel about love? What does love mean to you? First, take a moment to consider how you usually use the word.

Then write your definition of love by beginning with either 'LOVE IS . . .' or 'TO LOVE IS TO . . .' and complete the sentence with whatever thought comes to you.

_____

_____

_____

_____

One way of defining love is to describe it by saying what it is and what it is not. Perhaps you have just now used this method yourself.

A classic description of love appears in the Apostle Paul's First Letter to the Corinthians, 13:4-8 (Good News Bible):

> *Love is patient and kind; it is not jealous or conceited or proud; love is not ill-mannered or selfish or irritable; love does not keep a record of wrongs; love is not happy with evil, but is happy with the truth. Love never gives up; and its faith, hope and patience never fail. Love is eternal.*

How do you respond to this description? What do you feel and think about it? How does it compare with your own *experience* of love?

_____

_____

_____

_____

For many of us love is an elusive and emotionally-charged word which has a variety of meanings. As you proceed through the course, you may find that your definition of love changes with your experience.

Now we continue by asking you what you believe about love.

'Reality of Love' Graph

Choose one of the following statements which comes nearest to your general belief about the existence and reality of love.

1. Love as such does not exist on this planet. It is like 'security', a word used to describe an ideal state which is conspicuously absent in life.

2. Love has been expressed in the world by a few special teachers, such as Jesus Christ and the Buddha, but it is quite out of reach to us mere mortals.

3. I notice other people expressing love, but I am not sure I have ever felt it within myself, and so I have some personal difficulty in relating to it.

4. I know I am capable of giving and receiving love, and I can feel it within myself and many others.

5. I try to love freely, fully and fearlessly to the best of my ability.

6. I am pure love. All else is only fear, illusion and talk.

Having made your choice, mark an X on the graph below to indicate your present belief about love. It may be between two statements and numbers.

| 1 | 2 | 3 | 4 | 5 | 6 |

What did you feel as you were doing the exercise? What are you feeling and thinking now?

_____

_____

_____

_____

'Love' Experience Scan

Next we invite you to turn your attention inward to capture more of your feelings and thoughts about love. We call this exercise an Experience Scan, as it offers a quick and easy way to collect beliefs formed from your past experience. Pause 10-30 seconds, or whatever length of time seems comfortable and appropriate at every . . . to allow you to experience each step fully.

Close your eyes . . . Sit up straight . . . Take a few deep breaths . . . Relax . . . Allow your body, emotions and thoughts to become still . . . Become like a calm, quiet lake . . . When you are ready, say to yourself, 'LOVE IS . . .' and complete the sentence with a word or short phrase — whatever comes spontaneously to you. Do not *think* about it. Write down the first response which comes. Then do it again, this time allowing a new word or phrase to emerge. Write down the new response. If you blank out momentarily, simply begin again, knowing that something will soon come to you. Repeat the process again and again for at least ten minutes, or until you have filled the space below with columns of words.

LOVE IS . . .

Now examine your responses. Mark each response you regard as 'positive' with a plus (+) sign and each 'negative' one with a minus (-) sign.

Do you find any similarities or patterns in your responses? What observations can you make about them? Avoid judging your responses or yourself, but stay open to learning more about yourself.

_____

_____

_____

_____

_____

_____

We complete Part 2 by asking you to comment about your own general experience with love.

23

Your Relationship to Love

How do you relate to love? How loving are you? How loving are your relationships? With family? Friends? Co-workers? Authorities? The same sex? The opposite sex? What is your greatest challenge, problem or difficulty in bringing more love into your life? These are big questions. First, take a moment to consider what your experience has been, and then write about it as concisely as you can. Save details and 'stories' for another time. As we say in our workshop, *'Be deep and brief!'* But do use all of the space provided.

_____

_____

_____

_____

_____

_____

_____

_____

_____

_____

_____

_____

_____

_____

_____

_____

_____

_____

_____

_____

_____

You may find that the very act of writing about the way you relate to love prompts other feelings and thoughts to come to you over the next few days. If so, note that we provide space for you to record them in Session Two, Part 1 (pp. 45-6).

Next in Part 3 we give you our definitions of love.

PART 3. EXPLORING PERSPECTIVES

In this third part of every session, we each relate our own experience with the topic of the session.

EILEEN

The primary lesson to learn in life is to love. — Opening Doors Within

David and I have each had a lifetime of lessons about love, some of which we are still learning. So do understand that we are not putting ourselves forward as experts and saying we have all the answers. Far from it. An old adage is that people teach what they most need to learn. I am sure that it is not by accident that we have been learning and teaching about love for the past several years.

What is love? I hear about it. I speak about it. But what does it mean to me? I feel that love is one of the most misunderstood words in the dictionary. I realised very early that love is not just a word. It is an essence. It is a vibration. It is a power. It is life itself. Love is the most priceless energy in all the universe. Why? Love overcomes all fear. Love rises above all that would drag it down into the mire. It looks deeper than the surface into the innermost depth of the soul. Love is the balm that contains the power to heal and renew. It is the key to every door.

As I open my heart, I begin to understand the true meaning of love. A closed heart knows nothing of love. Love is a heavenly gift; it is free for all who are ready and willing to accept it. I can know love, I can feel it and yet I cannot hold onto it, for the more I try to possess it, the more it eludes me. Love is as free as the wind, and knows no limitations or barriers.

True love is never possessive; it never holds another person in bondage, but longs to see every soul free and unfettered, finding its rightful place in the perfect scheme of things. With love comes freedom. It is fear which binds and limits; it is love which cuts away all bonds and frees.

Love is an inner state of being. It does not have to be talked about, for it expresses in a thousand and one ways — a look, a touch, an action. Love is the universal language; it can be understood by all, for it is the language of silence.

I find love is so many things, and yet I know it is not something that can be bought, sold, weighed or measured. I can only give love. Love is in everyone and everything in varying degrees, and is waiting to be drawn forth. Love is not something apart from me; I am love. Love is trusting, accepting, believing without guarantee. Love is spontaneous and longs to express itself through joy, beauty, truth and even through tears.

Love lifts up. It brightens the way and lightens every task. It adds meaning to every relationship and joy to everything I do. It sings a happy song in me. Love lifts my spirits, renews my faith and blesses me all through the day.

Answering the call of love demands much courage and determination because vulnerability always includes a risk of being rejected. But without vulnerability love is impossible, and without love life is incomplete.

What does love mean to me? It is that indescribable, powerful energy which flows through my whole being out to all my fellow men and women, enabling me to see beyond the outer form to the divinity within each one, creating within me a feeling of oneness, wholeness and the 'peace of God that passes all understanding'.

DAVID

This is my commandment, that you love one another as I have loved you. — New Testament

The first association of love for me was with feelings, emotions and romance. Some Saturday matinee movies I was allowed to see as a young child had love scenes which, for me, merely delayed the action of the story-line. Love was something which grownups did and was of no interest or relevance to me whatsoever.

Later, as an adolescent, I discovered that love took on new and interesting dimensions, which I could finally relate to and experience for myself. Love changed from being an adjective (love scenes, love songs, love stories) to a noun (making love). In my teens, love meant having sex, and vice versa. I was utterly fascinated, and lost no time in exploring the sexual side of life. It became a way I could nurture myself and be nurtured.

Eventually a more personal, romantic connotation of love re-emerged for me (falling in love), having to do with the quality of relationship, and involving deeper feelings for my sexual partner. Much, much later, love took on the coloration of responsibility and service, the selfless performing of acts of loving-kindness towards others in need. 'Love thy neighbour' meant giving to people, and providing friendly and helpful support.

While love takes many forms, I have learned that the most important form of love is self-love — not egotism, but rather self-acceptance, self-appreciation, self-esteem. Without it, we cannot genuinely and fully love another person. We only remain needy and look outside ourself for confirmation, validation and love. I have come to realise that love is who I *am*, not what I have or do. Bringing more love into my life starts with being who I am, being me, being all of me.

As Eileen indicates in her sharing, love is complex and difficult to define. In our workshops and in this course we strive for simplicity and clarity, and therefore we use this definition: *'Love is compassionate acceptance of and respect for ourself and others.'* Thus bringing more love into my life means learning to take myself as I am and others as they are. It means learning to respect myself and others. It means acting with compassion, caring, warmth and understanding.

I ask myself about emotions, romance, feelings — where do they fit into a definition of love? I have come to agree with Martin Buber who says that love 'is not an emotion or a feeling. Feelings accompany love, but they do not constitute it.' Theologian Millar Burrows also suggests that love 'is not an emotion but an attitude of the will . . . To love one's neighbour is not to feel affection for him but to wish and seek his good.' Love is clearly more than just a feeling.

As a yardstick for myself, I define love even more simply by saying *to love is to allow,* thereby providing the title of this session. To the extent that I am able to allow myself to be as I am — that is, to accept myself without judgement or criticism — is the extent to which I truly love myself. It means I have to accept that I am all right just as I am, while acknowledging that I will always have room to grow, always have unrealised potential, always be in the process of becoming more of who I can be. It means I have to allow others to do and be the same.

I know *I can choose to accept and respect* myself and others. I know *I can choose to allow* myself and others to be as we are. Therefore I know I can *choose* to love, and I can *choose* to bring more love into my life.

What does love mean to me? I believe we are all created from pure love. Love is who we are. We are all born with the capacity to love and be loved. We are all here to express that love to ourselves and to one another.

PART 4. GAINING AWARENESS

In this part of each session, we explore your experience so that you may gain greater awareness of your own patterns of behaviour. Remember, with awareness comes the freedom and power of choice. The more awareness you gain, the more choice you have in how you conduct your life, that is, in establishing patterns which nourish you, and transforming patterns which limit you.

Expectations: Hopes and Fears

Participants in our workshops usually come bringing both hopes and fears about what could happen to them during or after the week. They sometimes have quite romantic and idealised hopes, fantasising the very best which could happen, and they also have quite catastrophic fears, imagining the very worst.

How about you? Do you have high hopes for the course? If so, it helps to know specifically what they are. One way of making your hopes clearer is to complete the following sentence in as many ways as you wish: 'I WILL BE VERY DISAPPOINTED, IF BY THE END OF THE COURSE . . .'

_____

_____

_____

_____

To find out whatever fears you may have about doing the course, complete this sentence in as many ways as you wish: 'I WILL BE VERY RELIEVED, IF BY THE END OF THE COURSE . . .'

_____

_____

_____

_____

We have learned that having positive expectations (hopes) or negative ones (fears) limits seriously your potential both for receiving whatever you want from the course, and also for avoiding whatever you do not want from it. Paradoxically, you must release all your expectations _so that_ you are open to receive whatever you want. Otherwise, if you hold onto your expectations tightly, then you are not free to accept the real gifts which the course has for you, whatever they may be.

'Wise and Loving Guide' Visualisation

We use guided visualisation throughout this course to enable you to do what we term 'the inner work' of preparing yourself to take a step forward in your life. This method is based upon the psychological law which says that images or mental pictures and ideas tend to produce the physical conditions and the external acts which correspond to them. (Refer to _The Act of Will_, Chapter 5, by Roberto Assagioli, M.D.) Put simply, every idea is a potential act at an initial stage. In Session Four we explore in greater detail the creative process of manifestation through visualisation.

This guided visualisation enables you to let go of your expectations and open up to your own inner wisdom, represented symbolically by a wise and loving guide. *We recommend that you pre-record this exercise to enable you to experience it freely and fully without interruption.* Refer to our taping suggestions in the section *Before You Begin* (p. 13). Pause 10-30 seconds, or whatever length of time seems comfortable and appropriate, at every . . . to allow you to experience each step fully. Avoid rushing through the exercise. Take your time.

Find a comfortable position, sitting up straight . . . Close your eyes . . . Take several long, slow, deep breaths . . . Relax your body completely . . . Release all of the tension . . . Allow whatever emotions you may be feeling to fade away . . . Do the same with your thoughts . . . Become like a calm, quiet lake, which mirrors perfectly the blue sky . . . Or the starry sky in the silence of the night . . . Be at peace, and yet remain alert . . .

When you are ready, allow to come to you the image or sense of a very large city, such as New York, London or Paris . . . It is a pleasant day . . . Experience yourself walking along the street in the city centre . . . Feel the solid pavement under your feet . . . See and hear the cars and buses . . . Observe that many other people are walking hurriedly along . . . Notice how preoccupied and impersonal everyone is . . .

Then find yourself walking into the lobby of a very tall building . . . Once inside, you notice several lifts or elevators, and you go to one and push the 'Up' button . . . The doors open and you walk into it alone . . . You push the button marked 'Roof-top', the doors close and as the lift begins to move, you feel perfectly comfortable, calm and safe . . .

The floor indicator shows that you are now moving past the first floor . . . Then past the second floor . . . Past the third floor . . . The fourth floor . . . The fifth floor . . . The sixth floor . . . The seventh floor . . . And beyond . . .

The lift begins to slow down, and then stops at the top floor . . . The doors open and you step out into an amazing sight: a roof-top garden complete with grass, bushes, trees and many different kinds of flowers . . . All of the blossoms everywhere are a dazzling white . . . The sun is shining brightly down upon you . . .

You walk along the neatly-trimmed paths and feel total peace and quiet here, far removed from the busy street you left only a few moments ago . . .

After a while, you come to a bench and sit down to rest . . . It is only now you notice that you have been carrying a package under your arm . . .

Soon you begin to have the feeling that you are not alone . . . You look up along the path ahead of you, and coming towards you is a wise and loving guide, someone who knows and loves you very much indeed, and with whom you feel quite safe and completely at ease . . .

The guide approaches, greets you warmly and asks you about your package . . . You reply, 'In here are all my expectations of the *Bringing More Love Into Your Life: The Choice Is Yours* course I am beginning . . . The guide then says, 'Please give them to me. They will only get in your way.' Willingly, you hand the package over . . .

Then the wise and loving guide says to you, 'Let me tell you something. Let me tell you the *real* purpose for your taking this course.' So in these next few moments, allow the guide to reveal this real, perhaps deeper, purpose to you . . .

Now you notice that the guide has another package, and you ask about it . . . The guide replies, 'In this package is the gift of this course for you,' and hands the package to you, adding, 'At any time during the course, you may open this package to learn what the gift is to you. Know also that you may return to this white garden as often as you wish and speak with me about any concern you may have. I am here to help you. As you have discovered, I know all about you, and am able and willing to answer any question you could possibly ask me about yourself.'

The guide now leaves you, and disappears among the growing things in the wondrous garden . . . In a moment, you arise from the bench with the new package containing the gift under your arm, and return to the lift . . . You push the 'Down' button, and the doors open . . . You walk into the lift and push the 'Ground Floor' button . . . The doors close, and the lift begins to descend . . .

In a few moments, the lift comes to a stop on the ground floor, the doors open and you step out into the lobby . . . You walk out onto the street, where once again you feel the solid pavement under your feet . . . Now, however, something seems to be quite different than before . . . The other people on the street are acknowledging and smiling at each other . . . The sun is shining down upon you all, and you feel safe, loving and peaceful . . . Even the traffic seems more a part of the scene . . . You make your way down the street, holding the package under your arm . . .

In your own time, allow everything to fade . . . Bring your attention back to the room where you are now . . . Open your eyes . . . Take a deep breath . . . And a gentle stretch . . .

Now write down anything you wish to remember from this exercise, especially your purpose for taking this course, its gift to you if you have already opened the package and any instance you noticed when your feelings were evoked.

_____

_____

_____

_____

_____

_____

Ladder of Life

The humorist Mark Twain said, 'Principles don't mean much on an empty stomach.' His statement, later to be echoed in the writings of psychologist Abraham Maslow, suggests that we have different kinds of needs, and that a priority exists whereby some needs have to be satisfied before others can be met.

Thus the principle of love (and the attendant need for acceptance and inclusion) will not mean much to us until we have taken care of more basic needs. Food in our stomach. Clothes on our back. Roof over our head.

We have devised a very simple ladder of qualities which puts love into a broader context with other personal needs. The ladder appears below.

UNITY
PEACE
LOVE
FREEDOM
CHOICE
AWARENESS
OPENNESS
TRUST
SECURITY

The *Contents* section shows that this course has separate sessions devoted to each of the first seven qualities. The issue of Session Two, *security*, comes first on our ladder. We have to be fundamentally safe and secure before we are ready to venture out, to dare, to risk.

Once we do feel safe, however, then the quality of *trust* becomes more available to us. It is difficult for us to trust when we do not feel secure. The ladder also suggests that we have to trust *before* we can love.

Trust then leads us to the third rung, *openness*. It is difficult for us to be open if we cannot trust — ourself, others, life, God. Having trust frees us to be honest and open.

The more open we are, the more aware we can be. The opposite is also true: the more closed we are, the more unaware we are of what is going on in our life. Therefore, the next rung of the ladder is *awareness*.

With awareness comes the power of *choice*. As we become aware of our behaviour patterns and blind spots, we have the choice to continue them if we feel they serve us, or to change them if they are too limiting.

Having choice empowers us and leads to greater *freedom*. How do we know? All we have to do is to consider when we do not feel empowered and free. It is when we feel we have no choice. Having choice liberates us and keeps us from feeling stuck, victimised or powerless.

Love is the seventh rung of the ladder. We cannot love when we do not feel free, that is, when we are limited by anxieties, fears and the unconscious behaviour patterns they create.

Love fosters *peace*. It is difficult for us to feel peaceful in the absence of love. Feeling love for ourself and others creates the peace.

Peace brings us a sense of *unity*, an interconnectedness with humanity, with all life, with the God within the very core of our being.

Note that this sequence of qualities is not altogether a linear, step-by-step process. For example openness may lead directly to freedom. The more open we are (that is, the more frank, unguarded and vulnerable), the freer we are. Note also that we can be on one rung of the ladder in one part of our life, such as employment, and on a completely different one in another part, such as relationships.

Learning About Love From Experience

This exercise shows us how to use our own experience to gain awareness.

Close your eyes . . . Sit up straight . . . Take a few deep breaths . . . Relax . . . Allow your body, emotions and thoughts to become still . . . Become like a calm, quiet lake . . .

When you are ready, allow to come to you a memory of a time when you felt very loving . . . Your love may have been directed towards yourself, another person, an animal, an object, a cause, God or something entirely different . . . It may be a recent experience, or one from long ago, perhaps even from your childhood . . .

Take your time . . . Wait patiently in the silence, knowing that something will soon come to you . . . Be willing to accept whatever comes without judging, censoring or rejecting it . . . Simply be ready to observe and examine it, with the purpose of learning more about it . . .

When a memory comes to you, allow specific details to come with it . . . Observe and explore the original experience with as many of your senses as you can . . . Re-live it . . . Let it be very real to you again, but avoid becoming lost in it . . . When you are ready, respond to the following questions . . .

How do you experience love? What does loving feel like to you?

_____

_____

_____

_____

Close your eyes again and reconnect with the remembered experience . . . How does loving register in your body, physically — what physical sensations accompany the experience of love for you? . . .

_____

_____

_____

_____

Close your eyes and reconnect . . . How does loving register for you emotionally — what emotions accompany the experience of love for you? . . .

_____

_____

_____

_____

Reconnect one last time . . . How does loving register for you intellectually — what thoughts, ideas or beliefs accompany the experience of love for you? . . .

_____

_____

_____

_____

Next create a new definition of love, only this time *base it entirely upon your own just-recorded personal experience of love*. Review your last four responses and use them as your own yardstick of whatever love means to you.

_____

_____

_____

_____

Finally re-read your original definition of love in Part 2 (p. 21). Write down any similarities and differences. How does it feel to use your own subjective experience in this way, that is, as a frame of reference and source of wisdom?

_____

_____

_____

_____

'Love Pure Forms and Distortions' Assessment

The quality of love can be experienced and expressed in many ways. Some ways can be considered pure, while others are distorted through our needs, desires and experience. Listed below are examples of both forms. In the blanks, put the number of the statement nearest to how you experience or express each quality.

1. I never experience or express this quality.
2. I rarely experience or express this quality.
3. I sometimes experience or express this quality.
4. I often experience or express this quality.
5. I always experience or express this quality.

PURE FORMS OF LOVE	DISTORTIONS OF LOVE
___ Acceptance	___ Attachment
___ Compassion	___ Conformity
___ Cooperation	___ Dependence
___ Inclusiveness	___ Exclusiveness
___ Openness	___ Fear of rejection
___ Receptivity	___ Jealousy
___ Respect	___ Neediness
___ Sensitivity to others	___ Possessiveness
___ Trust	___ Self-centredness
___ Union/Unity	___ Sentimentality

What did you feel as you were doing the exercise? What are you feeling and thinking now?

_____

_____

_____

_____

'Life Journey' Drawing

Draw a chronological journey or diagram of the highlights of your life, beginning with your birth and continuing until you were 15 years old. Include as many as possible of the significant (joyful and painful) relationships and events which come back to you. Be aware of any feelings or thoughts which come as you draw.

HIGHLIGHTS OF THE FIRST FIFTEEN YEARS OF MY LIFE

Examine your drawing. As a journey, how would you describe it? What is the overall quality, tone or impression of it?

_____

_____

_____

_____

What stands out about your drawing to you — what is the most significant part of it?

_____

_____

_____

_____

Do you find any similarities, patterns or repeating situations, events and ways of relating? What other observations can you make about your drawing?

_____

_____

_____

_____

Can you find any clues within the symbolism of the drawing itself as to when, why or how you have blocked yourself from love? For example what colours did you use? What sizes and shapes? What connections, separations or isolations among your images? How did you use the space?

_____

_____

_____

_____

Which people and events in your drawing were the most influential in shaping your present beliefs, attitudes and behaviour towards love?

_____

_____

_____

_____

Next in Part 5 we explore your past, present and future relationship with love, and begin to imagine ways of bringing more love into your life.

PART 5. DEVELOPING POTENTIAL

In this part of each session, we seek to go beyond your present awareness and experience, and offer you *new* possibilities, perspectives and growth.

Orientation Symbols and Drawings

We have an exercise, for which you need your drawing materials, which helps to orientate your position upon the map of love. In this exercise, you are asked several times to allow an image or sense which represents a specific topic to come to you, and then to explore it for the meaning it has for you. Some people feel that they simply make these images up in their own imagination, and therefore tend not to take them seriously. We believe that such images are valid and have much valuable information to give you when you are ready to use them.

For this same reason, give close attention to your dreams throughout the course. You may even wish to begin a dream diary, noting in elaborate detail each dream you have. At the very least, write down in Part 1 of each session images from your dreams and other symbols which are relevant to the theme and topics you are dealing with in this course, as they contain useful clues in your developing process.

Next review the 'Getting the Most from Visualisation' section in *Before You Begin*. Do it now before continuing.

As a reminder, pause from 10-30 seconds, or whatever length of time seems comfortable and appropriate, at every . . . to allow you to experience each step fully. Avoid rushing through the exercise. Take your time.

Find a comfortable position, sitting up straight . . . Close your eyes . . . Take several long, slow, deep breaths . . . Relax your body completely . . . Release all of the tension . . . Allow whatever emotions you may be feeling to fade away . . . Do the same with your thoughts . . . Become like a calm, quiet lake, which mirrors perfectly the blue sky, or the starry sky in the silence of the night . . . Be at peace and yet remain alert . . .

When you are ready, ask yourself the question, *'IN RELATION TO LOVE, WHERE AM I COMING FROM — WHAT HAS BEEN MY PAST EXPERIENCE?'* . . . Then allow an image or sense to come to you which represents an answer to this question . . . Take your time . . . Wait patiently in the silence, knowing that something will soon come to you . . . Be willing to accept whatever comes without judging, censoring or rejecting it . . . Simply be ready to observe and examine it, with the purpose of learning more about it . . .

As you begin to sense something, allow it to become more vivid . . . Note its size and shape . . . Its density and design . . . Its colour and texture . . . Explore it with as many of your senses as you can . . . Find the overall quality it suggests to you . . .

Then open your eyes, and express in a drawing below either the image itself or its quality . . . If nothing has come to you, open your eyes, hold the question in mind and begin to draw freely and spontaneously, letting something come to you in that way . . .

WHERE I AM COMING FROM

Write down the overall *quality* of the symbol and any other words, feelings or thoughts which came to you during the exercise, or which you are aware of now. What new insight or awareness does this symbol and its quality give to you?

_____

_____

_____

_____

Again close your eyes, take a few deep breaths and relax . . . Allow your body, emotions and thoughts to become still . . . Become like a calm, quiet lake . . .

When you are ready, ask yourself the question, *'IN RELATION TO LOVE, WHERE AM I NOW — WHAT IS MY PRESENT EXPERIENCE?'* . . . Then allow an image or sense to come to you which represents an answer to this question . . . Take your time . . . Wait patiently in the silence, knowing that something will soon come to you . . . Be willing to accept whatever comes without judging, censoring or rejecting it . . . Simply be ready to observe and examine it, with the purpose of learning more about it . . .

As you begin to sense something, allow it to become more vivid . . . Note its size and shape . . . Its density and design . . . Its colour and texture . . . Explore it with as many of your senses as you can . . . Find the overall quality it suggests to you . . .

Then open your eyes and express in a drawing below either the image itself or its quality . . . If nothing has come to you, open your eyes, hold the question in mind and begin to draw freely and spontaneously, letting something come to you in that way . . .

WHERE I AM NOW

Write down the overall *quality* of the symbol and any other words, feelings or thoughts which came to you during the exercise, or which you are aware of now. What new insight or awareness does this symbol and its quality give to you?

_____

_____

_____

_____

Again close your eyes, take a few deep breaths and relax . . . Allow your body, emotions and thoughts to become still . . . Become like a calm, quiet lake . . .

When you are ready, ask yourself the question, *'IN RELATION TO LOVE, WHERE AM I GOING — WHAT IS MY FUTURE DIRECTION?'* . . . Then allow an image or sense to come to you which represents an answer to this question . . . Take your time . . . Wait patiently in the silence, knowing that something will soon come to you . . . Be willing to accept whatever comes without judging, censoring or rejecting it . . . Simply be ready to observe and examine it, with the purpose of learning more about it . . .

As you begin to sense something, allow it to become more vivid . . . Note its size and shape . . . Its density and design . . . Its colour and texture . . . Explore it with as many of your senses as you can . . . Find the overall quality it suggests to you . . .

Then open your eyes, and express in a drawing below either the image itself or its quality . . . If nothing has come to you, open your eyes, hold the question in mind and begin to draw freely and spontaneously, letting something come to you in that way . . .

```
┌────────────────────────────────────────────────────────────┐
│                     WHERE I AM GOING                         │
│                                                              │
│                                                              │
│                                                              │
│                                                              │
│                                                              │
│                                                              │
│                                                              │
│                                                              │
│                                                              │
│                                                              │
│                                                              │
│                                                              │
│                                                              │
│                                                              │
│                                                              │
│                                                              │
│                                                              │
│                                                              │
│                                                              │
│                                                              │
└────────────────────────────────────────────────────────────┘
```

Write down the overall *quality* of the symbol and any other words, feelings, or thoughts which came to you during the exercise, or which you are aware of now. What new insight or awareness does this symbol and its quality give to you?

_____

_____

_____

_____

Once more, close your eyes, take a few deep breaths and relax . . . Allow your body, emotions and thoughts to become still . . . Become like a calm, quiet lake . . .

When you are ready, ask yourself the question, *'IN RELATION TO LOVE, WHAT AM I GOING TO NEED TO HELP ME TO GET THERE?'* . . . Then allow an image or sense to come to you which represents an answer to this question . . . Take your time . . . Wait patiently in the silence, knowing that something will soon come to you . . . Be willing to accept whatever comes without judging, censoring or rejecting it . . . Simply be ready to observe and examine it, with the purpose of learning more about it . . .

As you begin to sense something, allow it to become more vivid . . . Note its size and shape . . . Its density and design . . . Its colour and texture . . . Explore it with as many of your senses as you can . . . Find the overall quality it suggests to you . . .

Then open your eyes, and express in a drawing below either the image itself or its quality . . . If nothing has come to you, open your eyes, hold the question in mind and begin to draw freely and spontaneously, letting something come to you in that way . . .

WHAT I NEED TO HELP ME

Write down the overall *quality* of the symbol and any other words, feelings or thoughts which came to you during the exercise, or which you are aware of now. What new insight or awareness does this symbol and its quality give to you?

_____

_____

_____

_____

How do you feel about the images which came to you? What do you think about them?

_____

_____

_____

_____

How does it feel to use your imagination in this way to discover more about yourself?

_____

_____

_____

_____

Next in Part 6 we move from theory to practice, and invite you to make the quality of love more of a living reality for yourself.

PART 6. APPLYING IT

In this part of each session we encourage you to *use* your learning, to lift it from the pages of this course and to digest it, embody it and establish it in your everyday life.

Affirmation

In Part 1 we ask you to affirm, ' *I CHOOSE TO BRING MORE LOVE INTO MY LIFE, AND I AM BRINGING MORE LOVE INTO MY LIFE DAY BY DAY.*' Use this affirmation *throughout this course* in these ways: (1) Say the full affirmation aloud at different times throughout the day. (2) Write down the full affirmation on a large sheet of paper to be put up in your home where you will see it every day. (3) Write down the full affirmation on a small piece of paper to carry in your purse, wallet or pocket as a reminder of the deliberate choice you have made.

Models of Behaviour

Another way to begin to bring more love into your life is to observe people you admire who have been successful in their own expression of love, and note who they are and how they have done it. The idea is not to imitate them, but rather to identify the worthy *qualities* within them and their behaviour which seem to contribute to their success as loving individuals, and then to find ways to express these desirable qualities in your own life more often until they become a natural part of you.

To begin this process, close your eyes, take a few deep breaths, and relax . . . Allow your body, emotions and thoughts to become still . . . Become like a calm, quiet lake . . .

When you are ready, allow to come to you the names of three actual (not fictional) people whom you regard as especially loving, people who personify the quality of love to you . . . They may be from any time in history, or people whom you, yourself, have known . . . Write down their names below . . .

Then take time to find out the qualities about each person's expression of love which you admire (for example acceptance, compassion, openness, respect or trust) . . . Write down your observations about each one of these people and whatever makes these people special and admirable to you . . .

_____

_____

_____

_____

_____

_____

_____

_____

_____

_____

_____

Now review the qualities you have written for all of your models . . . Are there qualities which they have in common? . . . Select one quality which attracts your attention, one which you feel would help you bring more love into your life . . . Then refer to a dictionary and a thesaurus to get a sense of all its relevant meanings . . . Write down whatever you discover about this quality . . .

_____

_____

_____

_____

Would you like to have more of this quality in your life? . . . Imagine how life would be? . . . What differences might there be? . . . How would your relationships with the people around you change?

_____

_____

_____

_____

Finally, how might you bring more of this quality into your everyday life? . . . What specific actions could you take? . . . Are you willing to take them?

_____

_____

_____

_____

Word Cards

Another method of manifesting a desirable quality in your life is to write the name of the quality on cards and put them up in prominent locations in your home where you will see them several times a day: near your bed, on your desk, a door, a wall, the bathroom mirror, the refrigerator. Doing so develops the quality within yourself through subtle programming: the photographic film of your mind records each time you see the card and retains the image. With sufficient repetition, the quality begins to be enhanced, evoked and expressed in your life. Test it for yourself.

You can increase the effectiveness of this technique by reflecting on the meaning of the quality, feeling into the quality to the point of identifying with it in your imagination, repeatedly saying the quality aloud and writing the word many times — all of which reinforce your intention of bringing the quality into your life. Change the word periodically to avoid taking it for granted or becoming blind to it. Begin using this technique today with the quality you have chosen, and continue with it for the next thirty days. We ask you later in the course to report upon your experience of using this word card technique.

Brainstorming Possibilities

Next take some time to brainstorm ways you could bring more love into your everyday life. In brainstorming, the point is to allow many ideas to come to you as quickly as possible. Avoid evaluating, judging or rejecting any idea. Simply write down _everything_ as it occurs spontaneously to you.

Find out how many different ideas you can imagine, without stopping to consider how practical, effective, costly or comfortable they may be. Include absurd, fantastic, zany ideas as well, for they often hold the seeds of creative possibilities. Make sketches to help you remember images which come. Use the whole space below for your ideas. Take your time. Enjoy your creativity.

WAYS I CAN BRING MORE LOVE INTO MY LIFE

Examine your responses. Mark all of the ideas which are worth considering for implementation. Then choose one of them which you are willing to act upon, and write it down.

_____

_____

_____

_____

Identify a first step you can take to help bring it about. Be specific about when, where and how you plan to do it. Put your plan into action *before you begin the next session of this course*. Carry on step by step. You may be surprised how easy (or how difficult) it can be.

Suggested Reading

A completely different approach to begin bringing more love into your life is to read materials about love (both fiction and non-fiction, prose and poetry) which inspire you and evoke loving feelings within you — anything which keeps love an active presence in your life, for then love becomes more real and available to you.

In Part 6 of each session we recommend books and other materials which provide information, experience and support relevant to the specific topic of the session. Here are a few of our favourites.

1. *Inevitable Grace*, by Piero Ferrucci, presents a fascinating study of more than 500 exceptionally competent and creative people throughout history, and the lessons we can learn from how they lived their lives.

2. *Opening Doors Within*, our own book, presents a short inspirational piece of personal guidance for every day of the year.

3. *Daily Guideposts* is an excellent book (with all-new editions published annually) offering 365 human interest commentaries to start each day.

4. *Daily Word*, the monthly Unity magazine, offers daily inspirational messages. We each have subscribed to it for many years and find it very helpful.

Personal Goal

In Part 6 of each session, we invite you to select a personal goal for yourself, one relevant action to be taken before you begin the next session. Considering the possibilities, then making a choice, acting upon it and achieving it gives you positive reinforcement, and empowers and strengthens you in the process of bringing more love into your life.

Effective personal goals have these characteristics:

1. They are simple. Most complex tasks can be divided into smaller, more manageable parts, where successful outcomes are more likely. For example the goal, 'I will learn to love my parents,' could begin with the first step of a simpler goal, 'I will write a letter to my parents.'

2. They are specific. A goal needs to be precise enough for us to know definitely when we have achieved it. The general goal, 'I will be more loving,' would be difficult to assess. The more concrete goal, 'I will invite friends into my home at least twice a month,' is one which we can verify more easily.

3. They describe an action which can be observed. Thus, they require us to *do* something. 'I will read to my children every day,' is a demonstrable act, whereas, 'I will be more considerate of my children,' describes an attitude or inner state of being which may not be directly observable.

4. They reflect our values, priorities and desires, and therefore, as statements of intention, they have our full, unqualified support.

5. They are stated positively and emphatically, beginning with 'I will . . .' Now consider various simple, specific, observable actions you could take within the next few days which would be a step towards bringing more love into your life. Take your time. Then when you

Now consider various simple, specific, observable actions you could take within the next few days which would be a step towards bringing more love into your life. Take your time. Then when you are ready, choose one which seems important to you, one to take as a personal goal. Make a deliberate choice to achieve it. Write it down. We ask you to report your results with it in Session Two, Part 1.

_____

_____

_____

_____

Session Learnings

Turn back and review what you have done in this session. Then write down the three most important insights or learnings you have gained from it.

_____

_____

_____

_____

_____

Purpose

As we stated at the beginning of Part 2, the purpose of Session One is to find out how you feel about love and what it means to you, provide an orientation to love and explore ways of bringing more love into your life. To what degree has Session One achieved its general purpose for you?

_____

_____

_____

Congratulations! You have come to the end of Session One.

Please discuss your experience of this session with your support person *before you begin Session Two*.

In the next session we invite you to report on your personal goal, add names of loving people who may have come to mind as models, list relevant feelings, thoughts, dreams, images, personal interactions and other events which have occurred, and inspirational literature you may have read in the meantime.

As much as possible, try to stay aware of the process you have begun in the course, and the connection it has with daily life as you live it. Now take some time for yourself before you continue with Session Two.

CHOOSING TO FEEL SAFE

PART 1. MAKING CONNECTIONS

In our workshop, participants usually have only a few hours between sessions. It is always a very full and intense time for everyone including ourselves.

In this course, as you are not limited by such constraints, take a brief respite between sessions — long enough to begin to digest and apply in your daily life all that you are learning, and short enough to maintain the momentum of your ongoing exploration.

When you are ready to continue, begin by reviewing Session One to reconnect with your own process of development. Have you achieved the personal goal you set for yourself? How was it to choose, implement and accomplish something you value?

We notice that doing these exercises tends to prompt between sessions a variety of memories, feelings, ideas, insights, dreams, 'unfinished business', interactions and other relevant events in your inner and outer worlds. We regard all of these occurrences as an important part of your exploration, and therefore we reserve space at the beginning of each session for you to use as a personal journal.

Updating your unfolding process, *making connections with the theme, issues and exercises of this course*, helps you to recognise, accept, integrate and utilise these relevant happenings in your daily life more effectively, and also makes this book a more complete record for you.

_____
_____
_____
_____
_____
_____
_____
_____
_____
_____
_____
_____
_____
_____
_____

_____
_____
_____
_____
_____
_____
_____
_____
_____
_____
_____
_____
_____
_____
_____
_____
_____
_____
_____
_____
_____
_____
_____
_____
_____
_____
_____
_____
_____
_____
_____
_____

Next in Part 2 we explore what prevents you from loving freely and fully.

PART 2. TAKING STOCK

Purpose

The purpose of Session Two is to identify whatever blocks you from making the choice of bringing more love into your life.

This course holds the view that we are fashioned from pure love. Love is who and what we are essentially. Bringing more love into our life, therefore, starts with choosing to be more of our whole self. It means choosing to accept and respect ourself and others. It means choosing to allow ourself and others to be who we are, without making any judgements or demands.

It is not a question of waiting for external conditions — for the right moment, person, combination of events to come along — before we are able to love more fully. We do not have to wait for Cinderella or Prince Charming to sweep us off our feet. We do not have to wait for love to come *to* us. Expressing love is a matter of choice, a choice which is *always* ours to make.

If we are looking for more love in our life, what stops us from making this choice? The book *A Course in Miracles* states:

> *Your task is not to seek for love, but merely to seek and find all of the barriers within yourself that you have built against it. It is not necessary to seek for what is true, but it is necessary to seek for what is false.*

We agree with this observation, and base the general design of this course upon it. Therefore we begin to explore more closely whatever blocks you from making the choice of giving and receiving love more fully. First, consider why you do not have more love in your life now. Then write down your feelings and thoughts about it.

_____

_____

_____

_____

Complete this sentence spontaneously: *'I WOULD BE MORE LOVING IF ONLY . . .'*

_____

_____

_____

_____

If something *within you* were blocking you from being more loving, what might it be? Where or how might you have erected barriers within yourself against love?

_____

_____

_____

_____

'Reasons for Not Being More Open to Love' Check-list

People give different reasons for not being more open to love. Take a moment to consider each one of the following statements. Mark all of them which you have said to yourself at one time or another concerning the prospect of bringing more love into your life.

_____ I am very open to love, but the right person has not come along yet.

_____ I am happy the way I am. My life is very full and satisfying as it is.

_____ I am very busy now and have no extra time or energy for such things.

_____ I do not know what love is, so how can I give it?

_____ I am not lovable.

_____ I am not good enough. I do not deserve love.

_____ There is something wrong with me.

_____ No one could love me if they knew what I am really like.

_____ I do not know how to love.

_____ I am incapable of loving.

_____ I do not want all the bother, aggravation and trouble.

_____ Men/women want only one thing.

_____ I am afraid I might be manipulated, used or abused.

_____ I tried it once, and I am never going to let anyone get that close to me again.

_____ Love hurts.

_____ I might have to give up my freedom. I do not want to be tied down.

_____ I do not like making commitments.

_____ I am not ready for the responsibility.

_____ I am afraid I might be overwhelmed and lose my own sense of self.

_____ I am afraid I might be trapped for the rest of my life.

_____ I would rather be miserable by myself than miserable with someone else.

_____ I cannot trust others.

_____ I need to be in control to feel safe.

_____ I am too afraid of people.

_____ My love is too precious to be given away to just anyone and everyone.

_____ It is not my destiny or karma in this lifetime.

_____ I have decided to live a selfless life instead, and use all my time and energy to serve God.

If you have not marked any of the reasons above, or if you have others to add, write down your personal reasons for not bringing more love into your life.

_____

_____

_____

_____

_____

_____

_____

All of these statements, as honest and valid as they may appear to be, actually help us to *avoid* making the choice of bringing more love into our life.

'Blocks to Love' Experience Scan

We continue with an Experience Scan to explore whatever may lie behind these statements, and to discover more about your inner blocks and barriers to love.

Close your eyes . . . Sit up straight . . . Take a few deep breaths . . . Relax . . . Allow your body, emotions and thoughts to become still . . . Become like a calm, quiet lake . . .

When you are ready, say to yourself, *'WHAT STOPS ME FROM BEING MORE LOVING IS* . . . ,*'* and complete the sentence with a word or short phrase — whatever comes spontaneously to you. Do not *think* about it. Write down the first response which comes. Then do it again, this time allowing a new word or phrase to emerge. Write down the new response. If you blank out momentarily, simply begin again, knowing that something will soon come to you. Repeat the process again and again for at least ten minutes, or until you have filled the space below.

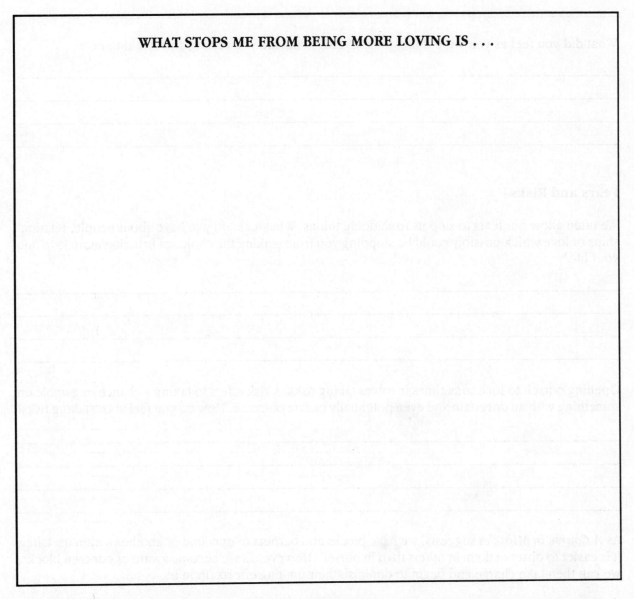

WHAT STOPS ME FROM BEING MORE LOVING IS . . .

Now examine your responses. Mark the ones which are especially meaningful or significant, or which otherwise draw your attention to them.

What is the overall quality, tone or impression of your responses?

_____

_____

_____

_____

What similarities or patterns do you find in them? What other observations can you make about your responses?

_____

_____

_____

_____

What did you feel as you were doing the exercise? What are you feeling and thinking now?

_____

_____

_____

_____

Fears and Risks

We often allow our fears to stop us from doing things. What fears do you have about people, relationships or love which possibly could be stopping you from making the choice of bringing more love into your life?

_____

_____

_____

_____

Opening ourself to love sometimes involves taking risks. A risk refers to taking a chance or gamble on something with an uncertain and even potentially unsafe outcome. How do you feel about taking risks?

_____

_____

_____

_____

As _A Course in Miracles_ suggests, we have blocks and barriers of one kind or another within us. Often it is easier to observe them in others than in ourself. However as we become aware of our own blocks, we can then take charge and begin to diminish their limiting effects upon us.

This course offers you many, many varied techniques to address your blocks to love, so you can do something about them whenever you are ready to do so.

PART 3. EXPLORING PERSPECTIVES

EILEEN

Turn every negative thought and emotion into positive. Simply refuse to accept any negativity ... You can transcend all negativity when you realise that the only power it has over you is your belief in it. As you experience this truth about yourself you are set free. — The Living Word

What are the blocks which stop the love flowing from me? I feel they are all the negative emotions, feelings and thoughts I experience, such as fear, jealousy, envy, self-pity, rejection and low self-esteem.

When I feel something in me is stopping me from loving, I have to take a good look at myself and find out what it is. I then go into the stillness of meditation to ask what I can do about it. I know that as long as the block is there in me I find it very difficult to love.

A good example of a block is low self-esteem. Much of my life I found it very difficult to love myself: my self-esteem was nil. So when someone suggested to me to affirm that I loved myself, I simply could not do it. I knew my faults and failings and weaknesses. I certainly could not say that I loved myself. I thought it was nonsense asking me to do such a thing.

I have had a great deal of un-learning to do in my life. I was brought up as a child never to say things such as 'I love myself', as it was considered a very selfish and self-centred thing to do. Old habits die hard.

Not long after this incident, I suddenly realised that by talking to the divinity within the core of my being, I could say I love myself. Accepting and loving my God-Self changed everything. I had to experience it for myself before it became a reality to me. It was a gradual process and did not come all at once.

The feeling of rejection can also be a big block for me, in fact one of the biggest. It closes my heart and stops the love flowing. I have found I can overcome this block by appreciating, loving and seeing the very best in myself. I also stop the self-pity, wasting time and energy feeling sorry for myself.

I have found a solution to the problem of negative feelings. It is sometimes difficult to do when I am in the midst of them and my heart is closed, but I realise the choice is always mine. I know that suppressing these feelings and emotions is not the answer. I cannot sweep them under the carpet and try to pretend they are not there. They are all part of me.

I want to be able to love all of myself, and even my negative emotions are part of the whole of me. It is not easy for me to love these negative parts. It would be much easier to ignore them, but I have tried to ignore them, and I have found that these negative emotions and feelings rear their heads and have to be dealt with again, sooner or later. I find it works for me to ask the God within me, that is, the highest level of my being, to help me to love these negative parts so they can be changed and transmuted.

It is like that part of the Bible which says, 'Ask, and it shall be given you; seek, and ye shall find; knock, and it shall be opened unto you' (Matthew 7:7). I have complete faith and trust in these principles. They work like magic because when I follow them I find I go through a change of consciousness from focusing upon the negative to the positive, and then I see the good in everything and everyone — including myself.

The more I use these techniques on my blocks, the more I stay open to love and to life.

DAVID

You have but two emotions, love and fear. — A Course in Miracles.

What blocks have I found within myself to giving and receiving love freely?

Much of my life has been governed by fear and insecurity. I imagine I must have had a very anxious childhood, for security issues have long been predominant in my life. As a child, I trusted our pet dogs more easily than I trusted most people. Of course I trusted people on a superficial level, but not with my innermost feelings and thoughts. For much of my life I lived in a plastic bubble, keeping everyone off at arms' length. I allowed no one to come into my inner sanctum, except my four-legged friends.

I have learned from experience that the first step in removing blocks is to find out exactly what they are so that I can begin to recognise them in operation. If I remain blind to my blocks, I can do nothing about them. They continue to have their limiting, sometimes even crippling, effects upon me.

The second step is to accept them as a part of me, and not to judge either them or myself for having them. (Otherwise, I feel guilt on top of everything else.) I have learned to honour my blocks, my defence mechanisms. They have helped me to cope, to survive. When I am ready, I can *choose* to let them go, one by one. I know that I must accept where I find myself upon the ladder of life, and that I can take all the time I need to move gently upwards.

One big change in my life is my attitude towards my fears. I remember vividly in my Psychosynthesis training doing a visualisation exercise in which I was asked to get a symbol for my own spiritual fulfilment. The image which came was the impressive statue of Jesus Christ with outstretched arms on Corcovado, overlooking Rio de Janeiro harbour. Then I was to visualise a pathway leading directly from where I stood at the bottom of a hill up to the top where the symbol was located. My task was to reach the symbol, knowing that along the way I would encounter distractions, blocks and other obstacles, representing my own personal barriers to spiritual fulfilment.

Beginning my imaginary walk up the hill, I soon discovered blocks which seemed to represent procrastination and self-indulgence, but the most formidable block I encountered was a daunting dragon. He was very frightening and had smoke and fire coming from his mouth and nostrils; most importantly, he was completely blocking the pathway. I stood paralysed and mute. When I was finally able to ask him who he was, he replied menacingly in measured words, 'I . . . am . . . your . . . fears.'

We continued talking, and after a while he asked me where I was going. I told him I needed to go to the top of the hill. His fearsomeness softened, and spreading his wings he said, 'Hop on my back, and I will take you to where you want to go.' I climbed on with some caution (Is this a trick? I asked myself), but I soon noticed he obeyed my every command, and so I began to relax. As we glided slowly up towards the statue, it transformed from solid stone to radiant amber light, and the visualisation ended as we flew into the statue, merging with the body of Christ.

This one exercise helped me enormously to realise that I can *use* my fears as tools in a creative way, rather than allowing them to stop me. I have learned that whether they limit me or serve me is strictly a matter of my own choice. Who would have thought that fears and other blocks are also blessings in disguise!

One of the special gifts of this peak experience for me is the great change it brought into my life. I still have fears, but I no longer am afraid of them, and so they have less power to stop me from doing what I want to do. The result is that I now have greater freedom and choice in my life — and more room for love.

PART 4. GAINING AWARENESS

Family History

As children we usually model ourselves unconsciously after our parents. We imitate the way they sit, stand, walk and speak. We adopt their habits, likes, dislikes, attitudes and beliefs. Therefore clues to the way we function as adults can often be found in our early home life and the people who served as models.

Take a few moments to reflect about your parents. (If one or both parents were missing from your childhood, consider whoever the significant adults were in your life at that time.) What were they like? How did they seem to you when you were small? How did they relate to each other? How did they relate to you? Return to your childhood now, and from that age re-experience your parents.

Then respond to these questions.

How much did your mother and father seem to love and accept themselves?

_____

_____

_____

How much did they seem to love and accept each other?

_____

_____

_____

How much did your mother and father seem to love and accept you?

_____

_____

_____

Did one of them seem more open, warm and loving? Which one? In what ways?

_____

_____

_____

How confident and secure, or anxious and fearful, were each of your parents?

_____

_____

_____

'Reality of Love' Graph

Which one of the following statements comes nearest to your parents' attitude towards love?

1. Love as such does not exist on this planet. It is like 'security', a word used to describe an ideal state which is conspicuously absent in life.

2. Love has been expressed in the world by a few special teachers, such as Jesus Christ and the Buddha, but it is quite out of reach to us mere mortals.

3. I notice other people expressing love, but I am not sure I have ever felt it within myself, and so I have some personal difficulty in relating to it.

4. I know I am capable of giving and receiving love, and I can feel it in myself and many others.

5. I try to love freely, fully and fearlessly to the best of my ability.

6. I am pure love. All else is only fear, illusion and talk.

Mark on the graph below to indicate where they would have placed themselves. Use 'M' for mother, and 'F' for father.

1	2	3	4	5	6

How does your assessment of your parents relate to your own response to the same statements and graph in Session One? (p. 22)

_____

_____

_____

_____

Be alert to the possibility that their beliefs and behaviour may have conditioned your own. We will ask you from time to time to compare your experience with that of your parents to gain insight into how they may have influenced you.

'Major Block to Love' Symbol and Drawing

One method we use regularly throughout the course to learn more about a given topic is to ask you to close your eyes, turn your attention inward and invite to come into your awareness an image or sense which symbolises or represents the topic. We then ask you to examine the symbol for whatever quality, meaning or message it suggests to you. Drawing the symbol then helps you to capture, clarify and assimilate the experience. Thus you bypass your cognitive mind and call upon other creative functions and sources of information and inspiration within you.

We now learn more about your major block to love by using this method.

Find a comfortable position, sitting up straight . . . Close your eyes . . . Take several long, slow, deep breaths . . . Relax your body completely . . . Release all of the tension . . . Allow whatever emotions you may be feeling to fade away . . . Do the same with your thoughts . . . Become like a calm, quiet lake, which mirrors perfectly the blue sky, or the starry sky in the silence of the night . . . Be at peace, and yet remain alert . . .

When you are ready, ask yourself the question, *'WHAT IS MY MAJOR BLOCK OR BARRIER TO BRINGING MORE LOVE INTO MY LIFE — WHAT PREVENTS ME FROM LOVING MORE FULLY?'* . . . Then allow an image or sense to come to you which represents an answer to this question . . . Take your time . . . Wait patiently in the silence, knowing that something will soon come to you . . . Be willing to accept whatever comes without judging, censoring or rejecting it . . . Simply be ready to observe and examine it, with the purpose of learning more about it . . .

As you begin to sense something, allow it to become more vivid . . . Note its size and shape . . . Its density and design . . . Its colour and texture . . . Explore it with as many of your senses as you can . . . Find the overall quality it suggests to you . . .

Then open your eyes and express in a drawing below either the image itself or its quality . . . If nothing has come to you, open your eyes, hold the question in mind and begin to draw freely and spontaneously, letting something come to you in that way . . .

MY MAJOR BLOCK TO LOVE

Write down the overall *quality* of the symbol and any other words, feelings or thoughts which came to you during the exercise, or which you are aware of now. What new insight or awareness does this symbol and its quality give to you.

_____

_____

_____

_____

Messages and 'Shoulds' Conditioning

We find that blocks and barriers to love often take the form of self-doubts, beliefs and fears which can be traced back to childhood conditioning.

We have already said that many of our attitudes and beliefs were formed quite early in life, taken unconsciously from others around us. We absorbed positive and negative messages, both directly in so many words (for example, a parent who may have said, 'You can't trust people!'), and indirectly through observation of behaviour (a parent's beliefs or actions which may have conveyed, 'Life is a struggle.')

Often these messages have an accompanying warning, either expressed or implied, which we call 'shoulds', because of the language these warnings usually use: 'You *should* always do this, or you *should* never do that.'

Unless we re-evaluate them later in life as mature, discerning adults, we take these messages and 'shoulds' for granted, and they form our attitudes, beliefs and other ways of being which simply continue automatically through habit, without ever having been a deliberate choice upon our part.

Consequently, we now continue to explore your childhood experience to find out some of the messages and 'shoulds' you absorbed at the time and how you feel about them now.

Close your eyes . . . Sit up straight . . . Take a few deep breaths . . . Relax . . . Allow your body, emotions and thoughts to become still . . . Become like a calm, quiet lake . . .

When you are ready, allow to come to you an image or sense of your mother, or whoever took the mothering role in your childhood . . . Ask yourself the question, *'WHAT MESSAGE AND 'SHOULD' ABOUT LOVE DID I LEARN FROM HER?'* either directly in so many words or indirectly by observation? . . . Second, *'HOW DOES THAT MESSAGE AND 'SHOULD' MAKE ME FEEL NOW?'* . . .

_____

_____

_____

_____

_____

_____

Close your eyes again . . . Take a few deep breaths . . . And relax . . .

When you are ready, allow to come to you an image or sense of your father, or whoever took the fathering role in your childhood . . . Ask yourself the question, *'WHAT MESSAGE AND 'SHOULD' ABOUT LOVE DID I LEARN FROM HIM?'* either directly in so many words, or indirectly by observation? . . . Second, *'HOW DOES THAT MESSAGE AND 'SHOULD' MAKE ME FEEL NOW?'* . . .

_____

_____

_____

_____

_____

_____

Close your eyes again . . . Take a few deep breaths . . . And relax . . .

When you are ready, allow to come to you an image or sense of a close relative from your childhood, perhaps a brother, sister, grandparent, aunt, uncle, or cousin . . . Ask yourself the question, *'WHAT MESSAGE AND 'SHOULD' ABOUT LOVE DID I LEARN FROM THAT PERSON?'* either directly in so many words or indirectly by observation? . . . Second, *'HOW DOES THAT MESSAGE AND 'SHOULD' MAKE ME FEEL NOW?'* . . .

_____

_____

_____

_____

Close your eyes again . . . Take a few deep breaths . . . And relax . . .

When you are ready, allow to come to you an image or sense of a religious leader or teacher from your childhood . . . Ask yourself the question, *'WHAT MESSAGE AND 'SHOULD' ABOUT LOVE DID I LEARN FROM THAT PERSON?'* either directly in so many words, or indirectly by observation? . . . Second, *'HOW DOES THAT MESSAGE AND 'SHOULD' MAKE ME FEEL NOW?'* . . .

_____

_____

_____

_____

_____

One last time, close your eyes . . . Take a few deep breaths . . . And relax . . .

When you are ready, allow to come to you an image or sense of a person or a situation from the mass media from your childhood, perhaps from radio, television, cinema, video, books or magazines . . . Ask yourself the question, *'WHAT MESSAGE AND 'SHOULD' ABOUT LOVE DID I LEARN FROM THAT PERSON OR SITUATION?'* either directly in so many words or indirectly by observation? . . . Second, *'HOW DOES THAT MESSAGE AND 'SHOULD' MAKE ME FEEL NOW?'* . . .

_____

_____

_____

_____

Examine the messages and 'shoulds' you learned about love as a child from others. Observe how you have said each one makes you feel now. Mark with a plus (+) sign the messages and 'shoulds' which you agree with now as an adult, and which you *choose* deliberately and freely to follow. Mark with a minus (-) sign those which you disagree with now, and which you *choose* deliberately to discard.

Then close your eyes, take several deep breaths, and relax . . . Visualise one at a time each person from whom you learned the messages and 'shoulds' you wish to discard. In your imagination, picture yourself handing them back to that person. Tell that person, *'HERE, TAKE THEM BACK. THEY ARE YOURS. THEY ARE NOT MINE. I DO NOT WANT THEM. I WISH TO BE FREE OF THEM. I CHOOSE NOW TO RETURN THEM TO YOU.'* Continue this ritual until you have given them all back to the appropriate people, and you feel that you have let go of all the unwanted messages and 'shoulds'.

'Shoulds' Scan

Finally, when you are ready, say to yourself, *'AS A LOVING PERSON, I SHOULD . . .'* and complete the sentence with a word or short phrase — whatever comes spontaneously to you. Do not *think* about it. Write down the first response which comes. Then do it again, this time allowing a new word or phrase to emerge. Write down the new response. If you blank out momentarily, simply begin again, knowing that something will soon come to you. Repeat the process again and again for at least ten minutes, or until you have filled the space below.

AS A LOVING PERSON, I SHOULD . . .

Next examine your responses. Mark with a plus (+) sign the 'shoulds' *which are now freely and fully your own choice*. Mark with a minus (-) sign the 'shoulds' which may represent someone else's beliefs or standards which you now *choose* to discard.

What valid and useful messages have you learned about love from these exercises?

_____

_____

_____

_____

What have you learned about the power of social conditioning upon you?

_____

_____

_____

_____

What have you learned about yourself?

_____

_____

_____

_____

Write down any feelings, thoughts and questions you wish to record.

_____

_____

_____

_____

_____

_____

Perhaps you now have a clearer sense of how you formed some of your beliefs about people, relationships, love and for that matter about the world and life in general. It is empowering and freeing to distinguish which of your beliefs and behaviours are a result of unconscious childhood conditioning, and which are a result of a free and deliberate choice on your part as an adult.

NOTE. The exercises and techniques in this course are quite adaptable. Consider them as *all-purpose tools* which you may use in a great variety of ways. For example, at another time you might wish to repeat the exercises in Part 4 to learn more about yourself in relation to other qualities which may be important to you, such as courage, faith, honesty, joy, peace, strength or trust.

Next in Part 5 we examine the role which fear plays in blocking you from making the choice to bring more love into your life.

PART 5. DEVELOPING POTENTIAL

Blocks, Shadows and Fears

Some people refer to their inner blocks as their 'shadow,' or the 'dark' side of themselves, making them appear mysterious, even ominous, and difficult if not impossible to master.

This course takes a more positive approach to resolving inner blocks and barriers. We are guided by Italian psychiatrist Dr. Roberto Assagioli, the founder of Psychosynthesis, who says in *The Act Of Will*:

> *Many people fear love, fear opening themselves to another human being, a group or an ideal. Sincere and honest self-examination and self-analysis, or an analysis conducted with the help of others, are the means of discovering and unmasking, and then getting rid of, these resistances and fears.*

He suggests that the way to deal with the 'shadow' is simply to walk side-by-side with it out into the light, that is, into the light of our awareness, for therein lies the power of choice. As we become aware of our blocks, recognising and accepting them as a part of ourselves, we can then choose to do something about them if we wish.

It is the specific intention of this course to help you conduct this 'sincere and honest self-examination and self-analysis', to identify and deal with your fears and resistances so that you may make the choice of bringing more love into your life.

'Fear' Check-list

We have entitled this session *Choosing To Feel Safe* because we have found that the primary reason most of us do not make the choice to love more freely and fully is that we feel unsafe and insecure in some way about people, relationships, love or life itself. We fear whatever might happen if we open ourselves to giving and receiving love more readily.

What is fear? It begins as a thought, anticipating the possibility of an unwanted happening of some kind. The thought is quickly followed by one or more of a range of emotional reactions — anxiety, dread, panic, terror — accompanied by feelings of uneasiness, vulnerability and worry.

Listed below are common fears which many of us have. Mark the fears which you imagine could be blocking you from making the choice of bringing more love into your life.

_____	Fear of being abused or used	_____	Fear of losing control
_____	Fear of being hurt	_____	Fear of losing sense of self
_____	Fear of commitment, responsibility	_____	Fear of manipulation
_____	Fear of entrapment	_____	Fear of powerlessness
_____	Fear of failure	_____	Fear of rejection
_____	Fear of intimacy	_____	Fear of the unknown

Write down other fears you have experienced regarding people, relationships and love.

_____

_____

_____

_____

Most of us have fears. Therefore the task is to recognise our fears and their effect upon us, then to accept them as a part of us and finally to diminish or eliminate their limiting influence upon us.

How much do your fears influence you? How strong are they? How limiting are they?

_____

_____

_____

_____

When and how do your fears make your relationship decisions for you? When and how do you allow them to stop you from being or doing something?

_____

_____

_____

_____

What is the worst part of having your fears? What is the best part?

_____

_____

_____

_____

How do you usually cope with an uncomfortable feeling such as fear? What methods work for you? What do you actually do?

_____

_____

_____

_____

Family Fear Patterns

Was there a typical family pattern regarding fear when you were a child? What messages and 'shoulds' about fear did you learn directly or indirectly from your mother and father?

_____

_____

_____

What specific fears did they have? How strong and limiting were their fears?

_____

_____

_____

_____

How did your mother and father express their fears? How did they each cope with them? What did they actually do?

_____

_____

_____

_____

Examine your responses so far here in Part 5. Do you find any similarities between your fear patterns and those of your parents? Often 'the apple never falls very far from the tree'. Is it true for you in this case? If so, take heart, knowing it is a behaviour pattern you have absorbed from others which you can begin to change whenever you are ready.

'Fear' Symbol and Drawing

Thus far we have been exploring your fear in general terms. Now we seek subjectively and symbolically the *specific* fear which stops you from bringing more love into your life. Identifying your fear is the first step towards resolving it.

Find a comfortable position, sitting up straight . . . Close your eyes . . . Take several long, slow, deep breaths . . . Relax your body completely . . . Release all of the tension . . . Allow whatever emotions you may be feeling to fade away . . . Do the same with your thoughts . . . Become like a calm, quiet lake, which mirrors perfectly the blue sky, or the starry sky in the silence of the night . . . Be at peace, and yet remain alert . . .

When you are ready, ask yourself the question, '*WHAT IS THE SPECIFIC FEAR WHICH STOPS ME FROM BRINGING MORE LOVE INTO MY LIFE?*' . . . Then allow an image or sense to come to you which represents an answer to this question . . . Take your time . . . Wait patiently in the silence, knowing that something will soon come to you . . . Be willing to accept whatever comes without judging, censoring or rejecting it . . . Simply be ready to observe and examine it with the purpose of learning more about it . . .

As you begin to sense something, allow it to become more vivid . . . Note its size and shape . . . Its density and design . . . Its colour and texture . . . Explore it with as many of your senses as you can . . . Find the overall quality it suggests to you . . .

Then open your eyes, and express in a drawing below either the image itself or its quality . . . If nothing has come to you, open your eyes, hold the question in mind and begin to draw freely and spontaneously, letting something come to you in that way . . .

THE FEAR WHICH STOPS ME FROM BRINGING MORE LOVE INTO MY LIFE

What is the specific fear which stops you from bringing more love into your life? Write down the overall *quality* of the symbol and any other words, feelings or thoughts which came to you during the exercise, or which you are aware of now. What new insight or awareness does this symbol and its quality give to you?

Functions of Fears

All of our personality patterns, including our fears and other blocks, have two primary functions. First, they *limit* us in some way. They hold us back, curtail our freedom, prevent us from changing and growing. In what specific ways does the fear you identified above limit you?

Second, our patterns *serve* us in some way. They help us to achieve whatever we want consciously or unconsciously (such as a sense of security, freedom or empowerment), and to avoid what we do not want (such as anxiety, pain or responsibility.) One method to find out how a personality pattern serves us is to ask ourself what we would lose or miss if it were *not* there as a part of us.

In what specific ways does the fear above serve you?

_____

_____

_____

_____

Fear also involves a loss of control, and usually another loss as well. For example, fear of entrapment concerns the loss of freedom. Fear of rejection concerns the loss of self-esteem. Fear of being over-whelmed concerns the loss of a sense of self. With the fear above, what are you at risk of losing?

_____

_____

_____

_____

Your response reflects the underlying issue at stake, the one which your fear is concerned with, and which needs to be addressed and resolved before you can feel safe and secure enough to make the choice of bringing more love into your life. To help you to address your fears and their underlying issues and concerns, this course presents more than 125 exercises and techniques which you may apply towards resolving your inner blocks and barriers, including your fears.

Fear and Taking Risks

Bringing more love into your life means facing your fears and taking risks. Risks have outcomes which can be desirable or undesirable, pleasant or unpleasant. Risks do not always have a 'positive' outcome. Our challenge then is to keep going and keep risking, as the risks which do not seem to work out give us as much as the ones which do, but in a different way.

When and how do you take risks? When and how do you avoid taking risks?

_____

_____

_____

_____

_____

_____

What messages and 'shoulds' have you learned from others about taking risks?

_____

_____

_____

_____

Here is a poem about risks by an unknown author.

> *To laugh is to risk appearing the fool.*
> *To weep is to risk appearing sentimental.*
> *To reach out for another is to risk involvement.*
> *To expose feelings is to risk exposing your true self.*
> *To place your true ideas, your dreams before a crowd is to risk their loss.*
> *To love is to risk not being loved in return.*
> *To live is to risk dying.*
> *To hope is to risk despair.*
> *To try is to risk failure.*
>
> *But risk must be taken*
> *Because the greatest hazard in life is to risk nothing.*
> *People who risk nothing, do nothing, are nothing.*
> *They may avoid suffering and sorrow,*
> *But they cannot learn, feel, grow, change, love, live.*
> *Chained by their attitudes, they are slaves.*
> *They have forfeited their freedom.*
> *Only the person who risks is free.*

Danish philosopher Søren Kierkegaard says clearly and simply: 'To risk is to lose your footing for a while. Not to risk is to lose your life.'

What is your reaction to these two observations about the need to take risks? What are your feelings and thoughts about them?

_____

_____

_____

_____

How willing are you to risk loving another person, and to risk another loving you? What do you imagine is the biggest risk you could take concerning love? What makes it a risk for you?

_____

_____

_____

What is the underlying issue or concern — what could you lose? What could you gain? What would it be like to have more love in your life?

_____

_____

_____

_____

Next in Part 6 we begin to address your blocks and barriers.

PART 6. APPLYING IT

Many of us might have the goal always to feel completely safe and secure. But such a goal is an illusion, as life just is not this way — even the most secure and well-balanced people often confront life in unsafe moments. Therefore our basic task is rather to (1) be true to ourselves; (2) create as much security and safety in our lives as possible; but (3) accept that we can be who we are even if we do not feel safe. It is ultimately a question of priorities and how we focus our attention and energy. The following exercise serves to illustrate this point.

Autogenic Training

Our blocks and barriers stop the natural flow of love within us. Our fears take control of us. Consequently many of us today suffer from pressure, tension and stress, often as a result of our insecurities, anxieties and resistance to making needed changes in our lives.

We know that stress can kill us through strokes and heart disease. Even before reaching that extreme, stress also drains off our vitality and clarity, producing fatigue and illness. Survival and other security issues can become more important to us, and we then have less time and attention to give to other rungs of the ladder of life including love.

This course therefore begins to address our blocks and barriers at the level of reducing physical and psychological stress in daily life so that we may have the time, attention and readiness to make the choice of bringing more love into our life.

In his book *90 Days to Self-Health,* C. Norman Shealy M.D. presents a system of mental exercises designed to help us learn to regulate our own body functioning at will. We can thus induce relaxation and reduce many of the symptoms of stress and anxiety, including muscular tension, headaches and insomnia. We have adapted the following exercise from Dr. Shealy, who credits the original 1930s' autogenic research of German psychiatrist J.H. Schultz and Wolfgang Luthe.

Find a comfortable position, either sitting up straight or lying down . . . Close your eyes . . . Take a few deep breaths . . . Relax . . . Allow your body, emotions and thoughts to become still . . . Become like a calm, quiet lake . . .

When you are ready, on each in-breath say to yourself (think the thought, feel the feeling), *'MY ARMS AND LEGS ARE . . .'* and on each out-breath, *'. . . HEAVY AND WARM . . .'* Actually feel the truth of the statement . . . Feel the heaviness . . . Feel the warmth . . . Know it is so . . . For two minutes say this statement to yourself over and over again, taking long, slow, deep breaths . . . As you do, realise it as an experienced fact . . .

Then on each in-breath say to yourself, *'MY HEARTBEAT IS . . .'* and on each out-breath, *'. . . CALM AND REGULAR . . .'* Actually feel the truth of the statement . . . Feel your heartbeat . . . Feel how calm it is . . . Feel how regular it is . . . Know it is so . . . For two minutes repeat this statement, taking long, slow, deep breaths . . . As you do, realise it as an experienced fact . . .

Then on each in-breath, say to yourself, *'MY BREATHING IS . . .'* and on each out-breath, *'. . . FREE AND EASY . . .'* Actually feel the truth of the statement . . . Feel the freedom . . . Feel the ease . . . Know it is so . . . For two minutes repeat this statement, taking long, slow, deep breaths . . . As you do, realise it as an experienced fact . . .

Then on each in-breath say to yourself, *'MY ABDOMEN . . .'* and on each out-breath, *'. . . IS WARM . . .'* Actually feel the truth of the statement . . . Feel the warmth in your abdomen . . . Know it is so . . . For two minutes repeat this statement, taking long, slow, deep breaths . . . As you do, realise it as an experienced fact . . .

Then on each in-breath say to yourself, *'MY FOREHEAD . . .'* and on each out-breath, *'. . . IS COOL . . .'* Actually feel the truth of the statement . . . Feel how cool your forehead is . . . Know it is so . . . For two minutes repeat this statement, taking long, slow, deep breaths . . . As you do, realise it as an experienced fact . . .

Then on each in-breath say to yourself, *'MY MIND IS . . .'* and on each out-breath, *'. . . QUIET AND STILL . . .'* Actually feel the truth of the statement . . . Feel how quiet and still your mind is becoming . . . Know it is so . . . For two minutes repeat this statement, taking long, slow, deep breaths . . . As you do, realise it as an experienced fact . . .

Then on each in-breath say to yourself, *'I AM CALM AND RELAXED . . .'* and on each out-breath, *'. . . AND FREE FROM ALL STRESS . . .'* Actually feel the truth of the statement . . . Feel the calm . . . Feel the relaxation . . . Feel the absence of stress . . . Know it is so . . . For two minutes repeat this statement, taking long, slow, deep breaths . . . As you do, realise it as an experienced fact . . .

Now put all seven statements together and repeat them in turn for another five minutes.

In subsequent periods, simply repeat all seven statements in turn for a total of twenty minutes. Use a kitchen timer to tell you when to stop.

As an experiment, do this exercise for twenty minutes twice a day for at least seven days, and notice the difference it makes in your stress level, sleep pattern, general health and sense of well-being. You may find its benefits so appealing that you choose to continue to make it a regular practice.

NOTE. Try this exercise only when you can choose freely to do it, rather than taking it on as another 'should' with its own added pressure.

Taking Risks

One method of dealing with fears is to confront them directly by taking manageable risks.

Here is an exercise to help you to identify and begin to transform your fears associated with taking risks in relationships.

Close your eyes . . . Sit up straight . . . Take a few deep breaths . . . Relax . . . Allow your body, emotions and thoughts to become still . . . Become like a calm, quiet lake . . .

When you are ready, say to yourself, *'IF I HAD THE COURAGE, I WOULD . . .'* and complete the sentence with a word or short phrase — whatever comes spontaneously to you. Do not *think* about it. Write down the first response which comes. Then do it again, this time allowing a new word or phrase to emerge. Write down the new response. If you blank out momentarily, simply begin again, knowing that something will soon come to you. Repeat it again and again for at least ten minutes, or until you have filled the space below.

IF I HAD THE COURAGE I WOULD . . .

What did you feel as you were doing the exercise? What are you feeling and thinking now?

_____

_____

_____

_____

Examine your responses. Mark the ideas which you feel are worth considering.

Now select one of them which you are willing to begin to put into action *within the next seven days*. Write it down, beginning with, *'I WILL . . .'*

_____

_____

_____

_____

What makes it a risk for you? What is the fear? What could you lose?

_____

_____

_____

_____

What would be the best possible outcome of taking this risk?

_____

_____

_____

What would be the worst possible outcome of taking this risk? How willing are you to accept such an outcome?

_____

_____

_____

_____

It is important for you to give your full 100 per cent support to any risk you choose to take. Affirm below, '*I AM COMPLETELY WILLING TO TAKE THIS RISK AND TO ACCEPT ITS OUTCOME.*' Then record any feelings and thoughts which writing your affirmation may prompt.

_____

_____

_____

_____

Next find a first step you can take to help bring it about. Be specific about when, where, and how you plan to carry it out.

Then take the risk. Put your plan into action *before you begin the next session of this course*. Be ready to report your experience of risking at the beginning of Session Three.

Ask yourself spontaneously several times a day, '*WHAT RISK DO I NEED TO BE TAKING RIGHT NOW?*' Whether or not you decide to take a risk is always your choice, but asking the question regularly helps you to become aware of creative alternatives in your life, and keeps you from feeling stuck.

Suggested Reading

1. *Feel the Fear and Do It Anyway,* by Susan Jeffers, says that taking action is the key to your success in handling fear, and that knowing you can handle anything which comes your way allows you to take risks. This book provides many ideas for increasing your sense of personal empowerment and fulfilment.

2. *Love is Letting Go of Fear,* by Gerald Jampolsky M.D., states: 'Although Love is always what we really want, we are often afraid of Love without consciously knowing it, and so we may act both blind and deaf to Love's presence. Yet, as we help ourselves and each other let go of fear, we begin to experience a personal transformation.'

3. *Risking,* by David Viscott says that you have to take risks for your life to get better. 'There is simply no way you can grow without taking chances. When you have an objective worth risking for, your actions become purposeful, your life begins to make sense, and then no risk can hold you back.'

Personal Goal

In addition to your chosen risk, consider various simple, specific, observable actions you could take within the next few days which would be a step towards bringing more love into your life. Then choose one which seems important to you, one to take as a personal goal. Make a deliberate choice to achieve it. Write it down. Remember, making and implementing choices empowers and strengthens you.

_____

_____

_____

_____

Session Learnings

Turn back and review what you have done in this session. Then write down the three most important insights or learnings you have gained from it.

_____

_____

_____

_____

_____

_____

_____

_____

Purpose

As we stated at the beginning of Part 2, the purpose of Session Two is to identify whatever blocks you from making the choice of bringing more love into your life. To what degree has Session Two achieved its general purpose for you?

_____

_____

_____

_____

Congratulations! You have come to the end of Session Two. Please discuss your experience of this session with your support person *before you begin Session Three.*

CHOOSING TO TRUST

PART 1. MAKING CONNECTIONS

Begin by reviewing Session Two to reconnect with your process of development. Have you achieved the personal goal you set for yourself? How was it?

Next write about your experience of choosing and taking a risk. How did your risk go? How did you feel at the time you took the risk? Any resistance? How do you feel about it now? What have you learned about yourself from the experience?

NOTE. If you have not taken your risk from Session Two yet, do not continue with Session Three until you have completed it. The course is designed to be taken one step at a time in sequence, with the exercises arranged to lead you to your desired objective. Otherwise by choosing not to do some of the exercises (even if you tell yourself that you will come back to them at a more convenient time), you may sabotage the very outcome you seek from this course.

Continue with these personal journal pages by *making connections with the theme, issues and exercises of this course*, recording whatever relevant memories, ideas, feelings, insights, dreams, 'unfinished business', interactions and other events in your inner and outer worlds have occurred since you completed Session Two. Include related reading you may have done, questions on your mind and any other observations and connections with the course you wish to make.

_____

_____

_____

_____

_____

_____

_____

_____

_____

_____

_____

_____

_____

_____

_____

_____

_____

_____

_____

_____
_____
_____
_____
_____
_____
_____
_____
_____
_____
_____
_____
_____
_____
_____
_____
_____
_____
_____
_____
_____
_____
_____
_____
_____
_____
_____
_____
_____
_____
_____
_____
_____

Next in Part 2 we take stock of how trusting you are.

PART 2. TAKING STOCK

Purpose

The purpose of Session Three is to explore personal trust within a spiritual context, and to present techniques to increase your trust in yourself and others.

'Trust' Assessment

In the last session you identified one or more blocks which stop you from making the choice of bringing more love into your life. Often such blocks make it difficult or impossible for us to trust ourself and others.

What is trust? Trust is a certainty, confidence or conviction in someone or something. Trust believes in, has faith in and depends upon someone or something. Trust usually develops only after our basic safety and security needs are addressed.

How trusting are you? Take a moment to consider each situation listed below. Then, in the blank, put the number of the statement which comes nearest to how you generally feel in the situation.

1. I am never trusting.
2. I am rarely trusting.
3. I am sometimes trusting.
4. I am usually trusting.
5. I am always trusting.

_____ With my mother.
_____ With my father.
_____ With family/other relatives.
_____ With people of the same sex.
_____ With people of the opposite sex.
_____ With lovers/mates/partners.
_____ With most friends.
_____ With most strangers.
_____ With people at school/at work.
_____ With supervisors/others in authority.
_____ With doctors/dentists/other health professionals.
_____ With salespeople/shop assistants/waiters.
_____ With people on the street/in large crowds.
_____ With foreigners/people in foreign countries.
_____ With the future.
_____ With God

Add up your ratings, divide by 16 and write your average rating here _____.

The higher your score, the more trusting you are, and therefore the more ready and willing you are to love and to be loved.

How do you feel about trust? What does trust mean to you?

_____

_____

_____

_____

How trusting are you? How does trust work in your life — or not?

_____

_____

_____

_____

Do you give trust freely and easily to others, or must it be earned? Where and how do you place limits upon your trust?

_____

_____

_____

_____

Would you like to be more trusting than you are? Are you willing to be more trusting?

_____

_____

_____

_____

Are you willing to take risks with giving your trust? If not, why not?

_____

_____

_____

_____

Why are you not more trusting than you are? What is the source or cause of your distrust?

_____

_____

_____

_____

What would it take for you to be more trusting generally, or for you to trust more easily than you do?

_____

_____

_____

_____

How trusting were your parents: of each other, of you, of people in general, of life, of God? What message and 'should' did you learn about trust from them?

_____

_____

_____

_____

Have you ever trusted someone, only to discover later that your trust was misplaced or betrayed? How did it make you feel? How did you react?

_____

_____

_____

_____

Write down the name of a person you trusted completely and who honoured and upheld your trust. How did it feel to be so trusting? If you have never trusted anyone completely, how does it make you feel to be this way?

_____

_____

_____

_____

Trust and Security

Personal trust is rooted in a sense of security. Where do you find security? What do you rely upon to keep you feeling safe? What makes you feel secure?

_____

_____

_____

How effective is it? How reliable is it? To what degree can you trust it?

_____

_____

_____

Trust and Belief About Life

Personal trust often relates to the beliefs people have about the nature of life. For example some people believe that everyone and everything in life are part of an organised, trustworthy divine plan which has order, meaning and purpose. Others hold the opposite view, that is, everything in life happens completely by chance in a totally random fashion, without any such order, meaning or purpose, and therefore without any basis for trust.

What do you believe? Do you find order and purpose in life? Or does it all seem rather random, haphazard and meaningless to you?

_____

_____

_____

_____

'Trust and Belief About God' Graph

Personal trust also relates to faith and the beliefs people have about God. Mark an X on the graph below to indicate your belief about God. It may be between two statements and numbers.

    1 = I am an atheist. I know that God does not exist; there is no God.
    2 = I am an agnostic. I do not know whether or not God exists.
    3 = I am a believer. I have faith and trust that God does exist; there is a God.
    4 = I am a human personality, and I have the divine spirit of God within me.
    5 = I am a pure, divine being, God-like, and I have a human personality through
        which I express and function.

1	2	3	4	5

Mark where your mother and father would have placed themselves. Be alert to the possibility that their beliefs and behaviour may have conditioned your own.

Trust and Belief in Yourself

One principle this course is based upon is that we cannot love others until we love ourself. In a similar way, we may have difficulty in trusting others, trusting life, trusting even God, because we have difficulty in trusting ourself. Do you always trust yourself completely? Or might there be one or more parts of yourself which you sometimes question, judge and do not trust?

_____

_____

_____

_____

In our workshop some people find these and the following questions quite thought-provoking. You may wonder why we include them in a course called *Bringing More Love Into Your Life: The Choice Is Yours*. If so, you may find that your queries are answered by the time you complete this session.

PART 3. EXPLORING PERSPECTIVES

EILEEN

Faith comes with practice. Live by faith until it becomes rocklike and unshakeable, and find the true freedom of the spirit. — Flight Into Freedom

Once I was reading the Bible and I read a passage which I had read many times, but this time the words seemed to stand out for me, and I wondered what they meant. These were the words of Jesus: 'If you have faith as a grain of mustard seed, you will say to this mountain, "Move from here to there," and it will move; and nothing will be impossible to you.' (*Matthew 17:20, Revised Standard Version*)

As I thought about these words and meditated upon them, I wondered what could be the highest and seemingly most insurmountable mountain standing in front of humanity right now, one which needs to be removed through 'faith as a grain of mustard seed'. The mountain which came to me was 'fear'. I feel there is so much fear in the world that it is like a canker, eating away all of the good, the positive, the beautiful, and leaving all of the negative and rotten. It is strangling humanity.

Fear is one of our greatest enemies. I know it can hold me back from doing what I need to do. But I realise that unless I am willing to face my fears, I can never get rid of them. I have found that as long as I try to avoid my fears, they can become like monsters, and when I have the courage to confront them, they begin to become more manageable, and sometimes even fade away into nothingness.

The way I deal with my fears is with faith and prayer. Faith is greater and more powerful than fear. I affirm my faith and trust that all is well with the world, that a vast plan is unfolding, that all is in the hands of the Creator and that whatever is happening in my life is for the very best.

How do I pray? To set the pace for the day, I have a time of attunement in the early morning on awakening, before my mind can become embroiled in all the events and activities of the day. I find my life then is like a clean canvas without a mark on it. For me, these first strokes upon waking need to be very clear and definite, full of love, inspiration and expectancy for the new day ahead.

I tap into the highest level of my being, the God-Self, and communicate with it. I have faith that all my needs are being wonderfully met, even before I communicate them. This is where faith in my contact with the God-Self is so necessary. When I start the day off in this way, I know the day will be full of wonders because I am living in harmony with divine laws.

An example of faith is my house. I was told from within that I was to have a small house built. I could not imagine how it was going to be done. Where was the money, and where were the hands to build it? In faith, I simply had to hold the vision of this house in my consciousness, and never let it go. Then when I mentioned it to my son who is a builder living in the USA, he said he would be willing to give two months of his time to come to Scotland and put my house up for me. What a wonderful start! Then an architect said he would do the design as a gift. Step by step, I watched the whole plan unfold. It is so uplifting to watch a vision on the inner levels coming into outer manifestation! It is the way the whole of the Findhorn Foundation was brought about over many years.

I have learned that God's guidance comes to each of us very clearly, if we but still ourselves to hear it. I have been told many times from within that Truth is simplicity itself, and therefore that the smallest child can understand and follow God's word. God's ways may sometimes be very strange, but they are not complicated. Simplicity is God's hallmark. I try to follow this principle and never let my life become too complicated. If it does, I know it is of my own making.

For me faith and prayer are something which need to be used and lived daily.

DAVID

Faith is believing what you know ain't so. — Mark Twain

When I arrived at the Findhorn Foundation, I was a professed agnostic. I remember once saying to a friend, 'I know more than I understand; and I understand more than I believe.' I told myself that I was open about becoming a believer, but only after I understood the nature of God and how life and the universe function. I have always had a tremendous need to know, to understand and be understood. I have learned that such a need can often be a control pattern, a means we use to avoid experiencing our feelings by functioning predominantly upon an intellectual level.

Then a dear friend gave me a wall plaque with a quotation by Saint Augustine which helped to clarify the relationship between understanding and believing for me. 'Understanding is the reward of faith,' he said. 'Therefore seek not to understand that you may believe, but believe that you may understand.'

I became vaguely aware of three principal stages in the development of faith. The first stage is when *we know about God* as an intellectual concept; the second stage is when *we believe in God* as an absolute conviction; and the third stage is when *we know God* as an experiential reality. In my mid-forties by this time, I was only barely entering stage one. However not by accident had I been led from the USA to this spiritual community in the north of Scotland, where my eight-year residence, filled with many valuable lessons and blessings, will always be a high point of my life.

One early learning involved trust. I had been in the community a very short time and was still getting to know the 300 resident members. I remember meeting and chatting amiably with one of the cooks at Cluny Hill College. Within minutes he said to me, 'From your handshake I sense that you have an issue with control; you feel you need to be in control of circumstances around you.'

Without pausing he continued matter-of-factly, 'Underneath this pattern usually lies an issue of trust. I imagine you do not trust others. If you did, you would not have to worry about control. Furthermore, you do not trust others because there is probably some part of yourself which you do not trust. I imagine it all goes back to your having low self-esteem and harbouring doubts about yourself.' He was right on all counts! I was dumbfounded. He had attuned to me and quickly brought it all out into the open for me to recognise.

Later, while still at the Findhorn Foundation, I enrolled in a short course in a transpersonal or spiritually-based humanistic psychology called Psychosynthesis. It was led by Lady Diana Whitmore who had come to Scotland from her London centre. My life has never been the same since that week, as seeds were planted which I will be harvesting gratefully for the rest of my life. So impressed was I that I eventually moved to London to do a three-year professional course at the Psychosynthesis and Education Trust. During my studies, I had several deeply moving experiences while participating in the exercises which form an important and integral part of the training.

I learned that these exercises, as simple as they may appear, can have very positive, powerful and permanent effects. They can connect, unite and inspire the intellect, the heart and the soul. I have deep love and respect for Psychosynthesis principles and techniques, for they have brought me closer to my own sense of Self, my own intrinsic spiritual nature. For me, they are as precious as pure gold, and therefore I present them in this course with great enthusiasm and reverence.

Accordingly I have come to add a fourth stage in the development of faith, which is when we experience that 'the Kingdom of God is within you' (*Luke 17:21, King James Version*), and not 'out there' somewhere, and that we are inseparably one with the divine and, therefore, that *we are God.*

PART 4. GAINING AWARENESS

Spiritual Development

This course places learning to love within a transpersonal context, one in which our continuing spiritual development is an essential part of the process. The basic task is to develop a stable, integrated personality by discovering, accepting and transforming behaviour patterns which block us from expressing our full potential. Giving such attention to ourself may be likened to a gardener preparing the ground, digging around and enriching it before the planting takes place.

Then when we plant the seeds of Spirit, they have a more fertile, conducive environment in which to take root, grow and flourish. This transpersonal task, the subject of this session, may be likened to the dove of Spirit descending into matter or physical form. It is meant to nurture and support the personality by providing direction and by expressing a host of pure, universal qualities, such as courage, inspiration, joy, love and wisdom.

Sources of Security, Faith and Trust

Some of us rely on elements in our *external* environment to give us a sense of security: money in the bank, a house, a job, investments or another person such as a parent or partner.

Some of us also consciously and unconsciously create life patterns to help us to feel secure and trusting, such as loading ourself down with work and responsibility, and staying busy compulsively from morning to night; or being relentlessly manipulative and needing to stay in complete control of every aspect of our life; or distracting ourself regularly with food, alcohol, drugs, sex and other counter-productive activities to avoid feeling how very insecure and unhappy we are.

Even if these externally-oriented manoeuvres worked well over a long period of time (and they do not), these behaviour patterns cannot provide a very fulfilling life for us. In the end they serve only as cover-ups and compensations, and they do nothing about our underlying feelings of insecurity, fear and anxiety which not only remain untouched, but often only continue to grow.

Therefore in this session we explore our *internal* environment and what it offers to provide a sense of security — specifically trust, faith, prayer and the divinity within our being, and how they relate to bringing more love into our life.

We begin this deepening process by asking you to consider your highest aspirations. What do you want to get out of life? What are your deepest longings? Take a moment to consider them, and then write them down. It is all right if they seem vague or abstract to you now. They may clarify at a later time.

_____

_____

_____

_____

Sooner or later addressing the topic of trust usually brings up other questions, such as the nature of faith, the meaning and purpose of life, and who or what is God. They are big questions and are not easy to answer. Asking ourself such questions is more important than getting the 'right' answer. Our beliefs about life and the universe affect us and how we relate to others.

Again, it is perfectly all right if you do not have ready and complete answers to the questions which follow in this session, but do stop, consider and then try to put something down for each one of them.

What do you feel is the origin, meaning and purpose of life?

_____

_____

_____

_____

What do you feel is the meaning and purpose of *your* life?

_____

_____

_____

_____

Who or What is God?

One common image of God which many people encounter in childhood is that of a Caucasian man with a long white beard who sits on a throne in the clouds. Some people think of God as being a benevolent father, always warm and loving, while to others he can be fearsome, angry and vengeful. In either case, he is a very human God created in their image with very human qualities and imperfections.

Other people think of God not as a person but as an abstraction, a concept, a symbol or a quality, such as love, truth or wisdom. Some regard God as an organising principle, a creator, a source. Still others consider God as simply a body of natural laws in perpetual and impartial operation.

Others say the notion of God is only a convenient fairy tale, conceived to explain the unexplainable, and to make life seem less pointless and more purposeful and worth living. To them God is not a living reality and therefore does not affect their feelings, thoughts and actions.

How do you feel about God? What does God mean to you?

_____

_____

_____

_____

In our workshops we find that some people have great resistance to both the word and the reality of God, and they deplore our frequent use of the term. We acknowledge that, like the word love, God is a very emotionally-charged word for many people, and also that it is a relatively meaningless word for many others because they have no personal awareness or experience of the reality behind it.

How about you? Have you experienced any difficulty or discomfort with our use of the word God? If so, are you aware of why you react to it in such a way? Is there another term you can substitute which is more comfortable for you?

_____

_____

_____

_____

The God-Self

We say that God is who we are, our basic essence, the highest level of our being — in other words, a number five on the graph in Part 2. It is the sacred, unchanging aspect of us which some people call the Indwelling God, the God Immanent or the Higher Self. Psychosynthesis calls it the Transpersonal Self. In this course we call it the God-Self.

We use God-Self to refer to the permanent part of us which is pure essence, pure Spirit, the vital source of our life which is unaffected by our mind's chatter or bodily conditions. Our God-Self is the love, the truth, the wisdom and the power within the very core of our being which animate, integrate and direct our personality and our life.

Opening Doors Within contains this description of the relationship between our God-Self and ourself:

> *You are the point of light within My Mind.*
> *You are the point of love within My Heart.*
> *When you can accept it, when you can see yourself*
> *As the microcosm of the macrocosm,*
> *You will never again belittle yourself*
> *Or think ill of yourself.*
> *You will realise that you are indeed*
> *Made in My image and likeness,*
> *That we are one,*
> *And that nothing and no one can separate us.*
> *If you feel any separation from Me,*
> *It is of your own making,*
> *For I never separate Myself from you.*
>
> *You are individually*
> *What I AM universally.*
> *Is it any wonder you have to be born again*
> *To accept the wonder of this truth?*
>
> *So many souls have strayed so far from Me*
> *And have separated themselves to such an extent*
> *That they have placed Me in the heavens*
> *At such great heights*
> *That I am unapproachable.*
>
> *I AM within you*
> *Hidden in the very depths*
> *Waiting to be recognised and drawn forth.*

What is your reaction to this description? How does your heart respond to it? What are your feelings saying to you?

_____

_____

_____

_____

How does your intellect respond to it? What are your thoughts saying to you?

_____

_____

_____

_____

Faith

Some people use the word faith to signify the religious doctrine they follow, or the church to which they belong. Others use the word to mean belief or trust. Some people use it to refer to the convictions they hold which have no evidence or proof to support them. How do you feel about faith? What does faith mean to you?

_____

_____

_____

_____

How does faith function in your life? What is your personal faith?

_____

_____

_____

_____

Write down one example when you did something in faith, and it turned out perfectly.

_____

_____

_____

_____

To what degree do you see (or are you willing to see) your God-Self's influence in everything which happens in your life?

_____

_____

_____

_____

To what degree do you accept (or are you willing to accept) that good comes from everything which happens to you?

_____

_____

_____

_____

To what degree do you accept (or are you willing to accept) that all your needs are being met *now?*

_____

_____

_____

_____

We say that faith is intuitive by nature, that is, it perceives the reality of something which is not evident, and then accepts it. Faith, if nurtured, leads to a sense of certainty.

Have you ever looked at other people and wished that you could have the same strong, unwavering faith they have? Now is the time to realise you do have that same capacity for faith.

One way to begin is to use the faith we do have, no matter how small or unsteady it may feel, because as we use it, it will increase, becoming stronger and stronger. In learning to swim, sooner or later we must take our foot off the bottom and begin moving through the water, or we will never learn to swim. The same holds true with faith. We need to experiment with it, try it out and find out if it works. This process is the essence of faith, and is the way in which it grows.

Put simply, to learn to trust it, test it!

When you do, hold a positive attitude, for occasionally you may stumble and fall and experience a seeming failure. If it happens to you, do not be daunted and tempted to give up. Rather, be like an infant learning to walk: simply learn the lesson, get up and start again.

Prayer

Some people use prayer as an urgent and desperate plea for help at the eleventh hour when all else has failed. For others prayer is simply quiet meditation.

Some people regard prayer as muttering little memorised (or read) messages automatically, with little or no meaning for the one who is praying. Still others believe prayer is direct communication with God.

How do you feel about prayer? What does prayer mean to you?

_____

_____

_____

_____

Do you take time to send out a prayer as a powerful tool when you are in need of help, or do you not bother to use prayer?

_____

_____

_____

_____

Do you have the faith that your prayers will be heard and answered?

_____

_____

_____

_____

Do you know to whom you are praying when you pray?

_____

_____

_____

_____

We say that prayer is talking to our God-Self, communing with the highest level of our being. Meditation is listening for our God-Self to talk to us.

In either case it is only a local call, not a long-distance one, so we encourage you to do both regularly!

A Letter to God

We conclude Part 4 with a step towards strengthening open and active communion with your God-Self.

Your goal is to write a personal letter in which you express all you need to say to God. Include whatever feelings, thoughts, doubts, fears, resentments, judgements, questions, requests and appreciations which are inside you and perhaps have been for a very long time. Hold nothing back. Express it all now.

Today's date _____

Dear God,

_____

_____

_____

_____

_____

_____

_____

Next in Part 5 we explore your relationship with your God-Self.

PART 5. DEVELOPING POTENTIAL

God is Love

Some people spend a lifetime in search of God.

Searching for the God-Self within your being is like searching for the air when all the time you are breathing it. It is like searching for the sun when all the time you are seeing, walking and living in its light.

God is the love in your heart, whatever love you may be capable of expressing presently. To find your God-Self, you need go no further than your own kind act or loving thought. As you share your love, you share God with all you meet.

One aspect of bringing more love into your life, therefore, is learning how to contact, know and express your God-Self. The letter you wrote in Part 4 was a step in this direction. We now offer you another way to commune with your inherent divinity.

The following exercise is in two parts. The first part asks you to find and explore a symbol for your God-Self. The second part asks you to set aside some time when you can be by yourself without interruption in a room with two chairs.

'God-Self' Symbol and Drawing

Find a comfortable position, sitting up straight . . . Close your eyes . . . Take several long, slow, deep breaths . . . Relax your body completely . . . Release all of the tension . . . Allow whatever emotions you may be feeling to fade away . . . Do the same with your thoughts . . . Become like a calm, quiet lake, which mirrors perfectly the blue sky, or the starry sky in the silence of the night . . . Be at peace, and yet remain alert . . .

When you are ready, allow to come to you an image or sense which represents your own God-Self, the highest level of your being . . . Take your time . . . Wait patiently in the silence, knowing that something will soon come to you which represents your God-Self . . . Be willing to accept whatever comes without judging, censoring or rejecting it . . . Simply be ready to observe and examine it, with the purpose of learning more about it . . .

As you begin to sense something, allow it to become more vivid . . . Note its size and shape . . . Its density and design . . . Its colour and texture . . . Explore it with as many of your senses as you can . . . Find the overall quality it suggests to you . . .

Then open your eyes, and express in a drawing below either the image itself or its quality . . . If nothing has come to you, open your eyes, hold the question in mind and begin to draw freely and spontaneously, letting something come to you in that way . . .

```

                              MY GOD-SELF
```

Write down the overall *quality* of the symbol and any other words, feelings or thoughts which came to you during the exercise, or which you are aware of now. What new insight or awareness does this symbol and its quality give to you?

_____

_____

_____

_____

Chair Exercise with Your God-Self

The next part of this exercise needs to be done when you have a room to yourself without interruption for at least half an hour. Record this exercise as you do it, for later re-play and study.

First arrange two chairs facing each other a comfortable distance apart. Sit on one of them. Imagine that your God-Self is sitting on the opposite chair. Your task is to speak aloud directly to your God-Self.

Close your eyes . . . Sit up straight . . . Take a few deep breaths . . . Relax . . . Allow your body, emotions and thoughts to become still again . . . Become like a calm, quiet lake . . .

When you are ready, take a moment to consider what you have to say to your God-Self. For example what do you need from life and from your God-Self? What feedback do you want to give to your God-Self? What questions do you have to ask?

Begin to talk to your God-Self. Bring outside whatever is inside of you. In the beginning you may feel a bit awkward or embarrassed about talking aloud to an empty chair. (If you wish, place a cushion there to represent your God-Self and talk to it.) This is a perfectly normal reaction at first. Simply acknowledge your feelings and carry on. As a way of starting, you may wish to repeat some or all of whatever you said in your letter. Then continue with new things to say for a few minutes.

Open your eyes, look at your God-Self in the chair facing you and begin to speak aloud now before continuing with further instructions below.

After a while, when it seems right to you, remain silent for a moment, take a few deep breaths and then write down whatever you are feeling and thinking.

_____

_____

_____

_____

Next move to the second chair and sit down . . . Close your eyes . . . Take a few deep breaths . . . Relax . . . Allow your body, emotions and thoughts to become still again . . . Become like a calm, quiet lake.

When you are ready, allow to come to you the symbol representing your God-Self which you drew on the preceding page . . . Remember the qualities it conveyed to you . . . Begin to experience these qualities within you . . . Then in your imagination portray, impersonate, take on the role of your own God-Self . . . Try it on like a coat . . . Identify with it . . . Become it . . . Be it . . . How do you sit? . . . How do you hold your head? . . . Place your hands? . . . Position your feet? . . . What tone of voice do you use to address this Personality sitting opposite you?

As the God-Self, you have been listening to the Personality through which you must express and function . . . It has expressed itself to you in both feelings and thoughts . . . It has told you what it needs and probably much more . . . How do you respond to this Personality? . . . What do you have to say to it? . . .

Open your eyes and begin to speak aloud now before continuing with further instructions below.

After a while, when it seems right to you, remain silent for a moment, take a few deep breaths and then write down whatever you are feeling and thinking as the God-Self towards the Personality sitting in front of you.

_____

_____

_____

_____

Next move back to the first chair again . . . Take a few deep breaths . . . And relax . . . Your God-Self has been talking directly to you . . . How do you feel about what has been said? . . . What are your thoughts? . . .

_____

_____

_____

_____

For the next ten minutes or more, whatever seems right to you, continue to carry on a dialogue between these two aspects of yourself, moving back and forth regularly between the two chairs and taking time to reconnect with each aspect before speaking. Let it be a give-and-take conversation, rather than long speeches. Stay in the moment, without thinking or planning ahead. Find out how spontaneous you can be. Feel your feelings and allow them to come out as well as your thoughts.

Continue your dialogue now before proceeding with the instructions below.

In your own time, bring the dialogue to an end, take a few deep breaths and a gentle stretch.

What did you feel as you were doing the exercise? What are you feeling and thinking now?

_____

_____

_____

_____

Take a moment to consider the nature of the *relationship* between your Personality and your God-Self. How would you describe the way in which they have interacted? For example their relationship may have been as that between parent/child, teacher/student, master/servant, oracle/seeker, or they may have related as partners or friends or in other ways.

_____

_____

_____

_____

What other observations can you make about how they related to each other?

_____

_____

_____

_____

In this exercise do you find any similarity or connection between your relationship with your God-Self and your relationship with either or both of your parents?

_____

_____

_____

_____

An old saying is that when we get our relationship with God right, everything else in our life will be right. While we would agree, we also know it is common practice to take whatever unresolved issues we may have with our parents (such as trust, love, power, responsibility or authority) and to project or transfer them unconsciously onto our other relationships, including that with God. We thus repeat unwittingly and endlessly the nature of our parental relationships with others.

Therefore in this context, to get our relationship with God right, we need to get our relationship with our parents right. It means taking time and effort to recognise, accept, transform and integrate whatever beliefs and behaviour patterns prevent us from having wholesome, satisfying relationships. Then we will be more open and free to accept the reality of our own divinity, our God-Self. Time spent in doing such 'parent work' is never wasted and may be facilitated by a trained counsellor in individual or group sessions.

Now write down any other feelings, thoughts or questions you wish to record.

_____

_____

_____

_____

_____

_____

_____

Inner Problem-Solving

Take a moment to consider a current issue, problem or concern in your life about which you would like to have more information. Summarise it below.

_____

_____

_____

_____

Write down whatever you have already done about it, if anything.

_____

_____

_____

_____

Write down what you could do about it, the various options or alternatives you have and whatever you are actually ready and willing to do.

_____

_____

_____

_____

At the Findhorn Foundation, whenever a need for information or a decision occurs, community members, after some thought and discussion, usually close their eyes, take a few deep breaths and allow the required information to come to them from their own inner source of wisdom. It has been the principal method used by individuals and groups for making decisions in the community for more than 30 years.

This process is called *attunement*, for it enables us to attune to or connect with other aspects of ourself in addition to our cognitive mind, and then to allow whatever information or help we need to flow through this connection. We value attunement highly and include it regularly in our workshops and in this course.

You have already used a form of attunement when you have asked for images or other senses to come to you in response to a particular question or issue. You can use the same basic process to help find information, make decisions and solve problems. Here again, the form of response varies from person to person, and may come as images, words, sounds, feelings, a knowing or a sensing and in other ways as well. You will need to experiment with it to discover in what form it works for you.

The key is for you to be completely relaxed and centred within yourself, so that you make a deep contact with your own inner source of wisdom. Like most skills it may take some practice to increase your speed, clarity and accuracy, but if you stay with it, you will discover countless applications for attunement.

Attunement Exercise

Find a comfortable position, sitting up straight . . . Close your eyes . . . Take several long, slow, deep breaths . . . Relax your body completely . . . Release all of the tension . . . Allow whatever emotions you may be feeling to fade away . . . Do the same with your thoughts . . . Become like a calm, quiet lake, which mirrors perfectly the blue sky, or the starry sky in the silence of the night . . . Be at peace, and yet remain alert . . .

This time allow yourself to relax even more deeply . . . Count backwards slowly from ten to one, and on each succeeding number, feel yourself going farther and farther into the very centre of your being . . . Feel yourself making a connection with your own inner source of wisdom, that pure, permanent centre deep within you which has the answer to any question you could possibly ask about yourself.

When you are ready, silently ask your inner source of wisdom for the information or help you need about your issue, problem or concern . . . Take your time . . . Wait patiently in the silence, knowing that something will soon come to you, knowing the help you seek is already on its way, perhaps in images, words, feelings or in other ways . . . Give it several minutes to emerge . . .

In your own time, allow everything to fade . . . Count slowly from one to ten, and on each succeeding number, feel yourself returning to your normal level of alert wakefulness again . . . Bring your attention back to the room where you are now . . . Open your eyes . . . Take a deep breath . . . and a gentle stretch . . .

Write down whatever you wish to remember from this exercise, especially noting inner responses you may have received to your issue, problem or concern.

_____

_____

_____

_____

_____

_____

_____

What are your feelings and thoughts about using this method to connect directly with your own inner source of wisdom?

_____

_____

_____

_____

Need for Discernment

Some people may question the appropriateness and validity of using attunement for information-gathering, decision-making and problem-solving. You may ask, where is it coming from? Is 'the source of my inner wisdom' the same thing as my God-Self? How can I tell whether or not I am just making it all up in my mind? What about my instincts, wishes, fears and other feelings — can't they influence whatever prompting comes to me in the silence? How can I trust any of it?

These questions are all valid and important ones, and they indicate the need for continuous discernment and discrimination.

On one hand, whatever experience we have in the silence is worth exploring, as, like a dream, no matter what its source it can provide useful information about ourself. Obviously a key issue is our proper interpretation and understanding of whatever comes to us. We write everything down as a record, and then, if appropriate and we choose to do so, test it out, and note the results. As with faith, to strengthen our attunement, we need to use it.

On the other hand, the source we contact at any one time in our attunement can be from various aspects of our own *inner* life, including sensations, desires, emotions, thoughts, imaginings and intuitions, all valid and necessary psychological functions, but not the same as our God-Self, described earlier in this session.

The source we contact can also come from *outer* influences. It is said we all live in a psychic ocean, and many people pick up impressions from the environment consciously or unconsciously.

Furthermore, the source can change from moment to moment, depending upon how still and attuned we are able to remain.

Consequently give yourself time to determine how valid an inner prompting may be before deciding to act upon it. Until you have learned to discriminate as to the source of a prompting, do not allow yourself to be drawn into taking immediate action without first checking it.

As with any skill, the development of attunement requires time, effort, patience and regular practice.

Review the exercises in this session. How might systematic practice with them help you to increase your *trust* in yourself and others?

_____

_____

_____

_____

PART 6. APPLYING IT

Improving Yourself

Many of us are trying to improve ourselves, reading this and that literature, going to various lectures and workshops, studying under a master or teacher or are part of this group or that community. These activities are signs that we are searching for something. We are hungry for spiritual food.

We can be served the most delicious food, but we ourself have to digest it and assimilate it if it is to nourish us. The same holds true with spiritual food. We can be served the most wonderful ideas, but what do we do with them?

Find out which food — which spiritual path — is right for you, and then nourish yourself with it. Watch it grow and flourish within you. It all starts within you. By doing your own exploring, thinking, meditating and praying, you will be nourished. Your faith and trust will grow.

Prayer

Prayer relaxes us into God's presence. How then to pray? Start where you are and pray as you can. If you have no method of prayer, try this simple one.

Find a quiet time and place. Every day set aside a definite period as your appointment with your God-Self — once, twice, as often as you can, but not so often that you will not keep it. Set aside a definite length of time — ten, twenty, thirty minutes; as long as you can, but not so long that you will not stay with it.

To begin your daily periods of prayer, become as still in your body as you can. Practise relaxing, either sitting up straight or lying out flat. Stay relaxed, and yet remain alert so that you do not go to sleep.

Become as still in your mind as you can. Practise peaceful thinking. Realise that every thought you think is a prayer, whether you are praying formally or not. Do not let your thoughts rule you. Rule your thoughts. Let no doubts, fears or other life-depleting thoughts enter in; if they do, deliberately fix your mind on positive, loving, constructive thoughts. Form them into affirmations. Repeat them over and over again, silently if you must, aloud if you can.

In your appointment with your God-Self, make your prayers God-centred. Feel how you are one with God, think how you are one with God, affirm how you are one with God. Feel God's love, God's power. Feel God working in, through and for you. As you pray, bring God into every part of your life so that you share everything: your hopes and dreams, faults and failings, accomplishments and successes.

Dialogue with your God-Self. Ask your God-Self specific questions as you did in the chair exercise, only now go within yourself. Wait patiently for the answers to come in one form or another, either right away or later during the day, or even after several days. Remember God is never in a hurry and yet is always on time!

Pray for and with others. Keep a prayer journal, and note for whom and what you pray; save space for noting results.

Try this method of prayer for the next 30 days. Test it for yourself. What do you have to lose! What do you have to gain?

Dialogue with Your God-Self

The letter you wrote and the chair exercise you did earlier in this session are external methods of communication. We now turn to an internal method of communication.

Find a comfortable position, sitting up straight . . . Close your eyes . . . Take several long, slow, deep breaths . . . Relax your body completely . . . Release all of the tension . . . Allow whatever emotions you may be feeling to fade away . . . Do the same with your thoughts . . . Become like a calm, quiet lake, which mirrors perfectly the blue sky, or the starry sky in the silence of the night . . . Be at peace, and yet remain alert . . .

When you are ready, allow to come to you an image or sense of your being in the room where you are now . . . In your imagination, see yourself sitting just the way you are . . . Begin to notice a very strong, very pure point of light glowing from within you . . . Let it become very clear, very definite and yet very soft, too . . .

This shining light is a symbol of your God-Self, the highest level of your being which loves you very much indeed . . . It is your God-Self, this radiant light within you, which fashions your life by creating all of your lessons, your opportunities, your many blessings . . . It loves you . . . It protects you . . . It supports you . . . It guides you . . . It wants only the very best for you in every way . . .

Here is your opportunity to commune silently with your God-Self . . . Express whatever feelings and thoughts you may have . . . Ask whatever questions you may have . . . Allow your God-Self to respond in the silence . . . Take the next few moments to be with your God-Self within the very core of your being . . .

Know that you can commune with your God-Self whenever you wish, simply by choosing to go into the silence . . . In your own time, allow everything to fade . . . Bring your attention back to the room where you are now . . . Open your eyes . . . Take a deep breath . . . And a gentle stretch . . . Now write down any feelings, thoughts and questions you wish to record.

_____

_____

_____

_____

_____

_____

_____

So far we have presented five methods to communicate with your inner centre of wisdom: (1) Wise and Loving Guide Visualisation, Session One, Part 4, (p. 27); (2) Writing a Letter to God (p. 84); (3) Chair Exercise with God (p. 87); (4) Attunement Exercise (p. 91); and (5) Dialogue with Your God-Self, above. Which of these methods have been the most helpful for you, and in what ways?

_____

_____

_____

_____

Optional Project: Writing Your Autobiography

If you wish to deepen your self-awareness, self-understanding and self-acceptance, we recommend that you write your autobiography, a comprehensive review and assessment of your life.

Writing your life story sharpens your skills of self-observation and introspection, allows information to emerge from both conscious and unconscious levels and helps you to trace issues and make connections with various parts of your life. It also provides an excellent channel for creative self-expression.

Here are some suggestions for writing your autobiography.

1. Write it out in longhand. The act of writing itself helps to trigger ideas.

2. Use a looseleaf notebook. It allows you to insert more material later.

3. Write about the events of your life in chronological order. It helps you to discover the origin and development of various personality traits, patterns and problems throughout your life.

4. Include a variety of events and issues such as your:

   A. **Childhood.** Pre-birth, birth, infancy, parents, earliest memories, brothers and sisters, early home-life, what growing up was like, early learnings about life.

   B. **Education.** Childhood, adult, specialities, courses, therapy, important growth experiences, challenges, relationship with your intellect and the world of ideas.

   C. **Health**. Diseases, serious illnesses, accidents, hospitalisations, operations, diet, addictions, exercise, sport, restrictions, relationship with your body.

   D. **Emotions.** Ease and frequency of expression of sadness, anger, joy, fear, depression, moods, stress, general mental health, relationship with your feelings.

   E. **Relationships.** Parents, siblings, schoolmates, co-workers, authorities, same sex, opposite sex, partners, social skills, challenges, introversion/extroversion.

   F. **Sexuality.** Development, acceptance, activity, best and worst experiences (and the qualities which made them the best and worst), fears, abuse, problems.

   G. **Spirituality.** Religion, faith, relationship to God, meditation, intuition, times of inspiration and fulfilment, sense of purpose, meaning, direction in life.

   H. **Values.** Ethical and moral standards, responsibility, commitment, service, aesthetics, joys, aspirations, priorities, balance between giving and receiving, your philosophy of life.

   I. **Work and Leisure.** Training and experience, job challenges and satisfactions, personal interests, hobbies, recreations, travels, balance between work and play.

5. Take your time writing. Let your life's story be as long as you want it to be. Allow your writing to extend over weeks and months if you wish. Welcome it as an exciting process of exploration and discovery, rather than as an ordeal to be completed as quickly as possible. Focus upon the journey, not the destination.

Do not be overwhelmed by the prospect of writing about your life experience. A journey of 10,000 miles starts with one step. You can start with one step, too. With one sentence, one paragraph, one page. Why not begin today!

Suggested Reading

1. *The Story of Your Life: Writing a Spiritual Autobiography*, by Dan Wakefield, offers a systematic approach to exploring our past and understanding our present. Through exercises such as drawing a favourite childhood room or describing a friend, we begin to understand the factors which help define our own spiritual journey.

Personal Goal

Consider various simple, specific, observable actions you could take within the next few days which would be a step towards bringing more love into your life. Then choose one which seems important to you, one to take as a personal goal. Make a deliberate choice to achieve it. Write it down. Remember, making and implementing choices empowers and strengthens you.

_____

_____

_____

_____

Session Learnings

Turn back and review what you have done in this session. Then write down the three most important insights or learnings you have gained from it.

_____

_____

_____

_____

_____

_____

_____

Purpose

As stated at the beginning of Part 2, the purpose of Session Three is to explore personal trust within a spiritual context, and to present techniques to increase your trust in yourself and others. To what degree has Session Three achieved its general purpose for you?

_____

_____

_____

Congratulations! You have come to the end of Session Three. Please discuss your experience of this session with your support person *before you begin Session Four.*

CHOOSING TO BE HONEST AND OPEN

PART 1. MAKING CONNECTIONS

Begin by reviewing Session Three to reconnect with your process of development. Have you achieved the personal goal you set for yourself? How was it?

Then, if you have chosen to take additional risks in bringing more love into your life since the beginning of the previous session, write about your experience: what you did, how successful you were and what you learned.

Continue with these personal journal pages by *making connections with the theme, issues and exercises of this course*, recording whatever relevant memories, ideas, feelings, insights, dreams, 'unfinished business', interactions and other events in your inner and outer worlds have occurred since you completed Session Three. Include related reading you may have done, questions on your mind and any other observations and connections with the course you wish to make.

_____

_____

_____

_____

_____

_____

_____

_____

_____

_____

_____

_____

_____

_____

_____

_____

_____

_____

_____

_____

_____

_____

Next in Part 2 we explore how you relate to the qualities of honesty and openness.

PART 2. TAKING STOCK

Purpose

The purpose of Session Four is to explore how you relate to honesty and openness in yourself and others, and to provide principles and methods to encourage you to be more honest and open in your life.

Two themes which run implicitly throughout this course are honesty and openness. They apply to how you respond to our questions and exercises, as well as to how you relate to yourself and others.

From the standpoint of the course, the more honest and open you are in applying yourself to the questions and exercises, the more you benefit. Unfortunately the converse is also true: the less honest and open you are, the less you benefit. We encourage you to be as honest and open as possible.

From the standpoint of bringing more love into your life, we focus upon these themes for another reason: these qualities are absolutely essential for healthy and whole relationships. They are needed for clear communication. They lead to insight and understanding. They foster trust. When they are missing, either by ignorance or by design, their absence blocks the free flow of love.

We begin by surveying your general attitude towards each of these qualities.

'Honesty' Graph and Assessment

Being honest is being truthful and authentic in word and deed, and therefore not devious, deceitful or false. Honesty reflects sincerity and integrity. Being honest is being candid, genuine and trustworthy.

How do you feel about honesty? What does honesty mean to you?

_____

_____

_____

_____

Mark an X on the graph below to indicate how honest you are. It may be in between two statements and numbers.

1. I am never honest, truthful and authentic with myself and others.
2. I am rarely honest, truthful and authentic with myself and others.
3. I am sometimes honest, truthful and authentic with myself and others.
4. I am usually honest, truthful and authentic with myself and others.
5. I am always honest, truthful and authentic with myself and others.

1	2	3	4	5

Mark where your mother and father would have placed themselves. Be alert to the possibility that their beliefs and behaviour may have conditioned your own.

In the blanks below, put the number of the statement above which comes nearest to how honest you feel you are generally in each situation.

_____ With my mother.	_____ With people of the opposite sex.
_____ With my father.	_____ With people at school or at work.
_____ With my family and other relatives.	_____ With most friends.
_____ With my lover or partner.	_____ With most strangers.
_____ With people of the same sex.	_____ With myself.

What is your greatest difficulty or challenge with honesty?

_____

_____

_____

_____

Are you always as honest as you can be with yourself and others? If not, what would it take for you to be more honest generally?

_____

_____

_____

_____

'Openness' Graph and Assessment

Openness builds upon honesty. Being open is being unguarded, vulnerable, accessible to new ideas, and therefore not withholding, blocked or closed. Being open is being impartial, receptive and visible.

How do you feel about openness? What does openness mean to you?

_____

_____

_____

_____

Mark an X on the graph below to indicate how open you are.

1. I am never open and vulnerable; I am always guarded and closed.
2. I am rarely open and vulnerable; I am usually guarded and closed.
3. I am sometimes open and vulnerable; I am sometimes guarded and closed.
4. I am usually open and vulnerable; I am rarely guarded and closed.
5. I am always open and vulnerable; I am never guarded and closed.

1	2	3	4	5

Mark where your mother and father would have placed themselves. Be alert to the possibility that their beliefs and behaviour may have conditioned your own.

In the blanks below, put the number of the statement above which comes nearest to how open you feel you are generally in each situation.

———— With my mother.   ———— With people of the opposite sex.

———— With my father.   ———— With people at school or at work.

———— With my family and other relatives.   ———— With most friends.

———— With my lover or partner.   ———— With most strangers.

———— With people of the same sex.   ———— With myself.

What is your greatest difficulty or challenge with openness?

————————————————————————————————————

————————————————————————————————————

————————————————————————————————————

————————————————————————————————————

Are you always as open as you can be with yourself and others? If not, what would it take for you to be more open generally?

————————————————————————————————————

————————————————————————————————————

————————————————————————————————————

————————————————————————————————————

What conditions or limits do you place upon your honesty and openness?

————————————————————————————————————

————————————————————————————————————

————————————————————————————————————

————————————————————————————————————

Now write down any other observations you wish to make about honesty and openness and the role they play in your life, *especially in relation to love.*

————————————————————————————————————

————————————————————————————————————

————————————————————————————————————

————————————————————————————————————

————————————————————————————————————

————————————————————————————————————

————————————————————————————————————

PART 3. EXPLORING PERSPECTIVES

EILEEN

The more open you are, the freer you are. — Foundations of a Spiritual Community

It is so easy to talk about being honest and open, but what happens when I come face to face with a difficult situation — the sort I would rather ignore or suppress completely? Only a short time ago I found myself in such a situation.

I was with three other people, all of whom I had known for a long time. Two of them I had always loved and respected, but the third person I had had difficulties with over the years. He wanted to do a video interview with two of us, and he had gone to a great deal of trouble setting up all of the equipment in my home.

I sat down to be interviewed, and only then did I realise I had a complete block with this person. I was feeling awful inside, as if my heart had closed up into a tight little wizened ball. What was I to do? Could I be honest and open about the way I was feeling?

I know there are different ways of handling such a situation. It can be done in love and understanding. It can be done in anger and resentment. I regret to say I took the latter way and made a real hash of it! In fact, I lost my temper and asked him to cancel the video and to leave my home. I stamped angrily out of the room and went into my bedroom.

As I did so, something happened to me. The words 'Ask, and ye shall receive' came to me. I found myself praying and asking for God's grace, asking for it over and over again. I soon found a peace and calm flowing through me.

In a few minutes I was able to go back into the next room and tell the person that we could go ahead with the video. We had a very straight talk, and I found that the emotional charge had gone. I was able to talk with him without any feeling of resentment or anger. It was then I realised that change can come 'in the twinkling of an eye'.

I had to learn some important lessons from this very unpleasant and difficult experience. First of all, there is a right and a wrong way to have a disagreement with another person, and I had chosen the wrong way by expressing my anger inappropriately. I know I was right to get my feelings out into the open as only then can something be done about them. But what also matters is *how* it is done.

I find it is important for me to keep open and to see the good which comes out of every situation. The video was made, and it is very good, despite everything. My relationship with the person concerned has changed completely. Being honest and open paid off, even if I did it in an unpleasant way.

What else did I learn? Putting prayer to the test when I was in a tight corner and seeing it work out perfectly by asking for and receiving God's grace. Seeing an example of change coming swiftly, and realising that I first had to make the choice to be open to it.

As a child I used to sulk and withdraw like a snail into its shell. I remember so well one time when my father sat down beside me and told me how he, too, used to sulk. He found as he grew up how it shut him off from other people, and that he knew he had to change. He learned that being honest and open is the way to do it. He suggested I watch myself any time I started to withdraw and feel sorry for myself, and so that is what I always try to do. I find it helps to stay open, no matter what I am feeling, for it allows healing to take place and the love to keep flowing.

DAVID

When in doubt, tell the truth. — Mark Twain

I prefer to think of myself as an honest person. Yet I know my honesty has varied according to circumstances, especially when my sense of self-esteem needed bolstering. Then I told people whatever I felt intuitively they would like to hear, regardless of whether it agreed with my own feelings, opinions or beliefs. I tried to gain their acceptance and approval, sacrificing my integrity and even losing my sense of self into the bargain.

The needs of diplomacy, the remnants of my 'Be a good boy!' childhood conditioning and deep insecurities have also played their part in the expression of honesty in my life. For many years I tried to be *all things* to all people. It was more than a fulltime job, and it never worked, at least not for long. I have come to learn that my task is to be *who I am* to all people. This is the essence of honesty and openness, a confirming echo of Hamlet's 'to thine own self be true'.

To me being open is being congruent, that is, presenting myself on the outside consistent with what I am on the inside, and thus living my life as if it were an open book. How much of an open book am I? During my residence at the Findhorn Foundation I learned a great deal about openness. For example there were times when I believed I was quite open and at peace with myself and the world, only to discover eventually that I simply had closed down and shut off to all of my feelings. I was not open, I was closed, and what I took for peace was actually numbness and deadness. I discovered that real openness brings feelings of aliveness, vitality and genuine contact and connection with the world around me.

I often encountered guests with questions about life in a spiritual community. I learned that there are no embarrassing questions, only embarrassing answers! Many times I was asked quite intimate questions about my faith, finances, personal habits, relationships and other aspects of community living. All questions were fair game.

In the beginning, I sometimes allowed others to answer the probing questions, or I deflected them with a question or with humour. In time, I simply gulped to myself as quietly as I could, and then carried on. Much later, when the gulp disappeared, I found I had reached a new level of openness. Then more comfortable about relating my past history, I found my next challenge was to express my feelings openly in the moment. Learning to be more open responsibly and sensitively is a never-ending process, with new challenges and lessons always emerging.

I soon became aware that we are all open books, no matter how much of ourself we may try to conceal. We all receive intuitive impressions of each other. We all see (or feel) past the words, past the actions, past the defences to the very heart, the very essence, of one another. We all are as transparent as glass. Then over one weekend I realised that every part of my past, present and even future is within reach intuitively to anyone who takes the time to attune to it. It was one of the most traumatic weekends of my life! After all, most people have their skeletons and monsters hidden away, and I have spent a good deal of my life keeping my own under lock and key. Imagine my anxiety when I discovered that everyone (whether they know it or not) has a pass key which can unlock any such door! Everyone has an intuitive radar which can penetrate our most elaborate defences!

Fortunately a few days later came the realisation of people's basic goodness, and that they accept and love me *despite* knowing all about me, sometimes perhaps even *because of it*. Openness then has become not a matter of *revealing* myself to others, but of simply *confirming* to them what they may already see, feel and know. I have learned over the years that rather than being instruments of strategy and defence, honesty and openness are a natural way of being, and accordingly make life much more simple, relaxed and fulfilling.

PART 4. GAINING AWARENESS

Relative Honesty and Openness

Now we continue to explore how honesty and openness function in your life and to search for whatever beliefs, practices and patterns you may have about these issues.

First what message and 'should' did you learn, either directly or indirectly, from your mother and father about honesty and openness?

_____

_____

_____

_____

Based on your self-assessment in Part 2, do you find that you are honest and open consistently, or does it seem to depend upon something outside yourself, such as the person, the situation, the time, the place, the issue?

_____

_____

_____

_____

Do you ever withhold revealing the entire truth, tell 'little white lies', or become intentionally general, indirect or vague? When? Why?

_____

_____

_____

_____

How obvious is deception and deceit to you? Can you sometimes tell when someone is not being honest and straightforward with you? How do you perceive or sense it?

_____

_____

_____

_____

What implications does your answer above have for you and your own practice of relative honesty and openness?

_____

_____

_____

_____

How do you prevent yourself from being more honest and open? What do you tell yourself?

_____

_____

_____

_____

What do you imagine is the worst thing which could happen if you were more honest and open?

_____

_____

_____

_____

Truth

Most people would say they generally tell the truth and try to live truthfully. But what is truth? How do you feel about truth? What does truth mean to you?

_____

_____

_____

_____

Here are two observations about truth. The first is a centuries-old statement by Xenophanes, quoted by Jean Hardy in her book, *A Psychology With a Soul: Psychosynthesis in Evolutionary Context*.

> *As for certain truth, no man has known it.*
> *Nor will he know it; neither of the gods,*
> *Nor yet of all the things of which I speak.*
> *And even if by chance he were to utter*
> *The final truth, he would himself not know it;*
> *For all is but a woven web of guesses.*

The second observation is by Sir George Trevelyan, British adult education pioneer.

> *Our greatest truths are but half-truths.*
> *Think not to settle down forever in any truth;*
> *Use it as a tent in which to pass a summer night,*
> *But build no house of it, or it will become your tomb.*
> *When you first become aware of its insufficiency, and*
> *See some counter-truth looming up in the distance,*
> *Then weep not but rejoice: it is the Lord's voice*
> *Saying, 'Take up your bed and walk.'*

What is your reaction to these two statements? What are your feelings and thoughts about them?

_____

_____

_____

_____

Honesty, Openness and Personal Disclosure

What is your attitude towards personal disclosure, that is, revealing information about yourself to others? Where and how do you draw the line in talking openly about yourself?

_____

_____

_____

_____

With whom and under what conditions are you willing and able to reveal details of your: 1) spiritual/religious beliefs? 2) political views and affiliations? 3) relationship history and challenges? 4) date of birth? 5) annual income and expenditures? and 6) sexual life? Or do you consider them all taboo, and too personal, intimate and private to discuss with others?

_____

_____

_____

_____

_____

_____

_____

_____

Honesty, Openness and Freedom

The more open you are, the freer you are. One method to discover the limits of your openness, therefore, is to find out when it is that you do not feel free. For example are there certain words or phrases which you do not feel free to use in front of other people? If so, write some of them here, and be aware of your feelings as you do.

_____

_____

_____

Another method is to write down at least three things that you cannot joke about, make fun of or laugh over (either by yourself or with others) — those parts of life which you regard as being too sensitive, serious, significant or sacred to be taken lightly.

_____

_____

_____

_____

These areas may be worth exploring as limits to your openness. If you treat these issues so carefully, where is the opportunity for change, development, flexibility, growth and renewal?

The book *Caring Enough to Confront*, by David Augsburger, presents the plea, 'Love me enough to tell me the truth.' Is there anything you do or did not feel free to say to your mother? Can you love her enough to tell her your own truth here and now? Write it down. Be specific, clear and direct!

_____

_____

_____

_____

Can you love your father enough to tell him your truth, perhaps something you never felt free to say to him? Write it down.

_____

_____

_____

_____

Is there something you do not feel free to say to others in your life right now — perhaps a relative, friend, co-worker, supervisor or partner? Someone who needs to hear your truth? Can you love them enough to tell them your truth here and now? Dare to be honest and open!

_____

_____

_____

_____

Is there something you do not feel free to say to *yourself?* Can you love yourself enough to tell yourself your own truth simply, clearly and directly?

_____

_____

_____

_____

Have you other personal feelings and thoughts you do not feel free to express openly, perhaps doubts about yourself, a relationship, the future, fantasies, hopes and dreams? Select one or two and write them down. Be aware of your feelings as you do so.

_____

_____

_____

_____

Emotional Honesty and Openness

It is important for us to feel, express and talk about our feelings freely, especially within our close relationships. Withholding feelings can be as dishonest as withholding thoughts, and doing so repeatedly often fosters a sense of separation and isolation. It helps us to be more secure, trusting and vulnerable with one another when we each know how the other generally feels and thinks. Being honest and open with our feelings as well as our thoughts is a gift we give to others.

How honest and open are you emotionally? How guarded are you? How freely do you allow yourself to feel, express and talk about your feelings?

_____

_____

_____

_____

Have you personal feelings you do not feel free to express openly — from joy, compassion, kindness, gratitude, happiness and peace, to sadness, resentment, anger, anxiety, hurt, pain? Would it help you to express them now as pure feelings? Would it help you to talk about them? Would it help to relate them to your support person or group? What would help you? Write about it here.

_____

_____

_____

_____

How freely do you cry? How often do you experience and express anger and other 'negative' emotions? (They are 'negative' only because they make us feel separate and disconnected from others.)

_____

_____

_____

_____

How do you prevent yourself from being more honest and open *emotionally*? What fears and concerns stop you? What then do you do with your unexpressed feelings?

_____

_____

_____

_____

Finally, review your written responses to all of the questions in Part 4.

What implications and directions do they suggest for bringing more love into your life?

_____

_____

_____

_____

_____

_____

_____

PART 5. DEVELOPING POTENTIAL

Meditation

We turn now to a series of meditation exercises which take you more deeply inside yourself.

Meditation has many different meanings and takes many different forms. How do you feel about meditation? What does meditation mean to you?

_____

_____

_____

_____

Meditation builds a pathway to the transpersonal or spiritual realms. It can take the form of disciplined thought or reflection upon an idea. It can also include other kinds of inner experiences.

First we present three simple forms of meditation as useful ways to discover more about yourself and honesty. Then we follow with two more exercises to help you discover more about yourself and openness.

NOTE. To gain full benefit from these exercises, take occasional breaks. Pace yourself. Take your time to digest one exercise before continuing with the next one.

Reflective Meditation

The reflective meditation uses the rational mind or intellect to consider a quality, symbol, seed thought or issue in all of its meanings and implications. It explores and reflects upon the topic deeply and thoroughly. Good concentration is required to keep the mind focused, as well as persistence to probe deeply and discover new and relevant dimensions of the topic.

The reflective meditation is not simply taking stock or observing passively, but rather it aims at understanding, interpreting and evaluating whatever we discover within ourself. It results in a clear idea about the given topic and greater knowledge about ourself. For example meditating reflectively upon ourself helps us to distinguish between the many changing parts of our personality and our pure, permanent, unchanging God-Self.

Now close your eyes . . . Sit up straight . . . Take a few deep breaths . . . Relax . . . Allow your body, emotions and thoughts to become still . . . Become like a calm, quiet lake . . .

When you are ready, begin to reflect upon the meaning of honesty . . . Allow yourself to delve into it widely and deeply . . . Consider your experience of it, and all of your feelings and thoughts about it . . . Address it from all angles . . . Contemplate it . . . Ponder it . . . Give your whole mind over to it . . . Think about what honesty is to you . . . Make notes for yourself below as you do so . . .

Give yourself at least ten minutes for this exercise . . .

MY FEELINGS AND THOUGHTS ABOUT HONESTY

What is the overall quality, tone or impression of your reflections? What are your feelings and thoughts about them?

_____

_____

_____

_____

What similarities or patterns do you find in your deliberations? What other observations can you make?

_____

_____

_____

_____

Receptive Meditation

The preceding reflective meditation actively uses our rational mind. However, in the following receptive meditation, our attention is directed upwards beyond the ordinary mind state and its awareness. It asks us to still the mind to await an inner response to an issue from another part of ourself. An example of this form of meditation is asking for an image or other sense to come to us in response to a question, as we have already done several times in the course.

An inner response or message is usually very brief, impersonal and meaningful. It may come in a variety of ways: a vision, intuition, illumination, inner hearing, words or even an urge to do something. It may also be experienced as a sense of inner contact with the God-Self.

We recommend that you always write down immediately whatever occurs to you during the meditation for better understanding and later reference. As you may have images or other senses come to you, have your drawing materials nearby.

Be aware that a relevant inspiration may come unexpectedly later, so do watch for it. For best results repeat the meditation daily on the same topic for at least seven days. Incidentally, meditating with a group of people usually improves results with all three forms of meditation.

Now close your eyes . . . Sit up straight . . . Take a few deep breaths . . . Relax . . . Allow your body, emotions and thoughts to become still . . . Become like a calm, quiet lake . . .

When you are ready, use your imagination to picture or sense yourself putting into a bowl all the words, thoughts and feelings you considered about the quality of honesty in the reflective meditation . . .

Visualise placing the bowl above your head, and allow the sun to shine brightly down upon it . . . Notice if any changes come about as a result of this action . . .

Then open yourself to receive images, words or other senses which convey _a deeper meaning_ of honesty . . . Allow them to come to you . . . Do not _think_ about it, or try to force anything to happen . . . Simply be receptive . . . Take your time . . . Take several minutes . . . Wait patiently in the silence for a deeper understanding of honesty to come quietly to you . . . Let it emerge slowly . . .

In your own time, allow your attention to return to the room where you are now . . . Open your eyes . . . Take a deep breath . . . And a gentle stretch.

Make any drawings and write down any feelings, thoughts and questions you wish to record.

DRAWINGS AND FURTHER NOTES ABOUT WHAT HONESTY MEANS TO ME

Now create your own definition of honesty based upon your experience in both the reflective meditation and the receptive meditation.

_____

_____

_____

_____

Creative Meditation

The creative meditation may be used for a variety of purposes, chief among them *self-creation,* for with it we may transform aspects of our personality. It uses the creative power of thought, and it is repeated regularly until the desired results are obtained.

The creative meditation consists of three elements: clear conception and formulation of the idea; use of the imagination to enhance the idea in images and symbols; and enlivening the idea with our own intention, feeling and desire.

Now close your eyes . . . Sit up straight . . . Take a few deep breaths . . . Relax . . . Allow your body, emotions and thoughts to become still . . . Become like a calm, quiet lake . . .

Imagine how honest you would like to be, how truthful, sincere and authentic with yourself and others . . . Let whatever you imagine be your free choice . . . Make certain you avoid all 'shoulds' . . . It is not meant to be a model of perfection . . . But rather a realistic and attainable ideal . . . Something which would be possible to achieve during your life . . . Something you are willing to be . . .

Then visualise yourself having this quality fully available to you . . . Picture yourself as being this ideal model of yourself in relation to honesty . . . How do you appear physically? . . . How does your face appear? . . . Your eyes? . . . Your stance? . . . The rest of you? . . .

Next, in your imagination, try on the ideal image like a coat . . . Identify with it . . . Merge with it . . . Become it . . . Be it . . . Experience what it is like to be this ideal model of yourself completely . . .

Then take a few minutes to visualise being in a number of everyday situations, possessing and acting out satisfactorily the qualities and attitudes of your ideal model . . . Bring your feelings into it as well . . .

Proceed through a typical day from morning to night and experience being this ideal . . . Picture scenes in which you interact successfully in the various personal and professional roles you play, involving perhaps your parents . . . partners . . . family . . . friends . . . schoolmates or co-workers . . . and other people in your life . . . Takeyour time . . . Make it as real and as vivid as possible . . .

In your own time, allow everything to fade, and bring your attention back to the room where you are now . . . Open your eyes . . . Take a deep breath . . . And a gentle stretch.

Now write down any feelings, thoughts and questions you wish to record.

_____

_____

_____

_____

_____

_____

_____

_____

'Block to Honesty' Symbol and Drawing

Next we continue our inner exploration to discover how you stop yourself from being more honest with yourself and others. Have your drawing materials nearby.

Now find a comfortable position, sitting up straight . . . Close your eyes . . . Take several long, slow, deep breaths . . . Relax your body completely . . . Release all of the tension . . . Allow whatever emotions you may be feeling to fade away . . . Do the same with your thoughts . . . Become like a calm, quiet lake, which mirrors perfectly the blue sky, or the starry sky in the silence of the night . . . Be at peace and yet remain alert . . .

When you are ready, ask yourself the question, *'WHAT IS MY MAJOR BLOCK TO BEING MORE HONEST — WHAT PREVENTS ME FROM BEING FULLY HONEST WITH MYSELF AND OTHERS?'* . . . Then allow an image or sense to come to you which represents an answer to this question . . . Take your time . . . Wait patiently in the silence, knowing that something will soon come to you . . . Be willing to accept whatever comes without judging, censoring or rejecting it . . . Simply be ready to observe and examine it with the purpose of learning more about it . . .

As you begin to sense something, allow it to become more vivid . . . Note its size and shape . . . Its density and design . . . Its colour and texture . . . Explore it with as many of your senses as you can . . . Find the overall quality it suggests to you . . .

Then open your eyes, and begin to express in a drawing below either the image itself or its quality . . . If nothing has come to you, open your eyes, hold the question in mind and begin to draw freely and spontaneously, letting something come to you in that way . . .

MY BLOCK TO BEING MORE HONEST

Write down the overall *quality* and any other words, feelings or thoughts which came to you during the exercise, or which you are aware of now. What new insight or awareness does this symbol and its quality give to you?

_____

_____

_____

_____

We recommend that you repeat the exercises with honesty you have done in Part 5, using the quality of openness. **NOTE.** We leave it to you to adapt and apply all of the exercises and techniques in this course in other ways which you feel may help you. We not only invite you to do so, we *encourage* you to look after yourself and prescribe for your own needs.

'Block to Openness' Visualisation and Drawing

We now shift our focus of attention from honesty to openness.

As with honesty, it helps to know how and why we prevent the free expression of openness in our life because then we can begin to address the block and change its limiting effects upon us. The following exercise helps you to identify your primary block. It invites you to use your imagination to evoke an image or sense which represents your inner block to openness.

The exercise then asks you to talk with the symbol to discover more about its role in your life. Treat whatever image comes (often appearing in the form of a person, an animal, or an object) as a Walt Disney cartoon character having the capacity to talk with you. Like encountering a stranger on a train or aeroplane, your symbol may or may not be very friendly, cooperative or communicative. Remain as detached and objective as possible, give it the freedom to be itself and learn whatever you can from it. It is all right if it seems as if you are making it up in your imagination.

NOTE. For maximum benefit you may wish to pre-record this exercise to enable you to stay with your own inner process without interruption. Pause 10-30 seconds at each . . . to allow you to experience each part fully. Avoid rushing through the exercise. Take your time.

Now close your eyes . . . Sit up straight . . . Take a few deep breaths . . . Relax . . . Allow your body, emotions and thoughts to become still . . . Become like a calm, quiet lake . . . When you are ready, imagine being out in the countryside in the middle of a beautiful meadow . . . It is a warm, pleasant day . . . Feel the ground under your feet . . . Feel the warmth of the sun shining upon your body . . . See the blue sky, the trees, grass and other plants . . . Hear the sounds of nature around you . . . Smell the fresh fragrance of the countryside . . . Feel the peace and contentment in this meadow . . .

Notice that on one side of the meadow is a dark forest . . . You find yourself beginning to walk along a footpath which leads you directly to the edge of the forest . . .

Then you begin to sense that within this forest is something which symbolises or represents whatever blocks you from being more open . . . Whatever keeps you guarded and closed . . . Whatever hinders you from bringing more openness into your life . . .

You call into the forest and invite to come out into the sunshine the symbolic block . . . Then you wait for something to appear from the dark forest, either an image or sense of some kind which represents your inner block to openness . . .

When it does come out into the light, take a few moments to examine it . . . What is its appearance? . . . What is it doing? . . . Then begin to dialogue with it . . . Find out as much as possible about it . . . How and why does it block you? . . . What does it need? . . . How does it serve you? . . . How does it limit you? . . . How may you begin to deal with it? . . . Take your time . . . Spend several minutes dialoguing with it . . . Learn all you can . . .

When the dialogue has come to an end, sense a beam of sunlight shining down upon you and the symbol, infilling and enfolding you both with its light and warmth . . . Notice if anything changes about either one of you . . .

Allow the symbol of your block to being more open to return to the deep, dark forest . . . You find yourself walking back to the place in the meadow where you first began . . . Feel the ground under your feet . . . Feel the warmth of the sun shining upon your body . . . See the blue sky, the trees, grass, and other plants . . . Hear the sounds of nature around you . . . Smell the fresh fragrance of the countryside . . . Feel the peace and contentment in this meadow . . .

Then, in your own time, allow the scene to fade, and bring your attention to the room where you are now . . . Open your eyes . . . Take a deep breath . . . And a gentle stretch.

Express in a drawing below either the symbol or the quality it represents to you. Allow your hand to move freely and intuitively.

MY BLOCK TO BEING MORE OPEN

Now write down any observations you wish to record about the block, what it needs, how to deal with it and anything else you have learned about it. Include changes which may have taken place. Also note words, feelings or thoughts which came to you during the visualisation, or afterwards while you were making the drawing.

_____

_____

_____

_____

_____

_____

_____

_____

_____

Evocation of Openness

In Session One, Part 6 (p. 40) we present one method of bringing a desired quality (such as love) into your life, that is, by the simple technique of writing the name of the quality upon a card and placing it in your home where you will see it often and where it will then be recorded on the photographic film of your mind.

Now we present an exercise for evoking a desired quality in another way. In this instance we use the quality of openness. Pre-record this exercise to enable you to stay with your own inner process. Avoid rushing the exercise. Take your time.

NOTE. If for physical reasons you are unable to participate fully in this exercise, simply hint or suggest as much as you can with your body. Or, if absolutely necessary, close your eyes and *imagine* or visualise it all happening.

Stand or sit on the floor facing a large mirror . . . Breathe deeply and relax . . .

First, for contrast, allow your body to express or dramatise the quality of 'closedness', the opposite of openness . . . Place your body in a highly uncomfortable posture, all knotted up, covering up or burying your head as if hiding away, with your arms and legs askew, shielding your body . . . Exaggerate it as much as you can to help you to get the feel of it . . .

As with the chair exercise in Session Three, you may feel awkward, self-conscious or embarrassed at first. When you acknowledge your feelings, they will soon disappear . . .

Look in the mirror at yourself, and observe whatever you see . . . Then close your eyes . . . Feel the actual physical tension and stress you are placing upon your body as you hold this closed position for another minute . . . Notice how much effort and energy it takes . . . Notice how it feels emotionally to be closed down . . .

Now relax . . . Feel the difference . . . Feel the contrast . . . Feel the relief . . .

Next open your eyes and allow your body to express or dramatise the quality of openness, the opposite of whatever you have been doing . . . From the field of Body Language, you may know it means not to cross your arms or legs, but rather to maintain a totally free, natural, unguarded position . . . Take on whatever seems to be the most appropriate physical characteristics of openness . . .

Experiment with various body positions, postures, movements, and gestures . . . Exaggerate everything you do . . . Make it all real, alive and fun . . . For example you may wish to express openness on your face with a smile and any other facial gestures which are meaningful to you . . . Allow yourself to be as spontaneous, intuitive and creative as you can be . . .

Look in the mirror at yourself and observe whatever you see . . . Then close your eyes . . . Feel the relaxation (the absence of tension) in your body . . . Feel the freedom . . . Notice how much less effort and energy it takes to be open . . . Notice how it feels emotionally to be open . . . Then begin slowly moving your entire body freely and rhythmically . . . Until at last you find yourself dancing openly . . . As you do, observe yourself occasionally in the mirror . . .

Once you are satisfied that your body is comfortably expressing openness, turn your attention to your thoughts . . . While continuing to move, begin to think about openness, and all it means to you . . . Reflect upon its benefits and blessings . . . Consider its value and usefulness . . . Appreciate and praise it . . . Realise how positive you are feeling about it . . . Desire it . . . Yearn for it . . . Feel how receptive you are to it . . . Choose to welcome it more and more into your life.

Then begin to evoke openness more directly while continuing to move about openly ... Affirm it aloud ... Repeat over and over again, *'I ALWAYS FEEL SAFE AND AT EASE TO BE COMPLETELY OPEN ...'* Feel the truth of the statement ... Feel the safety ... Feel the ease ... Feel the openness ... Know it is so ...

Now imagine situations or circumstances which normally would cause you to protect yourself by holding back, distancing yourself or closing down ... For example imagine being confronted by a difficult person ... A difficult problem ... Other anxious, insecure moments ... Then *see, feel* and *sense* yourself to be entirely open and safe ... Experience your own increased openness ... Acknowledge it ... Accept it ... Appreciate it ... Give thanks to your God-Self for it ...

Finally commit yourself to remaining this open throughout the rest of today, no matter what happens ... Model openness for others ... Be a living example of it ... Radiate openness to everyone you meet ...

Now write down any feelings, thoughts and questions you wish to record.

_____

_____

_____

_____

_____

_____

_____

_____

_____

_____

You may adapt this exercise to develop within yourself a wide variety of qualities, such as courage, joy, love, patience and peace. Repeat this exercise regularly until the desired quality has firmly taken root and is flourishing in your life.

Some people may question the long-term effect of this type of exercise. We would question it, too, if its purpose were simply to acquire a desired quality from *outside* ourself. However, this exercise and many others in this course are based upon the principle that we have *within us* countless qualities, including the quality of love, which exist in potential, ready to be developed.

A relevant analogy is that of the acorn which carries within it all potential parts of a mighty oak tree: its root system, trunk, branches, leaves, even more acorns. To evoke the oak tree from the dormant acorn, we simply provide it with a supportive environment, including proper ongoing nourishment.

Our task therefore is not to wish or otherwise search outside ourself for more — courage, joy, love, patience, peace — but rather *to evoke from within ourself the seeds of the desired quality which are already there,* and then to provide a supportive environment, including proper ongoing nourishment.

It is on this basis that we suggest you repeat this exercise regularly until the desired quality has firmly taken root and is flourishing in your life.

PART 6. APPLYING IT

Evening Review

One simple and effective method of exploring your attitudes and behaviour patterns regarding honesty and openness (and any other issues as well) is to set aside a few minutes each evening, ideally at bedtime, to review your day.

Take whatever time you have to give to it, whether a condensed two minutes, or an expanded fifteen minutes. However, avoid all pressure and stress. As with all our self-help exercises, choose to do the evening review because you want to do it, and not because you feel you 'should' do it.

In your imagination replay the entire day as though it were on a film or video. Do it in reverse time. Begin with the present moment and review the events of the evening, then earlier in the afternoon and then finally in the morning, until you return to the moment you awakened.

Recall face-to-face interactions, telephone calls, written messages and letters. Recall details of what and how you communicated with yourself and others, as well as what you may have held back consciously or unconsciously, with whom and why. Recall your actions (and inactions) and the statements they make about your relative honesty and openness.

Were there times when you were less than honest? Less than truthful? Less than sincere and authentic in word, thought, feeling and deed? Were there times when you were devious, deceitful or false? Were there times when you were less than open? Less than congruent and unguarded? Were there times when you were withholding, blocked or closed, either emotionally, mentally or spiritually?

Do you find any similarities or patterns of behaviour throughout the day? For example were you more honest or open with some people than with others? More open with your thoughts than with your feelings or actions? More honest than open?

If you spent the day completely alone, how honest and open were you with yourself? In your own decision-making? In whatever you said or thought to yourself throughout the day? How honest and open were you with your feelings?

How did the day compare with the 'ideal model' you visualised for yourself in the creative meditation? Did the blocks to honesty and openness which you identified in this session appear at any time during the day?

Were there any 'missed opportunities' to be more honest and open with yourself and others? If so, consider how you might wish to change things another time. However, avoid judging yourself — few people hit the bull's eye of the target every time. But in having the target, at least we know which way to face and where to aim. (We also know when we have missed the target!)

It is most important that you conduct the evening review objectively as a detached observer, quietly witnessing the day's successes and 'failures' without being pulled back into them again. Simply gain whatever awareness and insight you can from a given event, and then move on to the next one.

People often find that writing down their observations from an evening review is an added help to discovering more about their attitudes and patterns of behaviour.

As a way to apply your learning about honesty and openness, we invite you to conduct an evening review for the next seven days as part of the following exercise.

Adapting Techniques to Meet Individual Needs

We review below the principal techniques, exercises and resources introduced within the first four sessions of the course. Each of them may be adapted to help you develop more honesty and openness in your life.

Read through the entire list first, and then mark at least three of them (including the Evening Review) which particularly attract you and which *you actually commit yourself to try out and complete before you begin Session Five*. We leave it to your imagination to find ways to apply them to honesty and openness. Refer to the text where the techniques were first introduced for general instructions. Begin them all now. On the following page report your *results* with the techniques you choose.

_____ **Assessments,** to take stock of your experience with a given topic.

_____ **Attunements,** to contact your source of inner wisdom for inspiration and help.

_____ **Autobiography,** to explore, connect and express various parts of your past.

_____ **Autogenic Training,** to relax, and to be more receptive to other techniques.

_____ **Brainstorming,** to look for alternative solutions to problems.

_____ **Chair Exercises,** to bring your inner process out into the open.

_____ **Check-lists and Graphs,** to clarify and assess your experience with a topic.

_____ **Creative Meditations,** to manifest the ideal model of how your life can be.

_____ **Dialogues With Your God-Self,** to communicate directly with your inner centre.

_____ **Drawings,** to explore and express a topic creatively and graphically.

_____ **Evening Reviews,** to become aware of attitudes and behaviour patterns.

_____ **Evocation Exercises,** to establish and strengthen desired qualities within yourself.

_____ **Experience Scans,** to survey your attitudes, beliefs, feelings and thoughts.

_____ **'If I Had the Courage' Scans,** to identify fears and the risks to take to ease them.

_____ **Letter-Writing,** (to God, a parent, yourself), to express the unexpressed within you.

_____ **Messages and 'Shoulds' Scans,** to identify and let go of past conditioning.

_____ **Models of People,** to use as inspiration and for emulation.

_____ **Personal Goals,** to choose, implement and achieve desired outcomes.

_____ **Prayers,** to ask your God-Self for information, help and support.

_____ **Reading,** to gain new direction, inspiration and perspectives.

_____ **Receptive Meditations,** to evoke images and symbols, and to deepen awareness.

_____ **Reflective Meditations,** to foster understanding and evaluation of a topic.

_____ **Support Person or Group,** to give and receive encouragement, insight and help.

_____ **Visualisations,** to access, explore, enrich and ground your inner life.

_____ **Word Cards,** to evoke and develop desired personal qualities.

We encourage you to take increasing responsibility for your progress in the course (and in life) by choosing deliberately from our growing array of simple yet powerful and effective techniques and applying them to your personal concerns and challenges, including how to bring more love into your life.

DRAWINGS AND NOTES REPORTING RESULTS OF PART 6 EXERCISES

Suggested Reading

1. *Actualizations: You Don't Have To Rehearse To Be Yourself,* by Stewart Emery and Neal Rogin, helps us to create an environment in which our relationships become joyful, nurturing, satisfying adventures in mutual and personal growth.

2. *Focusing,* by Eugene T. Gendlin, Ph.D., offers a self-help technique to resolve personal problems by perceiving specific steps of contact, felt change and deeper levels of awareness within our physical body.

Personal Goal

Consider various simple, specific, observable actions you could take within the next few days which would be a step towards bringing more love into your life. Then choose one which seems important to you, one to take as a personal goal. Make a deliberate choice to achieve it. Write it down. Remember, making and implementing choices empowers and strengthens you.

_____

_____

_____

_____

Session Learnings

Turn back and review what you have done in this session. Then write down the three most important insights or learnings you have gained from it.

_____

_____

_____

_____

_____

Purpose

As stated at the beginning of Part 2, the purpose of Session Four is to explore how you relate to honesty and openness in yourself and others, and to provide principles and methods to encourage you to be more honest and open in your life. To what degree has Session Four achieved its general purpose for you?

_____

_____

_____

_____

Congratulations! You have come to the end of Session Four. Please discuss your experience of this session with your support person *before you begin Session Five.*

CHOOSING TO BE AWARE

PART 1. MAKING CONNECTIONS

Begin by reviewing Session Four to reconnect with your process of development. Have you achieved the personal goal you set for yourself? How was it?

NOTE. If you have not completed your Evening Reviews and at least two other techniques to develop more honesty and openness in your daily life (listed in Session Four, Part 6), we suggest that you do not continue with Session Five until you have completed them and reported your results on the page provided. To gain full benefit from the course, take it one step at a time, and complete *all* exercises before moving onwards.

Then, if you have chosen to take additional risks in bringing more love into your life since the beginning of the preceding session, write about your experience: what you did, how successful you were and what you learned.

Continue with these personal journal pages by *making connections with the theme, issues and exercises of this course*, recording whatever relevant memories, ideas, feelings, insights, dreams, 'unfinished business', interactions and other events in your inner and outer worlds have occurred since you completed Session Four. Include related reading you may have done, questions on your mind and any other observations and connections with the course you wish to make.

_____

_____

_____

_____

_____

_____

_____

_____

_____

_____

_____

_____

_____

_____

_____

_____

_____

_____

_____

_____

_____

_____

_____

_____

_____

_____

_____

_____

_____

_____

_____

_____

_____

_____

_____

_____

_____

_____

_____

_____

_____

_____

_____

_____

_____

_____

Next in Part 2 we explore personal beliefs which may have influenced or even blocked your bringing more love into your life.

PART 2. TAKING STOCK

Purpose

The purpose of Session Five is to explore some of your beliefs relevant to bringing more love into your life, to discover how these beliefs both serve you and limit you and to provide methods to help you change any beliefs which may block you from loving more freely and fully.

Awareness and Openness

In Session Two we explore some of your attitudes and beliefs (messages and 'shoulds'), as well as the fears they may have produced, which you absorbed as a child from significant adults around you. This session focuses more specifically upon your awareness, that is, how knowledgeable and understanding you are of your own experience and how it affects you.

The ladder of qualities presented in Session One suggests that openness leads to awareness. Many people are very open to learning about themselves and about life, and consequently they develop great personal knowledge, understanding and awareness. Others are not as open; they are either not ready, able or willing to learn. They may be focused upon the more basic issues of security and trust. As a result, it is more difficult for them to gain new awareness about their own inner and outer worlds.

You may have experienced this principle for yourself in Session Four during the Evocation Exercise. When you were feeling knotted up, closed down and cut off, where was your focus of attention? How aware, connected and in touch were you with the outer environment? Conversely, when you allowed yourself to be open, how much more able were you to observe, perceive and respond to your environment? Take a moment to consider your experience, and then write about it.

_____

_____

_____

_____

Now we explore some of your beliefs which may affect how you respond to love.

'Beliefs about Life' Graph

Some people believe life is to be enjoyed and celebrated. They are optimists and always look on the bright side of life, focusing upon whatever is right or good about things. They find the very best in everyone and everything.

Other people believe life is to be suffered and endured. They are pessimists and worriers, and always look on the dark side of life, focusing upon whatever is wrong or could go wrong. They find the very worst in everyone and everything.

What do you believe? Take a moment to consider your experience. Is life for you a celebration or a struggle? Do you see the best, or do you worry about whatever could go wrong? Be honest, but avoid judging yourself. It is all right to have negative feelings. Your experience is your experience.

125

_____

_____

_____

_____

Mark an X on the graph below to indicate your general beliefs about life.

> 1 = I believe that life is a struggle to be suffered and endured. I am a pessimist and a worrier, always looking on the dark side of life and seeing only the worst. I notice and focus upon whatever is wrong or could go wrong.

> 5 = I believe that life is to be enjoyed and celebrated. I am an optimist, always looking on the bright side of life and seeing only the best. I notice and focus upon whatever is right and good.

_____

| 1 | 2 | 3 | 4 | 5 |

Mark where your mother and father would have placed themselves. Be alert to the possibility that their beliefs and behaviour may have conditioned your own.

'Beliefs about People, Men and Women' Graph

People hold general beliefs about others. They make generalisations about people which usually come from past conditioning and personal experience. Some have quite positive beliefs about people: they like others, trust them, reach out to them and are comfortable, sympathetic and friendly with them. They have successful, intimate personal relationships.

Others have quite negative beliefs. They are afraid of people, do not trust them, are closed to them and are uncomfortable with them and even unsympathetic and unfriendly towards them. They do not have successful intimate relationships (even if they say they would like to have a deep, meaningful personal relationship).

What do you believe? Be honest, but avoid judging yourself. Take a moment to scan your beliefs about people in general, then about men and then about women. Record whatever thoughts come spontaneously to you.

_____

_____

_____

_____

_____

_____

_____

_____

Mark on the graph below to indicate your general beliefs about people, men and women. Use P for people, M for men and W for women.

    1 = I believe that they are usually unsafe, untrustworthy and difficult for me to be with.

    5 = I believe that they are usually safe, trustworthy and easy for me to be with.

1	2	3	4	5

Mark where your mother and father would have placed themselves. Be alert to the possibility that their beliefs and behaviour may have conditioned your own.

'Beliefs about Myself' Graph

One principle this course is based upon is that we cannot love others until we first love and accept ourself. Some people believe they are of great worth. They love themselves. They have a high level of self-acceptance, self-esteem and self-confidence. They are comfortable with themselves. They easily accept their humanness.

Other people believe they are of little worth. They do not love (or even like) themselves. They have a low level of self-acceptance, self-esteem and self-confidence. They are uncomfortable with themselves. They have doubts and fears about themselves, which they may express as arrogance, helplessness, self-pity or various other defensive and compensatory behaviours.

What do you believe about yourself and your own self-worth? Do you love yourself? First take a moment to consider your experience, and then write about it.

_____

_____

_____

_____

Mark an X on the graph below to indicate your general belief about your self-worth and self-acceptance.

    1 = I believe I am not a worthwhile person. I do not love or accept myself, and I feel bad about who I am. I am too _____
(ambitious, closed, frightened, helpless, hesitant, insecure or weak.)

    5 = I believe that I am a very worthwhile person. I love and accept myself exactly as I am. I feel good about myself, even though I know I am not perfect and will always have something more to learn.

1	2	3	4	5

Mark where your mother and father would have placed themselves. Be alert to the possibility that their beliefs and behaviour may have conditioned your own.

'Beliefs about Being Cause or Effect' Graph

Some people believe that we create our own reality, that is, we actively attract or manifest people, events, opportunities and lessons into our life as a direct result of attitudes and beliefs we hold within ourself. To these people *everything* which happens in our life is an extension of some part of our inner process, for which we must take full responsibility. Therefore we are the *cause* of everything which happens in our life.

Other people believe we have nothing personally to do with creating the people, events, opportunities and lessons which find their way into our life. To these people everything which happens to us is principally a random matter of conditioning, luck, coincidence or accident, and therefore we are not responsible for creating it. We are at the *effect* of everything which happens in our life.

How about you? Do you find any connection between your inner beliefs and attitudes and outer conditions and events, or not? In your life are you more of a cause or an effect? Take a moment to consider your experience and then write about it below.

_____

_____

_____

_____

Mark an X on the graph below to indicate your general belief about how life unfolds.

1 = I believe that random forces operating outside me, such as conditioning, coincidence, chance or accident, cause everything which happens to me, and therefore I take no responsibility for any of it.

5 = I believe that dynamic forces operating within me, such as attitudes, beliefs and my own outlook, cause everything which happens to me, and therefore I take full responsibility for creating everything in my life.

1	2	3	4	5

Mark where your mother and father would have placed themselves. Be alert to the possibility that their beliefs and behaviour may have conditioned your own.

What other personal beliefs may have influenced or blocked your bringing more love into your life?

_____

_____

_____

_____

_____

_____

_____

PART 3. EXPLORING PERSPECTIVES

EILEEN

As you think, so you are, and so you bring about.

I believe this principle completely. I know that I have attracted situations to myself, both positive and negative ones, by my thinking. At the time I would have liked to blame someone else, my situation or the environment around me. But when I have had the courage to be honest with myself, I have seen clearly that I have had only myself to blame.

How honest can I be with myself? It is not always easy. I personally get very annoyed when someone tells me that I have created a situation myself. For a long time I just could not accept it. Then I had an experience which made it very clear to me, showing me that I can always choose, that is, the choice is always mine as to how I create a situation.

I had been doing a great deal of travelling all over the world, giving lectures and workshops, with a certain amount of glamour attached to it all. I enjoyed meeting people and, what was more, I felt that I was loved, appreciated and respected far more when I was out in the world than when I was at the Findhorn Foundation, my own community, my own extended family.

I had reached the point where I wondered why I bothered to live in the community, as I felt that I was not needed there any more. Yet every time I meditated on whether or not I should stay, the inner guidance always came very clearly that my 'energy' was needed there.

Then one day I was sitting alone in my caravan feeling unwanted. In fact, I was a real misery. Out of the blue the thought came to me that I could *choose* to be loved, respected and appreciated right there in my own community. It was a very interesting thought. But I realised my just having the thought was not enough; I knew I would have to *do* something about it.

I went to a community meeting, and I shared with everyone there how I had had a real chip on my shoulder, and how I felt unwanted in the community, but also that I knew I had the opportunity to *choose* to be loved, appreciated and respected there. I was being honest about how I felt, and how I now wanted to change my attitudes and beliefs. Bringing my feelings out into the open made such a big difference!

Then I was tested again — did I really want to change? I was asked if I would participate in the big Transformation Game in the Universal Hall which would involve the whole community. I did not want to do it, but every time I meditated on it, the prompting which came was, 'Play the Game!' After a great struggle, I said I would. In the end it transformed my whole attitude and relationship towards the community. I came to realise how much I am loved, appreciated and respected there.

I emphasise that it all started with my *choosing* to have my life be different, *choosing* for it to be what I wanted it to be, and then *doing something* about it.

I know now that as I expect the very best in life, I draw it to me. So I expect the very best in everything and everyone, and I watch the very best come about. I expect my every need to be met, I expect the answer to every problem, I expect abundance on every level, I expect to grow spiritually. I accept no limitations in my life.

Now I find I can do anything at any time because I am drawing constantly from the God-Self within me, where there is always inspiration, and where nothing is impossible.

DAVID

You are all right, because God doesn't make any junk! — Anonymous

I first saw a poster with these words when I was in my forties. I wish I had seen and experienced its truth earlier in my life. Much earlier.

When children misbehave I imagine their parents usually say, 'Stop that!' or 'Don't do that!' My father would always preface his disciplinary words and actions by shouting angrily, 'What's the matter with you?' If I had had any doubt about my worth before, he cleared it away and confirmed my sense of low self-esteem which says, 'There is something the matter (or wrong) with me.' I spent much of my lifetime searching unconsciously for evidence to prove or disprove this doubt about myself. While one part of me reached out to others pleading, 'Please tell me I am all right,' another part of me looked for confirmation that I was not all right, and that there really was something wrong with me.

The first strong evidence of the latter was when I failed to speak proper English until I was five or six years old. Instead, I created my own language which my parents and older sister and brother were obliged to learn in order to communicate with me. The only word I remember is the word I used for my brother; his name is Harry; I called him 'Frafry'. I doubt that I used my unique language as a means of attracting attention; rather I feel it was a control mechanism I devised to protect myself. Imagine how different I must have felt! And the feedback I overheard from others! 'Don't worry, he'll grow out of it!' My English began to improve soon after I started school.

Dramatic proof that 'there is something wrong with me' came daily to me as a child because I sucked my thumb openly until I was twelve years old. It was not an act of defiance, rebellion or even habit, as much as it was something which I simply *had* to do, doubtless to decrease the high level of anxiety I must have felt. I endured enormous amounts of criticism, shaming and ostracism, not to mention hot pepper, mustard, adhesive tape on my thumb, even gloves — anything and everything my parents could imagine. Nothing worked. I needed to do it.

Even as an adult I never had to look very far to find more evidence to support my sense of low self-esteem. Over the years I have come slowly to several realisations. First I am convinced that I, myself, create all of my experiences. I attract them to myself as projections of my own inner life, my own belief system. Therefore I know that I need to take responsibility for every part of my life and not blame others for anything which happens to me. I have learned that because I create my own reality, I can also change it whenever I want to do so.

I discovered that I need to become aware of my past and its influence upon me *before* I can do anything about it. The point of awareness is the point of power, that is, when I can actually do something to bring about constructive change. The key is to recognise and acknowledge my past, without holding on to it as a sure guide for the future. I can affirm that 'I have a past, but I am more than my past'.

While I always *know* that I am a child of God, indeed that I am a God-Self fashioned from pure love, sometimes I *feel* small, finite and inadequate. In such cases, my experience is that my negative feelings always overpower my intellect — at least until I recognise and accept them and begin to deal with them clearly. It means I cannot allow my negative feelings to make my decisions for me.

Learning to love myself has been of great importance to me, as otherwise my sense of low self-esteem would have robbed me of any genuine or lasting sense of fulfilment, satisfaction and happiness. Yet I have come to accept that my low self-esteem served a number of strategic purposes: First it protected me, it helped me to survive. Later it showed me that it is possible for me to change fundamental and deeply-held beliefs. Best of all, it taught me that I can trust my own inner process — the love, light and wisdom of my being, my God-Self.

PART 4. GAINING AWARENESS

Awareness and Beliefs

The more we are aware of our personal experience at any given moment, the more we can *choose* to open our heart fully to give and receive love freely, and the less we need to be caught up in our fears, blind spots and behaviour patterns. Therefore learning to love means learning to stay aware, and not allowing ourself to lapse into old habitual, automatic, unconscious ways of feeling, thinking and behaving. One way to start this process is by exploring some of our beliefs.

What is a belief? It is something we accept as being true for us, something we trust and have confidence in, usually based upon our personal conditioning and experience.

Are you aware of all you believe? Or do your beliefs operate automatically, without much deliberate thought, review or even choice on your part?

Are you aware of where each of your beliefs came from, that is, how and when they were formed?

Are you aware of the great power and influence your beliefs have upon you, how they affect you physically, emotionally, mentally and spiritually?

Are you aware that you can change your beliefs — before they change you?

Personal Beliefs Review

Earlier in this session we sampled your beliefs in four relevant areas. Return to Part 2 now (p. 125) and review your beliefs and where you marked yourself on the graph for each one of these areas.

Then consider how each belief *serves* you in bringing more love into your life, and how each belief *limits* you in bringing more love into your life. Write down your findings.

1. Life

_____

_____

_____

2. People, men and women

_____

_____

_____

3. Myself

_____

_____

_____

4. Being cause or effect

_____

_____

_____

_____

Core Beliefs of Low Self-Esteem

At one time or another, most of us have doubts about ourself and our sense of worth. These doubts often come at a time when we feel we have made a mistake, done something we call wrong, stupid or bad, or seemingly 'failed' at something. Doubts may come when we feel judged or rejected or when we criticise ourself severely, even feel dislike or hatred for ourself. If such doubts become habitual, they form a belief, such as 'I am inadequate,' 'I am not good enough,' 'I do not deserve love,' 'I cannot do anything right,' or 'I am a failure.' Holding such a belief usually results in a poor self-image, low self-worth and little or no self-confidence.

We call this doubt or fear about ourself a _core belief_, as it lies at the core or centre of our sense of self. It serves as a basic and very effective block to the full expression of our self-esteem, self-acceptance and self-love.

As this course suggests that we cannot love others until we first love ourself, it is important to examine your beliefs about yourself, particularly your self-worth. For example what do you tell yourself at those times when you feel the least loving and accepting of yourself? What is your core belief about yourself? Here is one way to find out.

Now close your eyes . . . Sit up straight . . . Take a few deep breaths . . . Relax . . . Allow your body, emotions and thoughts to become still . . . Become like a calm, quiet lake . . .

When you are ready, allow yourself to experience that part of you which does not always like yourself very much . . . It may be the critic or judge inside of you . . . Take your time . . . Simply wait in the silence knowing that it will come to you . . .

Allow to come with it the thoughts and feelings, the doubts and fears which this part of yourself has about _your own self-worth_ . . . What does this part say to you? . . . What words does it use? . . . What is the worst thought, doubt or fear you have about your self-worth, your self-image? . . .

When you have found one or more of these thoughts or core beliefs about your self-worth, write them down.

_____

_____

_____

_____

Typical Operating Pattern

In our workshops we find that most people easily recognise and accept that they have one or more of these core beliefs of low self-esteem. We discover a typical operating pattern: first someone in our environment triggers the core belief by saying or doing something which makes us feel inadequate; next we have an emotional reaction; and then we take some kind of compensatory action.

Core beliefs and their operating patterns are like a musical juke-box. When a button is pushed, the corresponding record is selected, plays itself through, and then waits quietly until the next time the button is pushed, when it starts all over again. A similar stimulus/response pattern involving our core belief continues equally automatically for a whole lifetime unless we take notice of it and choose to change it.

How do our buttons get pushed? Core beliefs may be activated in response to major life events, such as when we lose a job, our partner ends the relationship or we 'fail' at some important task we set for ourself.

Our buttons are also triggered by everyday events, such as when we feel we are not being seen, heard, or understood, or when we perceive ourself judged, rejected or ignored by others.

Our initial emotional reactions may vary from anger to anxiety, from despair to depression, from help-lessness to hopelessness. Whatever the reaction, it results more from the core belief itself, rather than from the immediate circumstances and, as such, is part of the juke-box record of our behaviour pattern.

Also part of the pattern are the compensatory actions we then take. We may turn to food, alcohol, drugs, sex, sleep, work, service or achievement. We may substitute money, prestige or professional recognition for the personal recognition and self-acceptance which elude us.

Some people experience their core belief constantly as an ever-present influence in their life, while others seldom experience their core belief and its accompanying feelings of low self-worth. Rare is the person who has ever mastered completely this almost universal human pattern (no matter what they tell themselves and others about having worked through it.)

Our primary task is to learn to live more gracefully with our core belief of low self-esteem and not to allow it to dictate how we live our life.

Limiting Effects

From the Introduction and Session Three you know that we are all pure love. The core belief is only a shadow, and therefore is not real. However we take it very seriously because its limiting effects upon us are quite real.

What are these effects? We turn now to find out how core beliefs of low self-esteem may operate within your life and the effects they may have upon it.

Now close your eyes . . . Sit up straight . . . Take a few deep breaths . . . Relax . . . Allow your body, emotions and thoughts to become still . . . Become like a calm, quiet lake . . .

When you are ready, take a moment to consider the core belief of low self-esteem which you have written down. As a step towards transforming it, say it over to yourself a few times to help you to recognise and accept that it has been a part of you, probably for a very long time.

Then allow to come to you the most recent instance when you experienced your core belief, that is, when you actually believed and accepted your core belief as being true (rather than the doubt or fear it actually is). *Who* else was involved? *When* — what were the circumstances? *How* did it make you feel? *What* action did you take as a result? When the details are clear to you, record them in the blanks below.

I believed my core belief about myself with _____
_____ (Person)

when _____
_____ (Circumstances) _____

It made me feel _____ , and I reacted by
_____ (Emotion)

_____
_____ (Action)

Again consider your core belief of low self-esteem. Then allow to come to you another instance when you experienced your core belief, with someone else and under different circumstances.

I believed my core belief about myself with _____
_____ (Person)

when _____
_____ (Circumstances) _____

It made me feel _____ , and I reacted by
_____ (Emotion)

_____
_____ (Action)

Again consider your core belief of low self-esteem. Then allow to come to you an earlier instance when you experienced your core belief, with someone else under different circumstances.

I believed my core belief about myself with _____
_____ (Person)

when _____
_____ (Circumstances) _____

It made me feel _____ , and I reacted by
_____ (Emotion)

_____
_____ (Action)

Again consider your core belief of low self-esteem. Then allow to come to you an earlier instance when you experienced your core belief, with someone else under different circumstances.

I believed my core belief about myself with _____
_____ (Person)

when _____
_____ (Circumstances) _____

It made me feel _____ , and I reacted by
_____ (Emotion)

_____
_____ (Action)

One last time consider your core belief of low self-esteem. Then allow to come to you an instance from childhood, maybe even the very first time that you may have experienced your core belief.

I believed my core belief about myself with _____
_____ (Person)

when _____
_____ (Circumstances) _____

It made me feel _____ , and I reacted by
_____ (Emotion)

_____
_____ (Action)

Now examine all of your responses. What similarities or patterns do you find in the people who were involved — that is, what roles, categories or types were they, such as family members, friends, co-workers, authorities, people of the same or opposite sex, adults, children?

_____

_____

_____

_____

What similarities or patterns do you find in the circumstances?

_____

_____

_____

_____

What similarities or patterns do you find in the feelings provoked within you?

_____

_____

_____

_____

What similarities or patterns do you find in the actions you took?

_____

_____

_____

_____

From this exercise, to what extent do you recognise and accept that you may have a core belief of low self-esteem, one which follows a typical operating pattern in your life? Write down any feelings, thoughts and questions you wish to record.

_____

_____

_____

_____

Self-Image and Validation

What causes us to develop a poor self-image? One common explanation is that our self-image is the result of the validation we perceived from the significant people around us during the first two years of our life. For most of us, it means primarily our mother. Thus if we felt recognised, accepted and nurtured by our mother during this period, then we undoubtedly felt good about ourself and therefore developed a healthy self-image. However, if we did not feel valued, we may have concluded that it was our fault (something *was* wrong with *us*), for otherwise we would have been validated properly.

Harbouring this doubt about our worth in our infantile, two-year-old mind, we then began to look for further evidence to prove or disprove it. As a result, over the years we amass substantial evidence to 'prove' that the core belief of low self-esteem we have about ourself is true. Thus it becomes a perpetually self-fulfilling belief which, like the juke-box, repeats endlessly throughout our life unless we become aware of it and choose to do something about it.

Notice that this explanation does not suggest that our parents failed to love us. They may have been simply ignorant or inept about making us feel welcomed and worthwhile, or we ourself may have had difficulty in recognising or receiving their own unique expressions of love.

However it is also possible, as *The Drama of Being a Child* and other books by Alice Miller point out clearly, that for some of us, our parents actually did not love us, and consequently we suppressed our own needs and invented the core belief to avoid the deeper pain of that desperate realisation.

In any case, we offer you the likely supposition that since you were about two years old, you have been re-creating regularly one basic scenario, complete with a whole cast of characters, a variety of plots and circumstances, a range of emotional responses and a gamut of compensatory actions — all orchestrated unconsciously to 'prove' the apparent 'truth' of your core belief of low self-worth.

Limitations and Service Functions

As with all personality patterns, this core belief limits us, and it also serves us. On the one hand, it prevents us from experiencing our own goodness, our own wholeness; it keeps us from loving and accepting ourself and others. Consider for a moment how your own core belief of low self-worth limits you specifically. Then write down your findings.

_____

_____

_____

_____

On the other hand, our core belief also *gives* us something, it does something for us, or we would not allow it to continue to limit us. For example it may protect us, keep us safe, prevent us from having to take risks, making mistakes or failing. To discover how your core belief serves you, consider whatever (1) you might *lose* and (2) you might have to *do* or *be* if the core belief were *not* there as a part of you. Write down your findings.

_____

_____

_____

_____

The 'bad' news of Part 4 is that most of us have a core belief of low self-esteem operating in one way or another, which hinders us from bringing more love into our life.

The 'good' news of Part 5 and the rest of this course is that we can do something about our core beliefs. We can minimise their powerful influence and limiting effects upon our life. We can prevent them from blocking us from learning to love ourself and others, and from bringing more love into our life.

PART 5. DEVELOPING POTENTIAL

Taking Responsibility for Our Life

We all have been conditioned to some extent by parents, family, friends, teachers, the media, the church, the government, other social and political institutions and society at large. Such conditioning can be either desirable or undesirable, helpful or detrimental.

In any case, we need to take responsibility for our own attitudes and beliefs, no matter what their source may be or whether we formed them consciously or unconsciously.

Ken Keyes Jr. in his book *The Power of Unconditional Love,* says, 'You are not responsible for the programming you picked up in childhood. However, as an adult, you are 100 percent responsible for fixing it.'

It is the intention of this course to help you to 'fix' whatever blocks you from bringing more love into your life.

Our Beliefs Determine Our Experience

While you accept your beliefs as being true for you, they may not be true for anyone else.

Great diversity of belief exists in the world, making life interesting and varied, with always something new to discover, to be challenged by and to learn.

Ken Keyes Jr. also says, 'A loving person lives in a loving world. A hostile person lives in a hostile world. Everyone you meet is your mirror.' If we all live in the *same* world, how can that be?

It is because our beliefs are like tinted sunglasses through which we see the world; and the world, as a mirror, reflects back to us whatever belief we present to it.

What kind of world do you see? A loving world? A hostile one? Or something else entirely different?

The kind of world we see and experience depends upon which glasses we wear, that is, it depends upon our beliefs — even though we may tell ourself it is the other way around.

Rue Wallace Hass sums it up clearly and concisely: 'What you see is who you are.'

So what do you see? And who then are you?

It all depends upon the glasses you wear. It all depends upon your beliefs.

Re-Framing our Beliefs

Are you willing to try on a new pair of glasses?

Are you willing to consider updating your beliefs, perhaps even changing some of them?

It means taking a fresh approach. It means looking at things in a new way.

For example take a look at the figure below. What do you see?

Figure 1.

Whatever you see, continue to explore the drawing. Look at it in a new way. Allow it to change and be something else, something different. What do you see now?

You may first see the silhouette of two individuals in profile facing each other.

Or you may see a chalice or wine goblet.

Do you see both images? Keep looking at the figure until you find both the faces and the chalice. It is important that you see both images.

When you find them both, begin to switch your focus of attention back and forth several times between the faces and the chalice. Continue until you become aware of exactly *how* you manage to shift back and forth. What is the *inner* mechanism or process you use to cause your perspective to change instantly and totally from one image to the other?

Aware that both perspectives are present in the figure, we can remind ourself that the lower curve of the chalice is also the chins of the two people, or that the noses of the two faces are also the upper curves of the chalice. Or we can simply intend or command our awareness to shift to the other image. Our perspective can thus change with an act of will, that is, by our desiring and choosing for it to do so.

Some people refer to this process as *re-framing*, that is, taking a new look at something which is familiar to them, finding new perspectives, discovering new dimensions or exploring for new meanings and interpretations.

Notice that the drawing itself does not change; it remains constant. Only our perspective changes by the way in which we interact with the drawing. Notice also that we cannot see *both* images at the same time.

Now imagine how it would be if we were to go through life only having seen *either* the chalice *or* the two faces. Imagine how it would be if we were to have a strong attachment or personal investment in seeing only one of the images. Imagine how it would be if we were to fix upon that one image completely, thinking about it, reinforcing the image by holding tightly onto it in our awareness. Imagine how it would be if we were to be so convinced of the absolute certainty of the existence of only that one image that we became nearly incapable of seeing any other.

That is what can happen when we hold on to a belief rigidly. It is what can happen when we have looked through the same pair of sunglasses for so long that we forget we are even wearing sunglasses.

Time for Re-examination

Because you are applying yourself to this course now, it may be that the time has come in your life for you to re-examine some of your beliefs, especially those which you have taken for granted. It may be time to begin to re-frame the way in which you look at certain issues.

For example turn back to Part 2. now (p. 125) and note once again where you marked yourself on the four graphs.

Imagine what you would need in order to move up to a higher number on each one of the graphs. Imagine how your life might be different in each case. What would have to happen to make it possible? Might the process of re-framing help you to move up to a 5 on each graph, if you desired to do so?

By helping you to gain new awareness and understanding about yourself and about how your beliefs and behaviour patterns have been formed, we hope this course will enable you to change your core belief of low self-esteem and your other limiting beliefs, so that you may bring more love into your life.

We offer you many techniques throughout this course specifically to help you to re-frame your perspective about your core belief and yourself.

'Self-Appreciation' Scan

Most of us were conditioned as children not to talk about ourself and our sense of self-worth. Parents, teachers and others told us that we would be considered impolite, ill-mannered, immodest, conceited, egotistical, even arrogant and narcissistic if we were to talk about our 'good points'. Discussing our strengths, telling others what we like about ourself, or paying ourself a compliment are usually frowned upon, if not altogether taboo, in most parts of western society.

But honest self-appraisal and genuine self-appreciation are quite different from bragging and boasting.

The injunction 'Know thyself' surely means to recognise and accept both our strengths and our weaknesses, our 'positive' qualities as well as our 'negative' ones, our assets as well as our liabilities, and to be able to talk about them simply, clearly and objectively.

Therefore we invite you to take the next few moments to consider the various parts of yourself that you appreciate and love: habits, skills, qualities, traits, patterns, perspectives, feelings, ideas, ways of doing things. If you wish, you may do an Experience Scan using *WHAT I LOVE ABOUT MYSELF IS . . .'* or simply begin writing spontaneously.

NOTE. This is not to be a list of things you love *about life*, such as chocolate, dogs, roses, Mozart and the colour blue, but rather a list of what you love *about yourself*. Notice how you feel as you appreciate yourself. For example do you feel warm and relaxed? Awkward and uneasy? Shy and embarrassed? Continue your list until you have filled the entire space below.

WHAT I LOVE ABOUT MYSELF IS . . .

Examine your responses. Mark the ones which seem especially meaningful or significant or which otherwise draw your attention to them.

What did you feel as you were doing the exercise? What are you feeling and thinking now?

_____

_____

_____

_____

If you are a stranger to self-appreciation, find ways to introduce it into your daily life. You owe it to yourself to recognise and acknowledge yourself in sincere and positive ways. As you do so, you will also be contradicting your core belief of low self-esteem.

To begin with, you may wish to keep your self-appreciations to yourself, but eventually you will need to begin to voice them aloud to others. ('I appreciate the way I . . .' 'I am very good at . . .' 'I love my own . . .') Otherwise you take part in a conspiracy of silence, a social convention which limits you far more than it serves you.

As a simple step in this direction, telephone your support person now before going any farther and read to him or her the list of all the things you love about yourself. Write down your support person's response and your own feelings and thoughts which have been prompted.

_____

_____

_____

_____

Self-acceptance and self-appreciation are steps along the way towards the self-love which is essential for bringing more genuine love into our life.

Windows Of The Soul

The next step is to love yourself — *not* for these things you have listed — but for simply being yourself.

A common saying is that 'the eyes are the windows of the soul'.

Have you ever had the experience that as you gaze steadily into someone's eyes, you begin to penetrate their exterior and move more deeply into intimate contact with their inner being, their essential self, their God-Self? All of the outer traits become insignificant and fade away, and you feel in contact with the real person. It can be a very profound, revealing and moving experience, regardless of who the other person is and the nature of your relationship, for it is a fleeting yet unmistakable glimpse of the intrinsic sacredness of another human being.

We offer you that experience now. All you need is a mirror and total privacy. For maximum benefit you may wish to pre-record this exercise to enable you to stay with your own inner process without interruption. Avoid rushing through this exercise. Take your time.

Find a comfortable position, sitting closely in front of a mirror, or hold a hand mirror large enough to allow you to see your eyes clearly.

Now close your eyes . . . Sit up straight . . . Take a few deep breaths and relax . . . Allow your body, emotions and thoughts to become still . . . Become like a calm, quiet lake . . .

When you are ready, slowly open your eyes and look at yourself in the mirror . . . Look yourself in the eyes . . . What do you see? . . . Take a few minutes to establish direct genuine contact . . . Focus your attention upon one eye for a while, and then shift your gaze to the other one, rather than trying to see both eyes at once . . .

As you do, notice your inner response . . . How do you respond physically? . . . Relaxed? . . . Tense? . . . Full of energy? . . . How do you respond emotionally? . . . Cheerful? . . . Embarrassed? . . . Uneasy? . . . How do you respond mentally? . . . Curious? . . . Critical? . . . With increased mind chatter? . . .

Is it easy for you to maintain a comfortable gaze into your own eyes? . . . Or do you resist and find ways to take your attention away? . . . Make a deliberate choice to stay with the exercise and continue to maintain a steady, comfortable gaze into your own eyes, without either staring transfixed or looking away . . . Allow any embarrassment or discomfort you may be feeling to fade gently away . . .

Now penetrate more deeply into the eyes you see in the mirror . . . Look through and beyond them . . . Allow yourself to *feel* whatever lies beyond them . . . Stay with the experience for as long as you can . . .

When you are ready, say aloud, *'I LOVE AND ACCEPT MYSELF EXACTLY AS I AM . . .'* Continue to maintain deep eye contact with yourself in the mirror . . .

Notice your inner response . . . How do you respond physically? . . . Emotionally? . . . Mentally? . . .

When you are ready, repeat the statement aloud, *'I LOVE AND ACCEPT MYSELF EXACTLY AS I AM . . .'*

Take some time to be with this statement — the words, the idea, the feeling tone of it . . . Let it all sink deep within you . . .

Continue for a few moments to repeat the statement aloud, *'I LOVE AND ACCEPT MYSELF EXACTLY AS I AM . . .'* Keep it fresh . . . Avoid letting it become automatic or ritualistic . . . Maintain deep eye contact with yourself . . . Each time allow yourself to go farther inside yourself . . . Farther and farther . . . Farther than you have ever gone before . . . Connect with the very innermost part of yourself . . . Take all the time you need . . .

In your own time, allow your attention to return to the room where you are now . . . Take a deep breath . . . And a gentle stretch . . .

Now write down any feelings, thoughts and questions you wish to record.

_____

_____

_____

_____

_____

_____

_____

_____

_____

_____

_____

Repeat this exercise regularly as one simple and powerful method to re-frame your self-image.

Loyal Soldiers

In her book *The Unfolding Self: Psychosynthesis And Counselling* Molly Young Brown introduces a useful analogy applicable to the core belief of low self-esteem.

For years following the close of World War II, a Japanese soldier would occasionally be discovered hiding in the jungle of a South Pacific island. Unaware that the war was over, he had kept himself alive, waiting to be rescued. When found, he would be told he could stop hiding as the war was over, but the disbelieving soldier would respond sceptically, 'You are trying to trick me.' Eventually he would be subdued and repatriated to Japan, where he would be retired from active duty with full military honours as a hero for having served his country loyally, and would be re-integrated into civilian life.

Your core belief is a loyal soldier. It has served you well over the years. It has defended you. It has helped you to survive. It has kept you alive, perhaps through many battles and much pain.

But the war is over!

You have more options to protect yourself now than you did when you were two years old and first drafted your core belief into service. Out of hiding at last, your core belief need not be put to the firing squad for limiting you, but rather be retired with full honours for having served you well. It is time to transform and integrate it into your own sense of wholeness.

As you begin to address it, do not be surprised if you encounter a 'You are trying to trick me' disbelieving resistance from the part of you which believes your core belief to be true. After all, it has been serving you for many years. But in time, with loving patience, you will be able to persuade this part of you that the war is indeed over.

It will be a time when you can say, not as an affirmation, but as a real, heart-felt appreciation, 'I love and accept myself exactly as I am!'

'Needs' Symbol and Drawing

As we have indicated, core beliefs of low self-esteem and other beliefs and fears which limit you from bringing more love into your life do not develop overnight. They usually have been in evidence and reinforced over a very long time. Your desire, intention and choice are therefore needed to change them. Here is an exercise to identify whatever you need to help you to increase your self-acceptance and self-love.

Now find a comfortable position, sitting up straight . . . Close your eyes . . . Take several long, slow, deep breaths . . . Relax your body completely . . . Release all of the tension . . . Allow whatever emotions you may be feeling to fade away . . . Do the same with your thoughts . . . Become like a calm, quiet lake, which mirrors perfectly the blue sky, or the starry sky in the silence of the night . . . Be at peace and yet remain alert . . .

When you are ready, allow to come to you an image or sense which represents whatever you need to help you to increase your own self-acceptance and self-love . . . Take your time . . . Wait patiently in the silence, knowing that something will soon come to you . . . Be willing to accept whatever comes without judging, censoring or rejecting it . . . Simply observe and examine it with the purpose of learning more about it . . .

When you begin to sense something, allow it to become more vivid . . . Note its size and shape . . . Its density and design . . . Its colour and texture . . . Explore it with as many of your senses as you can . . . Find the overall quality it suggests to you . . .

Then open your eyes, and express in a drawing below either the image itself or its quality . . . If nothing has come to you, open your eyes, hold the question in mind and begin to draw freely and spontaneously, letting something come to you in that way . . .

WHAT I NEED TO HELP ME INCREASE MY SELF-ACCEPTANCE AND SELF-LOVE

Write down the overall *quality* of the symbol and any other words, feelings or thoughts which came to you during the exercise, or which you are aware of now. What new insight or awareness does this symbol and its quality give to you?

_____

_____

_____

_____

How might you use whatever this symbol represents to you to increase your own self-acceptance and self-love? What ideas for a 'next step' has it given you?

_____

_____

_____

_____

Next in Part 6 we offer more methods to help you to transform your core belief of low self-esteem.

PART 6. APPLYING IT

Affirmations

Our brain is a computer. Our mind is the programmer. Our life is the print-out.

Most of us have been programming ourself with a core belief of low self-esteem from the time we were two years old. Our resultant print-out has been filled with doubt, hesitancy, poor self-image and lack of assurance, confidence, acceptance and love.

So when we want to change the print-out, what must we do? Yes, of course, change the programming!

One effective means of changing the programming is with affirmations. *An affirmation is a positive, seed-planting statement or image in which we state or visualise clearly and precisely a desired outcome as if it were already so.* They are commands, given with authority, to our computer.

Examples of verbal affirmations are *'I AM BRINGING MORE LOVE INTO MY LIFE DAY BY DAY'*, and *'I LOVE AND ACCEPT MYSELF EXACTLY AS I AM'.* An example of a visual affirmation is the creative meditation ideal model of honesty in Session Four.

You may ask how repeatedly saying a sentence or visualising an image can change a life-long behaviour pattern. Affirmations are a means of switching our focus of attention similar to the way in which we switch our focus from one image to the other in the chalice/faces drawing in Part 5. Affirmations are a method used to re-frame a given situation, in this case our self-esteem.

We present three techniques to help you to re-frame your core belief of low self-esteem and to begin to love and accept yourself more fully.

Verbal Affirmations

Effective verbal affirmations have these characteristics:

1. They are stated positively and vigorously. ('I am always very confident now,' rather than 'I am no longer fearful.') They focus upon the new attitude we wish to create, rather than the old one we want to let go.

2. They are short, usually a dozen words or less. Most core beliefs are equally short ('I am in-adequate,' 'I am not good enough,' 'I cannot do anything right,' 'I am a failure'), and notice how effective they are!

3. They are stated in present tense, as if the desired outcome has already been achieved. ('I always feel very safe to be open to love now,' rather than 'I will feel increasingly safe to be open to love in the future.')

4. They begin with our name to keep them personal and connected to our own developing process. ('I, (Name) , always deserve love in my life.'

5. They are absolute. Using words such as *always, very* and *now,* and avoiding phrases such as *I can, I try to* or *I have the ability to,* help to close loopholes so that the part of us which believes our core beliefs to be true can find no room for exceptions.

6. They are limited to ourself and our own life because we cannot make affirmations on behalf of other people. ('I am always very loving and lovable,' rather than 'People always find me very loving and lovable.')

7. They are enhanced when we visualise the desired outcome as we write the affirmations and say them aloud.

The difference between an affirmation and a core belief is that the core belief is a lie which seems like the truth. An affirmation is the truth which seems like a lie!

Now we invite you to create a verbal affirmation which reverses or contradicts the core belief of low self-esteem which you identified in Part 4. It may mean simply stating the opposite. For example, if your core belief is 'I am not good enough,' your affirmation might be 'I am always good enough,' or 'I am absolutely perfect just as I am now.' Make it seem like the biggest lie you could possibly tell. It will be a stronger, more effective affirmation if you do!

Write it down several times, beginning with, 'I,   (Name)   , . . .' Each time as you write it, say it aloud and visualise the desired outcome to reinforce the re-programming of your computer, the re-framing of your self-esteem. Take your time. Keep it fresh and alive.

_____

_____

_____

_____

Almost all advertising influences us by using affirmations in a strategy of frequent repetition over a period of time. We use the same strategy. Avoid feelings of impatience and hurry, and give your affirmation the time it needs to take root. Repetition is the key. The original programming you wish to change did not develop overnight; nor is it likely to disappear overnight. With affirmations, as in advertising, persistence produces results.

Use your affirmation every day for the next seven days. Say it aloud several times a day. Set your watch, clock or timer to remind you to say it at least once an hour. Visualise the desired outcome each time you say it.

Here are some suggestions for reinforcing your affirmation:

● Say it occasionally as you make eye contact with yourself in a mirror.

● Write it down over and over again, while visualising the desired outcome.

● Write it on index cards, putting them up around your home or work place.

● Carry an index card with you in your pocket, wallet or purse as a daily reminder.

● Telephone your support person and others and say it aloud confidently.

● Find a picture or make a drawing which symbolises whatever you wish to achieve, display it prominently and hold it clearly in your awareness.

Continue to look for new and novel ways to remind yourself of your affirmation. Keep it a living presence in your life. Remember, you are re-framing. You are re-programming your computer. Most importantly, *you* are the one who is creating the outcome you desire.

Visual Affirmations

A graphic form of affirmation is the ideal model visualisation in which we picture in our imagination specific details of how we would like our life to be.

Now turn back to Session Four, Part 5 (p. 109) and review your experience of the creative meditation. Then re-play the ideal model technique in your imagination, substituting the quality of love for the that of honesty, and visualising how loving you would ideally like to be. After repeating this visualisation daily for the next seven days, write down your feelings, thoughts and observations about your experience.

_____

_____

_____

_____

Action Affirmations

The third affirmation technique is the reverse of the first two: it uses *outer* behaviour to produce a change in our *inner* state. With sufficient repetition over a period of time, we can actually change our inner state to match the outer behaviour we enact. We do it by 'acting as if' we already possessed the desired inner state.

People use this technique in everyday life. For example we know that we can change how we are feeling by such simple actions as singing or whistling, or by the way we dress, or by the way we speak, stand and move. The outer action is the catalyst for the inner change. By behaving as if we were feeling cheerful, confident, courageous or loving, eventually we become that which we enact. You may have experienced this process in Session Four when you used your body to enact characteristics of openness with the purpose of evoking this quality within yourself.

Take a moment now to consider outer, observable behaviours which to you reflect the quality of love. Begin with physical sensations, postures, gestures, movements and actions which you can enact privately, facing a large mirror. Apply them all towards yourself, 'acting as if' you loved and accepted yourself genuinely and fully, and you possessed a high level of self-confidence and self-esteem. Later, when you are comfortable with this technique, begin to identify specific outer, observable actions you can take when you are relating to others, 'acting as if' you loved them freely and fully, even (and especially) if you are feeling quite the contrary towards them at the time.

NOTE. By 'acting as if' we feel love for ourself or others when we may actually feel quite negative emotions, we are not being deceitful, hypocritical or inauthentic, *if* our intention is to identify with and evoke the highest level of our being, *despite* our negative or blocked feelings. While it is necessary for us to accept all parts of ourself, we do have the *choice* of which conflicting parts to energise and express — the positive or the negative, the highest or the lowest, the loving or the unloving. This important choice is *always* ours to make.

Practise enacting these outer, observable behaviours for at least five minutes each day for the next seven days. Report your experience with this technique below.

_____

_____

_____

_____

Suggested Reading

1. *Vivation,* by Jim Leonard and Phil Laut, says: 'Once you accept the idea that your reality is a projection of your mind, you begin to eliminate the tendency to feel like a victim and the desire to prove yourself right about your negative convictions. Accepting that your reality is the projection of your mind is giving yourself the opportunity to create for yourself the things you want in life.'

2. *I Deserve Love,* by Sondra Ray, shows how to use affirmations and presents hundreds of sample affirmations tailored for use in many different loving and sexual situations.

Personal Goal

Consider various simple, specific, observable actions you could take within the next few days which would be a step towards bringing more love into your life. Then choose one which seems important to you, one to take as a personal goal. Make a deliberate choice to achieve it. Write it down. Remember, making and implementing choices empowers and strengthens you.

_____

_____

_____

_____

Session Learnings

Turn back and review what you have done in this session. Then write down the three most important insights or learnings you have gained from it.

_____

_____

_____

_____

_____

_____

Purpose

As stated at the beginning of Part 2, the purpose of Session Five is to explore some of your beliefs relevant to bringing more love into your life, to discover how these beliefs both serve you and limit you and to provide methods to help you change any beliefs which may block you from loving more freely and fully. To what degree has Session Five achieved its general purpose for you?

_____

_____

_____

_____

Congratulations! You have come to the end of Session Five and the first half of the course. Please discuss your experience of this session with your support person *before you begin Session Six.*

CHOOSING TO ACCEPT

PART 1. MAKING CONNECTIONS

You are now beginning the second half of the course. Therefore review the first five sessions to reconnect with your process of development. Begin by turning back to Session One, Part 1, and review your primary purpose and specific objectives in taking this course. How do you assess your progress so far?

Have you achieved the personal goal you set for yourself in Session Five? How was it?

Next, if you have been using the evocative word cards introduced in Session One, Part 6 (p. 40), write down whatever your experience has been with them.

Then, if you have chosen to take additional risks in bringing more love into your life since the beginning of the preceding session, write about your experience: what you did, how successful you were and what you learned.

Continue with these personal journal pages by *making connections with the theme, issues and exercises of this course*, recording whatever relevant memories, ideas, feelings, insights, dreams, 'unfinished business', interactions and other events in your inner and outer worlds have occurred since you completed Session Five. Include related reading you may have done, questions on your mind and any other observations and connections with the course you wish to make.

_____
_____
_____
_____
_____
_____
_____
_____
_____
_____
_____
_____
_____
_____
_____
_____
_____
_____

_____

_____

_____

_____

_____

_____

_____

_____

_____

_____

_____

_____

_____

_____

_____

_____

_____

_____

_____

_____

_____

_____

_____

_____

_____

_____

_____

_____

_____

_____

_____

_____

_____

_____

_____

_____

_____

Next in Part 2 we explore the many different images you have of yourself.

PART 2. TAKING STOCK

Purpose

The purpose of Session Six is to experience that your personal identity is a composite of the many different images which you have of yourself, that these images are partial and ever-changing and that accepting all of them as a part of you is an important step in bringing more love into your life.

We all have many different images or identifications of ourselves. Each one is only a fragment, a partial image, because we are always changing and expressing different ones at different times. Each image we have of ourself then is only one piece of our total personal identity.

We have countless other pieces, other images — so many that it would be impossible to list them all. However, to give you a sense of them, we sample a few of the more obvious images we have of ourself.

'Gender Identifications' Check-list

We identify with our gender, and we have a sense of how it feels and what it means to be this way. Mark below all of the gender images you have of yourself at one time or another.

_____Female	_____Male
_____Girl	_____Boy
_____Woman	_____Man
_____Lady	_____Gentleman

'Family Identifications' Check-list

We identify with our family images. Mark below all of the images, whether real or assumed, you have of yourself.

_____Daughter	_____Son	_____Cousin
_____Granddaughter	_____Grandson	_____Orphan
_____Daughter-in-law	_____Son-in-law	
_____Niece	_____Nephew	
_____Sister	_____Brother	
_____Sister-in-law	_____Brother-in-law	
_____Aunt	_____Uncle	
_____Wife/partner	_____Husband/partner	
_____Mother	_____Father	
_____Mother-in-law	_____Father-in-law	
_____Grandmother	_____Grandfather	

Write down other family images you have of yourself.

_____

_____

Nationality Identifications

We identify with our nationality. Write down your original and any adopted nationality you may have. Include other similar images you have of yourself, such as planetary citizen, and the names which people coming from your community, state or region are called.

_____

_____

Political Identifications

We identify with our political persuasion, and have images of ourself as being a conservative, democrat, liberal, moderate, republican, revolutionary, socialist and others. Write down all of the political images you have of yourself, even if they are different ones at different times or with different issues.

_____

_____

Religious/Spiritual Identifications

We identify with our religious/spiritual persuasion, and have images of ourself as being an agnostic, atheist, believer, Buddhist, child of God, Christian, disciple, heretic, Hindu, humanitarian, Jew, meditator, Muslim, Protestant, Roman Catholic, seeker of Truth, servant of God, visionary and others. Write down all of the religious/spiritual images you have of yourself.

_____

_____

Work Identifications

We identify with our work, and have images of ourself as being an employee, self-employee, employer, unemployed or retired person, supervisor, colleague, subordinate and others. Write down all of the work images you have of yourself. Include all of the types of work you have had, for example as an administrator, civil servant, engineer, health professional, secretary, teacher or writer.

_____

_____

_____

_____

Special Interest Identifications

We identify with our hobbies and pastimes, and have images of ourself as being an artist, bird-watcher, camper, collector, cyclist, dancer, hiker, knitter, reader, sport spectator, swimmer, television viewer, theatre goer, volunteer and others. Write down all of the special interest images you have of yourself.

_____

_____

_____

_____

'Animal Trait Identifications' Check-list

We identify with our many attitudes, beliefs, desires, motives, needs, qualities and traits, and we have various images of ourself. Often we liken ourself to the best and worst traits of animals. We picture ourself as being 'free as a bird, sly as a fox, wise as an owl or strong as an ox'. Mark below all of the images or identifications which you may occasionally have of yourself.

_____ Alligator	_____ Crow	_____ Hog	_____ Rabbit
_____ Ape	_____ Deer	_____ Horse	_____ Rat
_____ Bat	_____ Dinosaur	_____ Jackal	_____ Scorpion
_____ Bear	_____ Dog	_____ Kangaroo	_____ Shark
_____ Beaver	_____ Dolphin	_____ Lamb	_____ Sheep
_____ Bee	_____ Duck	_____ Lark	_____ Shrimp
_____ Bird	_____ Eagle	_____ Leech	_____ Skunk
_____ Bull	_____ Eel	_____ Lion	_____ Snail
_____ Butterfly	_____ Elephant	_____ Lizard	_____ Snake
_____ Buzzard	_____ Ferret	_____ Magpie	_____ Sparrow
_____ Camel	_____ Fish	_____ Mole	_____ Spider
_____ Canary	_____ Flea	_____ Monkey	_____ Squirrel
_____ Carp	_____ Fly	_____ Moose	_____ Swan
_____ Cat	_____ Fox	_____ Mouse	_____ Tiger
_____ Chicken	_____ Frog	_____ Mule	_____ Turkey
_____ Clam	_____ Gazelle	_____ Ostrich	_____ Turtle
_____ Cock	_____ Giraffe	_____ Owl	_____ Vulture
_____ Cow	_____ Goat	_____ Ox	_____ Whale
_____ Crab	_____ Goose	_____ Parrot	_____ Wolf
_____ Crocodile	_____ Hawk	_____ Pig	_____ Worm

Write down other animal images you have of yourself.

_____

_____

_____

_____

Domestic Identifications

We identify with our home responsibilities, and have images of ourself as being a baby-sitter, book-keeper, cleaner, cook, chauffeur, dishwasher, do-it-yourselfer (perhaps including carpenter, electrician, painter or plumber), gardener, ironer, shopper and others. Write down all of the domestic images you have of yourself.

_____

_____

_____

_____

Physical Identifications

We identify with our physical body and sensations, and have images of ourself in physical terms, as being a person who is beautiful/plain, black/white, coordinated/clumsy, fast/slow, healthy/sick, strong/weak, tall/short, thin/fat, young/old and others. Write down all of the physical images you have of yourself.

_____

_____

_____

_____

Emotional Identifications

We identify with our emotions and feelings, and have images of ourself in emotional terms, as being a person who is angry, anxious, blissful, compassionate, depressed, elated, fearful, guilty, joyful, lonely, sad, serene and others. Write down all of the emotional images you have of yourself.

_____

_____

_____

_____

Mental Identifications

We identify with our minds and mental processes, and have images of ourself in mental terms, as being a person who is (un)analytical, (in)articulate, (un)clear, (un)educated, (un)intelligent, knowledgeable/ignorant, (il)logical, (ir)rational, (un)thoughtful and others. Write down all of the mental images you have of yourself.

_____

_____

_____

_____

Sexual Identifications

We identify with our sexual orientation and practice, and hold images of ourself as being an asexual, bisexual, celibate, deviant, heterosexual, homosexual, lesbian, nymphomaniac, seducer, stud, tease, transsexual, vamp, virgin, whore and others. Write down all of the sexual images you have of yourself.

_____

_____

_____

_____

'Behaviour Identifications' Check-list

We identify with our behaviour, and we have various behavioural images of ourselves. Mark below all of the identifications which you may occasionally have of yourself. You may test out questionable ones by saying to yourself, 'Sometimes I am a _____.'

_____Achiever	_____Creator	_____Idealist	_____Procrastinator
_____Activist	_____Critic	_____Innovator	_____Realist
_____Addict	_____Cynic	_____Insider	_____Rebel
_____Adolescent	_____Deceiver	_____Introvert	_____Receiver
_____Adult	_____Defender	_____Joker	_____Romantic
_____Adversary	_____Destroyer	_____Judge	_____Saboteur
_____Advisor	_____Devil	_____Leader	_____Sage
_____Ally	_____Dreamer	_____Listener	_____Saint
_____Angel	_____Dropout	_____Loser	_____Sceptic
_____Appreciator	_____Egotist	_____Lover	_____Sinner
_____Athlete	_____Enemy	_____Magician	_____Spy
_____Baby	_____Entertainer	_____Manipulator	_____Student
_____Beggar	_____Exaggerator	_____Monster	_____Success
_____Bigot	_____Extrovert	_____Mystic	_____Supporter
_____Bitch	_____Failure	_____Nuisance	_____Teacher
_____Bore	_____Fanatic	_____Observer	_____Thief
_____Catalyst	_____Fighter	_____Opponent	_____Tourist
_____Cheat	_____Fixer	_____Optimist	_____Tramp
_____Clown	_____Follower	_____Organiser	_____Tyrant
_____Comforter	_____Fool	_____Outsider	_____Victim
_____Communicator	_____Friend	_____Pacifist	_____Villain
_____Competitor	_____Giver	_____Parasite	_____Wallflower
_____Complainer	_____God	_____Perfectionist	_____Winner
_____Consumer	_____Gossip	_____Pessimist	_____Worrier
_____Controller	_____Helper	_____Pragmatist	_____Zealot

Write down other images you have of yourself which you have not yet listed in Part 2.

_____

_____

_____

_____

Now count up all of the images which you have marked or listed throughout Part 2. and write the total number here ___.

This number represents a very small fraction of the rich and ever-changing mosaic of your personal identity. It only hints at a colourful cast of characters you carry within you waiting to be accepted and integrated within your sense of self.

EILEEN

The old must die so that the new can come forth.

I used to wonder what these words meant. I could understand with the planting of a potato, for example, how the old potato has to die before new potatoes can grow from it, but for a long time I could not understand how this principle applied in my own life.

Now looking back over the years I can see clearly what it has meant. I have found over and over again when I have become secure and comfortable in an identity or role, that I have been forced by circumstances to let go of it to make room for something new to come into my life. Sometimes it has been extremely uncomfortable and even quite drastic and shattering, but I have found that each change of identity has actually meant a very positive time of growth and expansion for me.

For example, when I married for the first time, I became a wife, a housewife and later a mother of five children, and for many years these domestic roles were all I thought I was or could be. I was quite content with my lot at that time.

Then smash! Something happened to change my life. All of these roles were broken abruptly and I moved into a new, uncertain role with my second husband. My spiritual training was beginning and I had so many lessons to learn. It was a very painful time because there was so much resistance in me. For a while I lost my identity and became a recluse. Later I heard the 'still small voice' within me, and from then on I learned to live by the instructions I was given by my inner voice. My whole identity changed, and I can see now that the old identity had to die before the new one could come forth.

I began to feel secure in my new role as an oracle or channel receiving very simple teachings from my inner voice every night which I would read out the next morning to a small group which had formed. I continued to do so for years as we grew into a community. Then very unexpectedly one night I was told from within to stop reading my guidance out to the others, as it was time for them to do their own spiritual work by turning within to find their own inner source of wisdom, their own divine centre.

Smash! Again I lost my identity. It was a very bewildering time for me as I searched for a new role in the community. Eventually I became a member of the Core Group which oversees and guides the Findhorn Foundation. However some time later, after I had grown more comfortable in that role, I was told in meditation that it was time for me to withdraw from the Core Group.

Smash! Another identity shattered. Then our three children who had 'suddenly' grown up began leaving home one at a time. For the second time in my life I was no longer a mother on a day-to-day basis.

Smash! More soul-searching. Then my husband of 27 years left the community and me in search of a new role for himself. For the second time in my life, I was no longer a wife and partner.

Smash! Another period of bewilderment. It took some time to find my own self, my own identity. The result of all these identity 'crises' is that I have had to learn to stand on my own two feet and stand in my own light. I have had to learn what it is to be me. I have had to learn to put into practice the spiritual teachings I have received from within for more than 30 years.

Looking back, I can see how each identity change helped me to be more of myself, more of who I really am, more of all I can be. I give thanks now for every time I have had to 'die' to enable something new and more wonderful to come forth, and I realise that finding and expressing my wholeness is what life is really all about.

DAVID

Collaborate with the inevitable. — Roberto Assagioli, M.D.

For many years, while I was aware of some of my personal problems, I didn't know how to begin to deal with them. My turning point was the discovery of a Psychosynthesis method called Identification. It is a way of dealing with the partial images we have of ourself, even the negative ones we don't like.

One such image of mine is a trait which I had great difficulty in accepting as a part of myself. At times I feel the need to manipulate the environment around me — in both the best and worst senses of the term — not so that I may feel more powerful, dominating or important, but rather to feel more in control of things and safe.

The method of Identification leads to our becoming the partial image, that is, taking it on and expressing it in order to find out more about it and accept it. The method invites us to imagine the image as a separate person, with its own name, personality, feelings, thoughts and behaviour. The image becomes one of our inner cast of characters, or subpersonalities as they are called.

So when I closed my eyes, identified with my need for manipulation and asked for a symbol to represent it, out came 'Mr. Manipulator', who looks like a shadowy cloak-and-dagger spy. Through dialoguing with him in my imagination, I learned that he is very skilful at controlling people. He is clever, works long hours and has a vast array of ingenious strategies and tricks to get what he wants. He is not a very pleasant person, but he knows his job, and he does it very well.

I can also be judgemental, so another subpersonality of mine is 'The Judge', who in my imagination looks like an English court judge in a powdered white wig and long black robe. With him, everyone is always guilty. He is quick to point out shortcomings, oversights and mistakes of all kinds, and he always brands the perpetrator as being wrong or even bad. He delights in judging people, events and especially other subpersonalities of mine.

Both of these men say they work for a third subpersonality, a 'Frightened Child', who is very anxious, insecure and afraid of everyone and everything. 'Mr. Manipulator' keeps the environment familiar, predictable and under reasonable control for her. 'The Judge' holds most people off at arm's length with his judgements, thus creating a safe distance between my 'Frightened Child' and others. I have learned that subpersonalities often cooperate and collude with each other in this way.

At first I was uncomfortable with bringing such parts of myself out into the open. I didn't want to recognise or accept that they were a part of me. I wanted to focus only upon what I thought were my good parts, while either denying, or relegating to a closet or the basement, all the rest. I didn't want to give them any attention for fear that they might grow and perhaps overwhelm me. 'See only the best' and 'Let sleeping dogs lie' were my guiding mottoes then. However I discovered very quickly how freeing it is to make friends with all of the 'people' inside me. Using the model of subpersonalities, I could at long last not only recognise and accept parts of myself I had never been able to acknowledge before, but also begin to integrate them more into my own sense of self. I also learned that not all subpersonalities are unpleasant, unsavoury or difficult. They can be quite obviously positive and enhancing. For example I have discovered within me 'The Diplomat', who seeks to make connections with others and to put them at ease; 'The Teacher', who delights in introducing people to new experiences; and 'Mother Hen', who feels responsible for looking after others.

The method of Identification has shown me that I always need to be willing to re-define myself, finding and expressing new parts, insights and dimensions of my personal identity, rather than considering myself as a set package of fixed proportions. This method is surely one of the most helpful and effective personal growth techniques I have ever found.

PART 4. GAINING AWARENESS

The Session Six title, *Choosing To Accept,* means accepting ourself as we are without judgement, criticism or condemnation. It is accepting others as they are without wanting them to be any different.

Acceptance is not denial, tolerance or resignation. We can certainly change the parts of ourself we wish to improve, but only after we accept them.

Otherwise the parts of ourself which we do not recognise and accept — our positive qualities as well as negative ones — we tend to project onto others; and therefore we do not see others as they are, we see only our own projections. Consequently as we are more able to accept ourself, we are more able to see and accept other people clearly and genuinely. Thus accepting all parts of ourself is a necessary step towards bringing more love into our life.

Identification

One powerful method which aids self-acceptance is known as *Identification*. It invites us to explore various parts of ourself directly and fully. It entails facing them squarely, examining them freely from all sides and accepting them completely as a part of us. Identification is the essential first part of a two-part process. We present the second part in Session Seven.

Identification takes several forms. One common form has five steps, all of which you are familiar with from some of the exercises we have already done. The first step asks us to visualise a relevant need, desire, trait or attitude in symbolic form, such as a person, animal or object. The second step then asks us to explore the symbol for whatever qualities it expresses to us. The third step invites us to make a drawing of the symbol as a means of anchoring it within our own awareness.

The fourth step calls for us to interact and dialogue with the symbol to learn more about the part of us it represents. Finally the fifth step asks us to become the symbol, that is, to imagine ourself as actually being the symbol, identifying with it completely, to gain insights about how this part of us feels, thinks and behaves.

'Personal Identity' Symbol and Drawing

Select a personal identity from Part 2 which you would like to find out more about, and write it down.

_____

Then find a comfortable position, sitting up straight . . . Close your eyes . . . Take several long, slow, deep breaths . . . Relax your body completely . . . Release all of the tension . . . Allow whatever emotions you may be feeling to fade away . . . Do the same with your thoughts . . . Become like a calm, quiet lake, which mirrors perfectly the blue sky, or the starry sky in the silence of the night . . . Be at peace and yet remain alert . . .

When you are ready, allow to come to you an image or sense which represents the personal identity you have selected . . . Take your time . . . Wait patiently in the silence, knowing that something will soon come to you which represents this personal identity . . . Be willing to accept whatever comes without judging, censoring or rejecting it . . . Simply be ready to observe and examine it, with the purpose of learning more about it . . .

As you begin to sense something, allow it to become more vivid . . . Note its size and shape . . . Its density and design . . . Its colour and texture . . . Explore it with as many of your senses as you can . . . Find the overall quality it suggests to you . . .

Then open your eyes and express in a drawing below either the image itself, or its quality . . . If nothing has come to you, open your eyes, hold the question in mind and begin to draw freely and spontaneously, letting something come to you in that way . . .

MY PERSONAL IDENTITY OF _____

Write down the overall *quality* of the symbol and any other words, feelings or thoughts which came to you during the exercise, or which you are aware of now. What new insight or awareness does this symbol or its quality give to you?

_____

_____

_____

_____

We continue with the fourth and fifth stages of the exercise. Close your eyes . . . Sit up straight . . . Take a few deep breaths . . . Relax . . . Allow your body, emotions and thoughts to become still . . . Become like a calm, quiet lake again . . .

When you are ready, allow the image or sense of your personal identity to return to you . . . Begin to dialogue with it . . . Find out as much as possible about it . . . Its history . . . How long it has been a part of you . . . What it needs . . . How it serves you . . . How it limits you . . . How you might deal with it . . . Take your time . . . Spend several minutes interacting with it . . . Learn all you can . . .

Then, in your imagination, try on this symbol like a coat . . . Merge with it . . . Become it . . . Feel what it is like to be this symbol completely . . . As this symbol, what are your feelings? . . . What are your thoughts? . . . What are your needs? . . . What are your motivations? . . . Take your time to explore this part of yourself *from its own point of view* . . .

Finally allow yourself to separate from this symbol and return your awareness to your whole self once again . . .

In your own time, allow everything to fade . . . Bring your attention back to the room where you are now . . . Open your eyes . . . Take a deep breath . . . And a gentle stretch . . .

Now write down your feelings, thoughts and questions you wish to record from your dialogue and identification with your personal identity. Note especially how it serves you, how it limits you and whatever it says it needs.

_____

_____

_____

_____

_____

_____

_____

_____

_____

Subpersonalities

One form of Identification is imagining a symbol of one of our personal identities and then *becoming* it to learn more about it from inside itself, as above.

The various images of ourself which we carry around with us (some of which you tabulated in Part 2) can be called *subpersonalities*, as they are parts of our personality, but obviously not the whole of it. The technique of subpersonalities is another form of Identification.

Each subpersonality has its own personality and behaviour. For example, whenever we are feeling helpless and victimised (and therefore expressing our 'Victim' subpersonality), we stand, sit, feel, think, move, talk and act differently than we do whenever we are feeling assertive, strong and powerful (perhaps expressing a 'Leader' subpersonality).

Subpersonalities may be likened to musicians in an orchestra. They each have their part to play and their contribution to make to the whole. For many people, however, it is an orchestra without a leader, and so most of the musicians consider themselves to be star soloists. They have their own music to perform and take the spotlight away from all the others whenever they can.

Conflicts abound. Rather than all playing the same music and blending harmoniously, they sound collectively more like the pre-concert tune-up. They are undisciplined and uncoordinated. They need a leader, someone to take charge, to direct and harmonise their talents and all they have to offer to the whole.

In the same way parts of ourself compete for attention and expression. For example the part of us who wants to buy flowers for our table may be confronted by the practical part who says the flowers will only wilt in a few days, so why be so foolish! Or one part of us wants to be in a committed, loving relationship, while another part wants freedom and independence above all else.

One common conflict for many people occurs between our 'Mystic' subpersonality and our 'Pragmatist'. Our 'Mystic' part says, 'All you need to do in life is to put your faith and trust in God, set all of your worries aside and go with the flow. You can always depend on God to provide for all of your needs and to take good care of you.'

Our 'Pragmatist' counters with, 'Nonsense! You can't pray your troubles and responsibilities away, and leave everything for God to do. Besides God doesn't have to pay the rent, or put food on the table. *I* am the one who has to do it!'

Our 'Sceptic' subpersonality may appear from nowhere, declaring, 'What makes you two so sure there even is a God?' Within no time, we may have constellations of other subpersonalities joining forces and taking sides in the debate, leaving us in a state of utter confusion. With no obvious conductor on the scene, the orchestra falls apart.

Clearly we need a leader to resolve such conflicts and to harmonise and coalesce all the many parts of ourself. The discovery of our leader is the subject of Session Seven, and the employment of our leader is outlined in Session Eight.

Transpersonal Qualities

Our God-Self draws upon many transpersonal qualities or universal principles which it seeks to express. The 'Angel Meditation Cards', developed at the Findhorn Foundation, depict a few of these archetypal qualities. There are many others, of course, but this list gives a sense of the many pure qualities which are standing by, waiting for us to experience and express, so that we may fulfil our own sense of purpose in life.

Abundance	Efficiency	Inspiration	Release
Adventure	Enthusiasm	Integrity	Responsibility
Balance	Expectancy	Joy	Simplicity
Beauty	Faith	Light	Spontaneity
Birth	Flexibility	Love	Strength
Brotherhood	Forgiveness	Obedience	Surrender
Clarity	Freedom	Openness	Synthesis
Communication	Grace	Patience	Tenderness
Compassion	Gratitude	Peace	Transformation
Courage	Harmony	Play	Trust
Creativity	Healing	Power	Truth
Delight	Honesty	Purification	Understanding
Education	Humour	Purpose	Willingness

Such a quality or principle lies at the core of each subpersonality, whatever its outer behaviour may be. For example an aggressive 'Bully' subpersonality may have at its core the quality of Power. A 'Judge' subpersonality may have at its core the quality of Discrimination. A 'Sentimentalist' subpersonality may have at its core the quality of Love. Thus all subpersonalities may be regarded as *distortions* of these pure qualities which are hidden gifts waiting to be found and claimed.

Therefore, if we try to eliminate a seemingly 'undesirable' aspect or subpersonality from our behaviour (for example the part of us who judges), we actually deprive ourself of the real gift it has to offer us. The challenge is to recover the gift by making the best use of our subpersonality, and enabling it to express itself in a more coordinated, positive, helpful way. As we consciously recognise, accept and express a subpersonality, and claim the gift at its core, it becomes integrated into the whole of us, rather than remaining a disconcerting, disconnected fragment.

Referring to drives, urges, needs and other distinctive forms of personal behaviour as subpersonalities helps us to:

- Form them and give them structure.
- Bring them more clearly into our awareness.
- Deal with them constructively and systematically.
- Reclaim and express positive parts of ourself.

Our task is not the negative one of judging and making any part of ourself 'wrong' or 'bad', and subsequently trying to dispose of it. Rather it is the positive task of reforming and harmonising it with other parts of ourself, and therefore activating the positive quality it brings to our life. This starts with recognising and accepting the subpersonality completely, that is, embracing it fully as it is, without judgement, criticism or embarrassment. As we learn to accept all parts of ourself, we are more able to accept all parts of others, a vital (for some) step towards giving and receiving love unconditionally.

'The House in the Meadow' Subpersonality Visualisation

This Identification exercise helps us to learn more about our subpersonalities. Before proceeding, turn back now and review 'Getting the Most from Visualisation' in the *Before You Begin* introductory section of the course.

Choose a part of yourself which you would like to find out more about, perhaps a desire, need or other aspect of your behaviour or another personal identity from Part 2, and write about it here.

_____

_____

_____

_____

Now close your eyes . . . Take a few deep breaths . . . Relax . . . Allow your body, emotions and thoughts to become still . . . Become like a calm, quiet lake again . . .

When you are ready, imagine being out in the countryside, in the middle of a beautiful meadow . . . It is a warm, pleasant day . . . Feel the ground under your feet . . . Feel the warmth of the sun shining down upon your body . . . See the blue sky, the trees, grass and other plants . . . Hear the sounds of nature around you . . . Smell the fresh fragrance of the countryside . . . Experience the peace and contentment here . . .

After a while, you notice that at the far side of the meadow is a house, and that you are standing upon a footpath which leads directly to it . . . You decide to examine the house more closely, and so you begin walking towards it . . .

As you come nearer to the house, you see a sign saying 'The House of My Subpersonalities' . . . You hear sounds coming from the house as you begin to walk around it, first along one side, then along the rear, then along the other side, until at last you come once again to the front of the house . . .

You walk up to the front door, knock upon it, and then call through the door into the house, asking the subpersonality who represents the part of yourself which you wish to explore to come outside to talk with you . . . Then you move back a few steps, and wait . . .

A moment later the door opens and out comes the subpersonality who represents the part of yourself which you wish to explore . . .

What does it look like — what is its appearance? . . . Try not to judge, censor or reject it . . . Simply observe and examine it, with the purpose of learning more about it . . .

Treat your subpersonality, no matter what it is, as a Walt Disney cartoon character having the capacity to talk with you, and begin to dialogue with it . . . Find out as much as possible . . . Its history . . . How long it has been a part of you . . . Whatever its needs are . . . How it serves you . . . How it limits you . . . The quality or principle at its core which it offers to you . . . How you might deal with it . . . Take your time . . . Spend several minutes interacting with it . . . Learn all you can . . . Begin your dialogue now . . .

When your dialogue has come to an end, sense a beam of sunlight shining down upon you and your subpersonality, filling and enfolding you both within its light and warmth . . . Notice if any changes appear in either one of you . . .

Say goodbye to your subpersonality and allow it to go back inside the house . . . Be aware that you may return to this house any time you choose and talk with this subpersonality or any other one you desire . . .

You begin to walk along the footpath which leads from the meadow to where you first began . . . As you do, feel the ground under your feet . . . Feel the warmth of the sun shining down upon your body . . . See the blue sky, the trees, grass and other plants . . . Hear the sounds of nature around you . . . Smell the fresh fragrance of the countryside . . . Experience the peace and contentment here . . .

In your own time, allow the scene to fade . . . Bring your attention back to the room where you are now . . . Open your eyes . . . Take a deep breath . . . And a gentle stretch . . .

Now write down any feelings, thoughts and questions you wish to record from your dialogue with the subpersonality. Note especially how it serves you, how it limits you, what its needs are and the quality at its core which it offers to you.

_____

_____

_____

_____

_____

_____

_____

_____

_____

_____

_____

To complete the exercise, close your eyes again . . . Sit up straight . . . Take a few deep breaths . . . Relax . . . Allow your body, emotions and thoughts to become still . . . Become like a calm, quiet lake . . .

When you are ready, allow to come to you the quality which this subpersonality offers to you. How often do you experience this quality presently in your life?

_____

_____

_____

Which part of yourself stops you from having more of this quality? How? Why?

_____

_____

_____

How do you imagine life would be for you if you had more of this quality available? What differences might there be, especially in your relationships?

_____

_____

_____

Would you like to have more of this quality in your life? If so, how might you begin to do it? What 'next step' are you open and willing to take?

_____

_____

_____

Take a few moments now to visualise yourself taking this step successfully and having more of this quality in your life . . .

Then, in your own time, allow everything to fade . . . Bring your attention back to the room where you are now . . . Open your eyes . . . Take a deep breath . . . And a gentle stretch . . .

Now write down any feelings, thoughts or questions you may wish to record.

_____

_____

_____

Next in Part 5 we explore as a subpersonality that part of you which blocks you from bringing more love into your life.

PART 5. DEVELOPING POTENTIAL

Review Part 2 and look for images which you either (1) omitted, even though you are aware that they are a part of you, or (2) included, but have difficulty in accepting as a part of you. List them below.

_____

_____

_____

_____

These subpersonalities would seem to be calling for your attention — and your acceptance. Use the following exercise and the suggestions in Part 6 to become better acquainted with these parts of yourself.

'The House in the Meadow Revisited' Visualisation

In Session Two you identified a major block to bringing more love into your life. In Session Five you identified a core belief of low self-esteem which may seriously limit your giving and receiving love fully. By now you may have also gathered additional feelings, thoughts and other clues about how you stop yourself from bringing more love into your life.

We invite you to return to the house in the meadow to meet the part of you which blocks you from bringing more love into your life. This time we offer several questions for you to ask the subpersonality. After visualising the subpersonality, pose the first question. Immediately after you receive an inner response, open your eyes, write down a summary of the response and read the next question. Then close your eyes, re-visualise your subpersonality and ask the next question. Most people find that they develop a rhythm and shift easily between the inner and outer perspectives.

You may wish to pre-record this exercise so that you may participate in it more freely. Pause on the tape 10-30 seconds, or whatever time seems comfortable and appropriate, at every . . . to allow you to experience each step fully. Avoid rushing through the exercise. Take your time. Give yourself at least 30 minutes to complete this exercise.

Now find a comfortable position, sitting up straight . . . Close your eyes . . . Take several long, slow, deep breaths . . . Relax your body completely . . . Release all of the tension . . . Allow whatever emotions you may be feeling to fade away . . . Do the same with your thoughts . . . Become like a calm, quiet lake, which mirrors perfectly the blue sky, or the starry sky in the silence of the night . . . Be at peace and yet remain alert . . .

When you are ready, imagine being out in the countryside, in the middle of a beautiful meadow . . . It is a warm, pleasant day . . . Feel the ground under your feet . . . Feel the warmth of the sun shining down upon your body . . . See the blue sky, the trees, grass and other plants . . . Hear the sounds of nature around you . . . Smell the fresh fragrance of the countryside . . . Experience the peace and contentment here . . .

After a while, you notice that at the far side of the meadow is a house, and that you are standing upon a footpath which leads directly to it . . . You decide to examine the house more closely, and so you begin walking towards it . . .

As you come nearer to the house, you see a sign saying 'The House of My Subpersonalities' . . . You hear sounds coming from the house as you begin to walk around it, first along one side, then along the rear, then along the other side, until at last you come once again to the front of the house . . .

You walk up to the front door, knock upon it and then call through the door into the house, asking the subpersonality who represents the part of yourself which blocks you from bringing more love into your life to come outside and talk with you . . . Then you move back a few steps, and wait . . .

A moment later the door opens, and out comes the subpersonality who represents the part of yourself which blocks you from bringing more love into your life . . . Try not to judge, censor or reject it . . . Simply observe and examine it, with the purpose of learning more about it . . .

What does this subpersonality look like — what is its appearance?

_____

_____

_____

_____

Begin to dialogue with it. Ask it who it is. Does it have a name? If not, give it a descriptive name of your own by the end of the exercise.

_____

_____

_____

_____

Find out about its history. Ask this subpersonality how old it is — how long has it been a part of you? Where did it come from? When? How? Who else was involved?

_____

_____

_____

_____

What are its needs? Ask it.

_____

_____

_____

_____

What is its underlying motivation — why does it do the things it does?

_____

_____

_____

_____

How does this subpersonality stop you from bringing more love into your life?

_____

_____

_____

_____

Ask it what quality or principle it has at its core to offer to you.

_____

_____

_____

_____

How does this subpersonality serve you — what would you lose or miss if it were not a part of you?

_____

_____

_____

_____

How does it limit or restrict you? Ask it.

_____

_____

_____

_____

What is it afraid of — what does it fear? Does it have any enemies?

_____

_____

_____

_____

What risk does this subpersonality need to take? Ask it what could happen ideally if it were to take this risk and succeed.

_____

_____

_____

_____

_____

_____

_____

Continue to dialogue with your subpersonality for the next several minutes. Allow both of you to ask and answer questions for each other and to discuss mutual concerns. Write down the main points as they emerge.

_____

_____

_____

_____

_____

_____

_____

_____

_____

_____

_____

When your dialogue has come to an end, you sense a beam or column of sunlight shining down upon you and your subpersonality, filling and enfolding you both within its light and warmth . . . Notice if any changes appear in either of you . . .

You become aware that the column of light is actually a radiant lift or elevator, and that you and your subpersonality, standing within it, begin to rise slowly upwards . . . You feel perfectly comfortable, calm and safe, as though it were a normal, everyday occurrence . . . You continue to ascend, and the ground begins to fall faster away from you . . .

Soon you can see not only the whole house clearly, but all of the meadow . . . Higher and higher the two of you rise within the column of light until the entire countryside becomes a vast magnificent panorama, stretching out before you in all directions as far as you can see . . .

Now you begin to enter a bank of fleecy white clouds . . . Soon all of the earth below fades from view, as you become completely enveloped by the clouds . . .

A moment later you rise above the clouds and witness an amazing sight: a beautiful, immaculate garden in full blossom . . . It is a place of safety, love and support . . . As you step from the column of light onto a neatly-trimmed garden path, you feel total peace and contentment . . .

After a while, you see coming towards you a wise and loving guide, someone who knows and loves you very much indeed, and with whom you feel quite safe and completely at ease . . . The guide says to you, 'I am here to help you. Speak with me about the concerns you have. I know all about you, and am able and willing to answer any question you may have about yourself and your subpersonalities.'

Begin to talk with this wise and loving guide about your subpersonality for the next several minutes . . . Allow all three of you to ask and answer questions for each other and to discuss mutual concerns . . . Discuss what your subpersonality needs and how best to deal with it . . . Continue to write down the main points as they emerge . . .

_____
_____
_____
_____
_____
_____
_____
_____
_____
_____

When the dialogue has finished, the guide gives you a tangible gift to help you deal with this sub-personality, perhaps a symbolic reminder of some kind . . .

You thank the guide for the gift and say goodbye . . . You return with your subpersonality to the column of light . . . The two of you enter it once again and begin to descend slowly and safely . . . Soon you enter the bank of clouds, and the beautiful garden fades from view . . .

A moment later you emerge below the clouds where you see the familiar countryside stretching out before you . . . As you continue to descend, the ground comes up to greet you . . . In only a few moments, you and your subpersonality stand firmly upon the ground again, near the front door of the house in the meadow . . . Notice if any changes appear in either one of you . . .

You ask your subpersonality if it has anything more to say to you, any final questions or comments . . . You say anything you need to say to it as well . . .

Then you say goodbye to your subpersonality and allow it to go back inside the house . . . Be aware that you may return to this house any time you choose and talk with this subpersonality or any other one you desire . . .

You begin to walk along the footpath which leads from the meadow to where you first began . . . As you do, feel the ground under your feet . . . Feel the warmth of the sun shining down upon your body . . . See the blue sky, the trees, grass and other plants . . . Hear the sounds of nature around you . . . Smell the fresh fragrance of the countryside . . . Experience the peace and contentment here . . .

In your own time, allow everything to fade . . . Bring your attention back to the room where you are now . . . Open your eyes . . . Take a deep breath . . . And a gentle stretch . . .

Write down any feelings, thoughts and questions you wish to record from this visualisation. Include the token gift which the guide may have given you to deal with this particular subpersonality.

_____

_____

_____

_____

_____

_____

_____

_____

To complete the exercise, close your eyes again . . . Sit up straight . . . Take a few deep breaths . . . Relax . . . Allow your body, emotions and thoughts to become still . . . Become like a calm, quiet lake . . .

When you are ready, allow to come to you the quality which this subpersonality offers to you. How often do you experience this quality presently in your life?

_____

_____

_____

Which part of yourself stops you from having more of this quality? How? Why?

_____

_____

_____

How do you imagine life would be for you if you had more of this quality available? What difference might there be, especially in your relationships?

_____

_____

_____

Would you like to have more of this quality in your life? If so, how might you begin to do it? What 'next step' are you open and willing to take?

_____

_____

_____

Take a few moments now to visualise yourself taking this step successfully and having more of this quality in your life.

Then, in your own time, allow everything to fade . . . Bring your attention back to the room where you are now . . . Open your eyes . . . Take a deep breath . . . And a gentle stretch . . .

Now write down any feelings, thoughts or questions you may wish to record.

_____

_____

_____

_____

Use this Identification exercise regularly to explore any part of yourself you want to deal with more consciously and creatively.

To what degree do you accept that parts of *yourself* are stopping you from bringing more love into your life? What are your feelings and thoughts about it?

_____

_____

_____

_____

To what degree do you accept that they are only *parts* of yourself, and not *all* of yourself?

_____

_____

_____

_____

To what degree do you accept that you can exercise control over them and can change them so that you may bring more love into your life?

_____

_____

_____

_____

To what degree are you open and willing to begin to change them now?

_____

_____

_____

_____

Next in Part 6 we present suggestions for using the technique of subpersonalities.

PART 6. APPLYING IT

How many subpersonalities is it possible to have?

The American psychologist Gordon Allport states that the English language has some 18,000 designations for distinctive forms of personal behaviour, and that this figure is greatly exceeded when they appear in combination! So we have virtually an unlimited number of subpersonalities to draw upon to express our own uniqueness.

The Technique of Subpersonalities

We offer the following suggestions for using the technique of subpersonalities to bring you greater awareness and self-acceptance. Practise these four exercises for at least the next seven days. Report your results on the following page *before you begin Session Seven*. Note also when and how you may have experienced resistance to doing any or all of these exercises, and what you did about it.

1. Morning Preview. Each morning consider which of your subpersonalities might be useful for you to identify with and express at certain times or places during the day. Then remember to do it.

2. Disidentification. Say to yourself regularly, 'I am more than whoever "I" think "I" am in any given moment, for I know that "I" change from one subpersonality to another.'

3. Identification. Say to yourself regularly, '*Who* (what part of me — which subpersonality?) is experiencing and reacting to this person or situation now?' Also be aware of which of your subpersonalities is speaking whenever you use the word 'I'.

4. Evening Review. Each evening, review your day to find which subpersonalities were most active and in what specific circumstances. Also review the past to find out when a given subpersonality has been active and in what circumstances. Look for repeating patterns.

Additional Techniques

Here are some more ideas to try if you wish.

1. Creative Meditation. Use this visualisation to establish and manifest how you would like a given subpersonality to be ideally. (See Session Four, Part 5, p. 112)

2. House in the Meadow. Use subpersonalities to deal with other subpersonalities. For example go to the house in the meadow and ask to dialogue with the subpersonality who can best help you to deal with a problem subpersonality.

3. Chair Exercise. Subpersonalities are often found in pairs, expressed as polarities (Extravert/Introvert, Leader/Follower, Success/Failure, Tyrant/Victim, Optimist/Pessimist). Do a chair exercise to learn more about one or more of your subpersonalities. (See Session Three, Part 5, p. 87) Then identify with the polar (perhaps more dormant) subpersonality to discover how it feels, thinks and acts, as a means of strengthening, balancing and blending it with the other (perhaps more dominant) subpersonality. *Suggestion:* Begin with a dialogue between the subpersonality who wants to bring more love into your life and the one who is afraid to bring more love into your life.

NOTES AND DRAWINGS REPORTING RESULTS OF PART 6 EXERCISES

Suggested Reading

Subpersonalities: The People Inside Us, by John Rowan, is a comprehensive book for people interested in their own personality and how it helps or hinders their everyday life.

Personal Goal

Consider various simple, specific, observable actions you could take within the next few days which would be a step towards bringing more love into your life. Then choose one which seems important to you, one to take as a personal goal. Make a deliberate choice to achieve it. Write it down. Remember, making and implementing choices empowers and strengthens you.

_____

_____

_____

_____

Session Learnings

Turn back and review what you have done in this session. Then write down the three most important insights or learnings you have gained from it.

_____

_____

_____

_____

_____

_____

_____

Purpose

As stated at the beginning of Part 2, the purpose of Session Six is to experience that your personal identity is a composite of the many different images which you have of yourself, that these images are partial and ever-changing and that accepting all of them as a part of you is an important step in bringing more love into your life. To what degree has Session Six achieved its general purpose for you?

_____

_____

_____

_____

Congratulations! You have come to the end of Session Six. Please discuss your experience of this session with your support person *before you begin Session Seven*.

CHOOSING TO BE FREE

PART 1. MAKING CONNECTIONS

Begin by reviewing Session Six to reconnect with your process of development. Have you achieved the personal goal you set for yourself? How was it?

Then, if you have chosen to take additional risks in bringing more love into your life since the beginning of the preceding session, write about your experience: what you did, how successful you were and what you learned.

Continue with these personal journal pages by *making connections with the theme, issues and exercises of this course*, recording whatever relevant memories, ideas, feelings, insights, dreams, 'unfinished business', interactions and other events in your inner and outer worlds have occurred since you completed Session Six. Include related reading you may have done, questions on your mind and any other observations and connections with the course you wish to make.

_____

_____

_____

_____

_____

_____

_____

_____

_____

_____

_____

_____

_____

_____

_____

_____

_____

_____

_____

_____

_____

_____

Next in Part 2 we begin to explore the *real* you.

PART 2. TAKING STOCK

Purpose

The purpose of Session Seven is to identify and experience your basic sense of self (and the freedom it brings), and to learn methods to resolve inner conflicts which prevent you from bringing more love into your life.

'Who Are You?' Check-list

Who are you? The real you? Who is underneath all the images, identifications and roles? Where is the 'conductor' of your orchestra of subpersonalities? What inner conflicts stop you from bringing more love into your life, and what can you do about them to set yourself free? These questions and their answers form the basis of Session Seven.

We experience ourself in different ways at different times. However we tend to identify ourself *primarily* in one of the ways described below. Rank the following statements in order from 1 to 5, with 1 being how you *least often* experience yourself and 5 being how you *most often* experience yourself.

_____ **I am my body.** I am very much in touch with my body and its physical sensations. It gives me the solid sense of being alive. I and my body are one. I live in an outer, physical world, and I contact and embrace life mostly through my body. The real me would not exist without it. My body is basically who I am.

_____ **I am my emotions.** I am very sensitive to my emotions, and I feel them intensely. They make me feel alive. I and my emotions are one. I live in a passionate, affective world, and I perceive life mostly through my emotions. The real me would not exist without them. My emotions are basically who I am.

_____ **I am my desires.** I am very motivated by my drives. They empower me and give me a satisfying sense of being alive. I and my desires are one. I live in a spontaneous and ever-changing world of human drives and impulses, and I experience life mostly through trying to satisfy my desires. The real me would not exist without them. My desires are basically who I am.

_____ **I am my mind.** I know I am very attuned to my mind and its thoughts and ideas, and I think that intellect, knowledge and understanding are very important. They let me know I am alive. I and my mind are one. I live in a rational, cognitive world, and I am aware of life mostly through my mind. The real me would not exist without it. My mind is basically who I am.

_____ **I am my roles.** I am very engaged in many activities and portray many different roles. They affirm my being alive. I and my roles are one. I live in a multifaceted world and play many parts which I perform for the benefit of myself and others. I experience life mostly through my roles. The real me would not exist without tnem. My roles are basically who I am.

Now underline all of the individual statements in each of the descriptions above which apply to you and your experience of yourself.

'Who Am I?' Experience Scan

In Session Six we explore various ways in which we describe ourselves. We continue this exploration in search of the real you.
.

Now close your eyes . . . Sit up straight . . . Take a few deep breaths . . . Relax . . . Allow your body, emotions and thoughts to become still . . . Become like a calm, quiet lake . . .

When you are ready, say to yourself, *'WHO AM I? I AM . . . ,'* and complete the sentence with a word or short phrase — whatever comes spontaneously to you. Do not *think* about it. Write down the response. Then do it again, this time allowing a new word or phrase to emerge. Write down that response. If you blank out momentarily, simply begin again, knowing that something will soon come to you. Repeat it again and again for at least ten minutes, or until you have filled the space below.

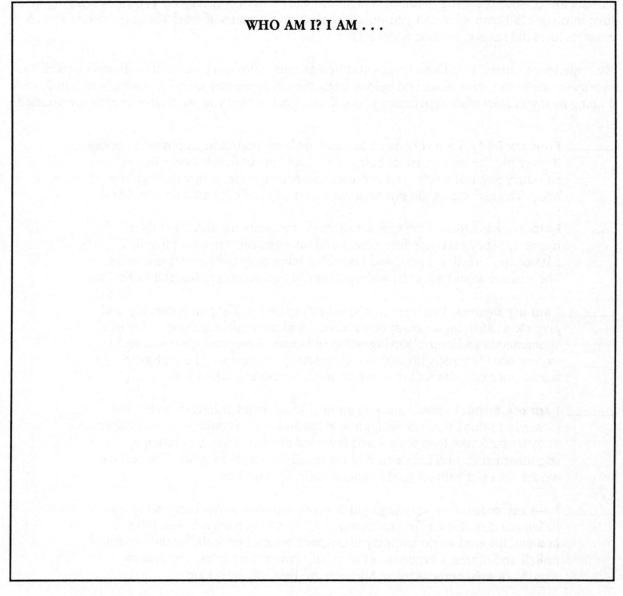

WHO AM I? I AM . . .

Now examine your responses. Mark the five with which you most strongly identify, that is, the responses which are the nearest, the most accurate or the best descriptions of *who you basically are*, the responses which seem the most significant, meaningful and important to you.

Self-Observation

Most of us have the ability to report accurate, discerning, objective observations about ourself and others, free of judgement, criticism or evaluation. Write down a few descriptive observations about your own physical self: your body and how you use it, its sensations and how you experience and express them. Avoid judging, criticising or evaluating yourself. Be completely factual, detached and objective.

_____

_____

_____

_____

Write down a few descriptive observations about your emotions and feelings, and how you experience and express them. Avoid judgement. Be detached.

_____

_____

_____

Write down a few descriptive observations about your desires, and how you experience, express and satisfy them. Avoid criticism. Be factual.

_____

_____

_____

_____

Write down a few descriptive observations about your intellect and its thoughts and ideas, and how you experience and express them. Be discerning.

_____

_____

_____

_____

Finally write down a few descriptive observations about the various roles you play in life, and how you experience and express them. Be objective.

_____

_____

_____

_____

Now ask yourself _who_, what part of you has been observing yourself? _Who_ has been reporting? _Who_ is aware of all these things you have said about yourself? _Who_ witnesses? _Who_ is detached and objective?

_____

_____

_____

_____

Now contact your support person and ask for feedback about how detached, discerning and objective your observations have been, and how free from judgement, criticism or evaluation. Write down a summary of your support person's comments, and any response you may have to the comments or to this exercise.

_____

_____

_____

_____

Inner Conflict

Inner conflict between two or more opposing points of view often delays or prevents us from getting what we want. It can bring confusion, ambivalence and indecision.

How about you? How does inner conflict affect you? How do you usually deal with it? How do you try to resolve it? (Or do you do nothing, hoping that it will resolve itself?)

_____

_____

_____

_____

_____

_____

_____

_____

What do you imagine is the basic conflict within you which prevents you from bringing more love into your life?

_____

_____

_____

Affirm below, _'I AM WILLING TO RESOLVE THIS CONFLICT OR ANY OTHER CONFLICT WITHIN ME WHICH STOPS ME FROM LOVING FREELY AND FULLY.'_ Then record any feelings or thoughts which writing your affirmation may prompt.

_____

_____

_____

_____

Next in Part 3 we relate our own thoughts about these issues.

PART 3. EXPLORING PERSPECTIVES

EILEEN

It is this (Christ) consciousness which is drawing more and more souls together
so that you all may become aware of the Christ within. — Opening Doors Within

Who am I? What am I doing? Where am I going? Many of us ask ourself these questions (often prompted by our own doubts, fears and inner conflicts) from time to time. I know I have.

Once in meditation when I asked the question 'Who am I?' I was told to use an affirmation. At the time I did not like the idea of an affirmation, as I felt it was brain-washing, so I put the guidance aside. But every time I meditated on this question, I was given the same answer.

Eventually I asked which affirmation to use and I was given this one: 'I am a beautiful Christ-filled being.' I was shocked! How could I go around saying such a thing! I wouldn't dare! People would think I was going 'round the bend'.

But the inner prompting was so insistent that, in the end, I decided I would try it when I was alone and no one could hear me. So at first I started to mumble half-heartedly, 'I am a beautiful Christ-filled being.' But as I kept on using this affirmation over a period of time, I began to see what was happening, and what it really means to use an affirmation.

To begin with, all that was coming from me was just words, empty words which did not mean anything to me. However, as I continued using this affirmation, the words seemed slowly to become alive. Then later I realised that I was becoming the words. Eventually I came to know and accept that I am indeed a beautiful Christ-filled being.

In fact we all are beautiful Christ-filled beings, but we each need to recognise it and accept it. Now I can make this statement without any hesitation because I know it is the truth. I also know from this experience that affirmations used properly are very powerful tools.

Then I asked myself the question in meditation, 'What am I doing on this planet at this time?' The answer I received from within was 'To serve God and humanity.' As I meditated upon this response, I realised that to serve God is to see God's hand in everything and to give God the honour and glory for it at all times.

I felt I understood that first part, but I wondered about serving humanity. The inner prompting I received was that the greatest gift I can give people is to turn them within to find the God within themselves so that they can live, move and have their being from their own divine centre.

That is what I always try to do now in my lectures, workshops, books and tapes — direct people to explore more deeply inside themselves until they come to the very core of their being, to their own God-Self.

I feel that it is important for each of us to take time to go into the stillness to find answers to these questions and to the other doubts, fears and inner conflicts we may have about ourself. I am sure the answers which come to everyone are all very different. It doesn't matter. What matters is putting into practice whatever prompting is received in the stillness.

DAVID

When troubles hover, go to cover! — Professor Edward Stasheff

In the early days of television, long before videotape, most programmes were broadcast live. Even with rehearsal, mistakes abounded, many of them quite hilarious. Human performers as well as animals would move unexpectedly out of camera range and disappear from sight, leaving viewers bewildered until the camera could catch up with the action again.

Back then, as a broadcasting student at the University of Michigan, I learned an important lesson for TV directors: 'When troubles hover, go to cover.' It means when unexpected difficulties arise during a live programme, have the cameraman put a cover shot or wide-angle picture of the entire scene on the air as quickly as possible. With a bigger picture, no matter what happens, all the action will be in full view, and therefore nothing will be missed at home by the viewer.

Now, thirty years later, I find the axiom has taken on new meaning. When I am faced with personal or professional problems, I try to remember to step back and put things quickly into a bigger picture, a wider perspective, so that everything is in full view, and I can be aware of it all and not miss what is *really* taking place.

I step back by observing myself directly and objectively in the moment, and by asking myself questions. What am I experiencing right now? What am I aware of? What are my feelings? My thoughts? *Who*, what part of me, is experiencing it? Why is it happening now? What is the lesson for me to learn? What message is my God-Self giving me through this experience? What is the hidden gift or benefit for me to find in it?

Focusing quietly on these questions and the answers which often come in the silence keeps me from becoming blocked by worry and confusion. I find that the issue is not automatically resolved. My feelings and thoughts about it certainly do not change instantly. But stepping back, observing, asking myself questions and seeing it as part of a bigger picture provides me with sufficient distance that I do not feel as threatened, victimised or overwhelmed by it as I once might have done.

Remembering to ask these questions about an outer difficulty or inner conflict gives me solid ground to stand on. It helps me examine options and choose to act. It helps me ultimately to benefit from the difficulty if possible, rather than be drained or defeated by it. It makes the situation more manageable. With a change in my own perspective, the difficulty can often turn into an opportunity.

This process of stepping back and looking for the bigger picture is called 'disidentification'. It means I do not need to *become* my problems, conflicts, feelings or thoughts, and confuse them with who I really am, that is, my essential spiritual nature. It leads me to the sense that 'I *have* the problem', rather than 'I *am* the problem'.

I have experienced the wisdom in Roberto Assagioli's assertion: 'We are dominated by everything with which our self becomes identified. We can dominate, direct and utilise everything from which we disidentify ourselves.' Thus my physical sensations, feelings, desires, thoughts, roles and other identifications need not control me, as they once did. I now have found a way to regulate and use them more effectively. I have learned that the simple act of stepping back and observing myself objectively opens the door to increased freedom and joy of the spirit.

Therefore I am no longer satisfied with only part of the picture, the part I already know about. I do what I can now to get *everything* in full view. I go to the bigger picture and find the perspective, understanding and support which can help me move more swiftly and easily through difficulties. When all else fails, I try to remember Prof Stasheff's good advice: when troubles hover, go to cover!

PART 4. GAINING AWARENESS

Identification and Disidentification

First, turn back to Session Six, Part 2 (p. 151) and to Part 2 of this session (p. 177) and review all of the various images and identifications you have of yourself. Do it now before continuing.

We imagine one of your identifications might be, 'I am American,' or 'British' or 'German'. If so, a nationality-based identification indicates only where you were born, the country you pay allegiance to or perhaps a cultural predisposition, but it is not basically *who* you are. You are *more than* this part of you.

Another one of your identifications might be, 'I am a secretary,' or 'a supervisor' or 'a teacher'. If so, a work-based identification indicates only your training, career field, competencies or whatever you do for a living, but it is not basically *who* you are. You are *more than* this part of you.

You might also have said, 'I am a dreamer,' or 'an introvert' or 'a perfectionist'. If so, a behaviour-based identification indicates only personal attitudes, habits and traits, but it is not basically *who* you are. You are *more than* this part of you.

We say in Session Six that the method of *identification leads us to step into the partial image*, take it on and become it to learn more about it, recognise it, accept it and learn how to express it and the gifts it offers more effectively. It is one stage of a two-stage process.

All of these images are not only partial ones, but they also can change, and therefore they are not basically *who* we are, because our essential Self is always the same — pure, permanent and unchanging. From infancy to adulthood, this centre within ourself is constant, always remaining the same.

It is the detached, impartial observer within us who has been aware of everything we have ever experienced throughout our entire life. It is this *'more than'* place within ourself which we call our personal Self or 'I'.

Here in Session Seven we explore the second stage of the process. Once we have fully acknowledged and identified with a part of ourself, the method of *disidentification leads us to step back from the partial image*, disconnect from it, move some distance away from it — not so that we can deny, avoid, suppress or stop it — but rather so that we can observe it, gain greater perspective about it and, if we have not already done so, recognise it, accept it and harmonise it more effectively with other parts of ourself.

One way for us to experience this permanent centre within ourself, then, is to take one step back from everything we identify with so that we can experience who we are when we are not being all of these other things.

The task is to peel off *all* of these partial images we have of ourself, like so many layers of an onion, to reveal our centre, our core, the permanent place within us which does not change. To find out who we are, we simply remove temporarily all of who we are *not*, that is, all of our partial images and identifications, all of our subpersonalities and roles.

Self-Awareness Exercise

The following exercise, formulated originally by Roberto Assagioli, helps us first to examine aspects of our personality while maintaining the point of view of the observer, recognising that *the observer is not that which he or she observes*. It then leads us to become aware of our personal Self or 'I'.

You may wish to pre-record this exercise so that you may participate in it freely and fully without interruption. Avoid rushing through it. Take your time.

Find a comfortable position, sitting up straight . . . Close your eyes . . . Take several long, slow, deep breaths . . . Relax your body completely . . . Release all of the tension . . . Allow whatever emotions you may be feeling to fade away . . . Do the same with your thoughts . . . Become like a calm, quiet lake, which mirrors perfectly the blue sky, or the starry sky in the silence of the night . . . Be at peace and yet remain alert . . .

When you are ready, affirm the following statements slowly and thoughtfully.

'I have a body but I am more than my body. My body may find itself in different conditions of health or sickness, it may be rested or tired, but that has nothing to do with my Self, my real 'I'. I value my body as my precious instrument of experience and of action in the outer world, but it is only an instrument. I treat it well, I seek to keep it in good health, but it is not my Self. I have a body, but I am more than my body.

'I have emotions, but I am more than my emotions. My emotions are diversified, changing, sometimes contradictory. They may swing from love to hatred, from calm to anger, from joy to sorrow, and yet my essence — my true nature — does not change. 'I' remain. Though a wave of anger may temporarily submerge me, I know that it will pass in time; therefore I am not this anger. Since I can observe and understand my emotions, and then gradually learn to direct, use and integrate them harmoniously, it is clear that they are not my Self. I have emotions, but I am more than my emotions.

I have desires, but I am more than my desires. Desires are aroused by physical and emotional drives, and by other influences. They are often changeable and contradictory, therefore they are not my Self. I have desires, but I am more than my desires.

I have a mind, but I am more than my mind. My mind is a valuable tool of discovery and expression, but it is not the essence of my being. Its contents are constantly changing as it embraces new ideas, knowledge and experience. Often it refuses to obey me! Therefore it cannot be me, my Self. It is an organ of knowledge in regard to both the outer and the inner worlds, but it is not my Self. I have a mind, but I am more than my mind.

I engage in various activities and play many roles in life. I must play these roles and I willingly play them as well as possible, be it the role of son or father, wife or husband, teacher or student, artist or executive. But I am more than the son, the wife, the artist. These are roles, specific but partial roles, which I am playing, agree to play and can watch and observe myself playing. Therefore I am not any of them. I am Self-identified, and I am not only the actor, but the director of the acting.

After disidentifying my Self, the 'I', from the contents of consciousness, such as sensations, emotions, desires, thoughts and roles, I recognise and affirm that I am a centre of pure Self-awareness and will, capable of observing, directing and using all of my psychological processes and my physical body.

'I have a body, but I am more than my body.

'I have emotions, but I am more than my emotions.

'I have desires, but I am more than my desires.

'I have a mind, but I am more than my mind.

'I have roles, but I am more than my roles.

'I am I, a permanent centre of pure Self-awareness and will.'

Most people take a long time to develop this kind of Self-awareness, and so it is perfectly all right and quite natural if you have not immediately experienced (to your satisfaction) the sense of your own personal Self. As with all of the exercises in this course, you will gain greater benefit by regularly repeating it until it does become real to you.

Disidentification has many values. It helps us to (a) step back from whatever we are feeling, thinking and identifying with; (b) observe, use and harmonise all parts of ourself; (c) experience who we are, a permanent centre of pure Self-awareness and will; and (d) rest, nurture and heal ourself.

However the goal is not for us to be totally disidentified one hundred per cent of the time. Rather it is to help us accept and express the gifts of *all* parts of ourself in ways which lead to self-mastery and wholeness.

'Personal Self' Symbol and Drawing

When we step back completely from all of our partial identifications, that which remains is our centre — not simply another image, subpersonality or role — but our basic Self, our pure essence, who we really are.

What is your inner experience of your personal Self? Finding a symbol for it and drawing it is a step towards discovering more about it.

Now close your eyes . . . Sit up straight . . . Take a few deep breaths . . . Relax . . . Allow your body, emotions and thoughts to become still . . . Become like a calm, quiet lake . . .

When you are ready, allow to come to you an image or sense which represents your personal Self, the pure, permanent, unchanging, aware centre within you . . . Take your time . . . Wait patiently in the silence, knowing that something will soon come to you . . . Be willing to accept whatever comes without judging, censoring or rejecting it . . . Simply be ready to observe and examine it, with the purpose of learning more about it . . .

As you begin to sense something, allow it to become more vivid . . . Note its size and shape . . . Its density and design . . . Its colour and texture . . . Explore it with as many of your senses as you can . . . Find the overall quality it suggests to you . . .

Then open your eyes, and express in a drawing below either the image itself or its quality . . . If nothing has come to you, open your eyes, hold the question in mind and begin to draw freely and spontaneously, letting something come to you in that way . . .

```
┌─────────────────────────────────────────────────────────┐
│                    MY PERSONAL SELF                       │
│                                                           │
│                                                           │
│                                                           │
│                                                           │
│                                                           │
│                                                           │
│                                                           │
│                                                           │
│                                                           │
│                                                           │
│                                                           │
│                                                           │
│                                                           │
│                                                           │
│                                                           │
│                                                           │
│                                                           │
│                                                           │
│                                                           │
│                                                           │
│                                                           │
│                                                           │
└─────────────────────────────────────────────────────────┘
```

Write down the overall *quality* of the symbol and any other words, feelings or thoughts which came to you during the exercise, or which you are aware of now. What new insight or awareness does this symbol and its quality give to you?

_____

_____

_____

_____

Personal Self-Realisation

It can be reassuring to realise that our basic essential Self remains the same throughout our life, regardless of what is happening around us. To deepen your experience of your personal Self, we present the following two exercises, devised originally by Diana Whitmore.

First, review the various observations you made about yourself in the 'Self-Observation' section of Part 2 of this session (p. 179), all of the descriptions of your body, emotions, desires, mind and roles. Do it now before continuing.

Then close your eyes . . . Sit up straight . . . Take a few deep breaths . . . Relax . . . Allow your body, emotions and thoughts to become still . . . Become like a calm, quiet lake . . . When you are ready, ask yourself *who*, what part of me, wrote these descriptions originally? . . . *Who* was aware then? . . . *Who* is re-experiencing them now? . . . *Who* is aware now? . . . *Who* am I? . . .

Then allow to come to you any memory from your early childhood . . . It may be a pleasant or an unpleasant one . . . Take your time . . . Wait patiently in the silence, knowing that something will soon come to you . . . Be willing to accept whatever comes without judging, censoring or rejecting it . . . Simply be ready to observe and examine it . . .

When you begin to sense something, allow specific details to come back to you . . . How old are you? . . . What clothes are you wearing? . . . Where are you? . . . What time of day is it? . . . What time of year? . . . Is anyone else around? . . . What is happening? . . . What do you see? . . . What can you hear? . . . How do you feel? . . . Observe the original experience with as many of your senses as you can . . . Allow it to be very real for you again, but avoid becoming lost in it . . . Write down a summary of it . . .

_____

_____

_____

Ask yourself: *Who*, what part of me, had this experience originally? . . . *Who* was a child then? . . . *Who* is re-experiencing it now? . . . *Who* is aware now? . . . *Who* am I? . . .

Then allow to come to you any memory from your teenage years . . . Take your time . . . Wait patiently in the silence, knowing that something will soon come to you . . . Be willing to accept whatever comes without judging, censoring or rejecting it . . . Simply be ready to observe and examine it . . .

When you begin to sense something, allow specific details to come back to you . . . Observe the original experience with as many of your senses as you can . . . Allow it to be very real for you again, but avoid becoming lost in it . . . Write down a summary of it . . .

_____

_____

_____

Ask yourself: *Who*, what part of me, had this experience originally? . . . *Who* was an adolescent then? . . . *Who* is re-experiencing it now? . . . *Who* is aware now? . . . *Who* am I? . . .

Then allow to come to you any memory from the past week . . . Take your time . . . Wait patiently in the silence, knowing that something will soon come to you . . . Be willing to accept whatever comes without judging, censoring or rejecting it . . . Simply be ready to observe and examine it . . .

When you begin to sense something, allow specific details to come back to you . . . Observe the original experience with as many of your senses as you can . . . Allow it to be very real for you again, but avoid becoming lost in it . . . Write down a summary of it . . .

_____

_____

_____

Ask yourself: *Who*, what part of me, had this experience originally? . . . *Who* is re-experiencing it now? . . . *Who* is aware? . . . *Who* am I? . . .

Then allow to come to you any memory of a time of great crisis or personal pain in your life, perhaps an experience which might even be blocking you now from bringing more love into your life . . . Take your time . . . Wait patiently in the silence, knowing that something will soon come to you . . . Be willing to accept whatever comes without judging, censoring or rejecting it . . . Simply be ready to observe and examine it . . .

When you begin to sense something, allow specific details to come back to you . . . Observe the original experience with as many of your senses as you can . . . Allow it to be very real for you again, but avoid becoming lost in it . . . Write down a summary of it . . .

_____

_____

_____

_____

Ask yourself: *Who*, what part of me, had this experience originally? . . . *Who* lived through it? . . . *Who* is re-experiencing it now? . . . *Who* is aware? . . . *Who* am I? . . .

Then allow to come to you any memory of a peak or special experience you have had, a time when you were greatly inspired, profoundly moved or rapturously uplifted . . . Take your time . . . Wait patiently in the silence, knowing that something will soon come to you . . . Be willing to accept whatever comes without judging, censoring or rejecting it . . . Simply be ready to observe and examine it . . .

When you begin to sense something, allow specific details to come back to you . . . Observe the original experience with as many of your senses as you can . . . Allow it to be very real for you again, but avoid becoming lost in it . . . Write down a summary of it . . .

_____

_____

_____

_____

Ask yourself: *Who*, what part of me, had this experience originally? . . . *Who* felt the specialness then? . . . *Who* is re-experiencing it now? . . . *Who* is aware? . . . *Who* am I? . . .

Then allow to come to you an experience which may take place for you sometime in the future . . . Take your time . . . Wait patiently in the silence, knowing that something will soon come to you . . . Be willing to accept whatever comes without judging, censoring or rejecting it . . . Simply be ready to observe and examine it . . .

When you begin to sense something, allow specific details to come to you . . . Observe the experience with as many of your senses as you can . . . Allow it to be very real for you, but avoid becoming lost in it . . . Write down a summary of it . . .

_____

_____

_____

_____

Ask yourself: *Who*, what part of me, is imagining this future experience now? . . . *Who* is aware now? . . . *Who* may experience it in the future? . . . *Who* has a future? . . . *Who* will be aware then? . . . *Who* am I? . . .

Realise that it has been one basic part of you, the same 'you', who has had all of these experiences . . . It is this singular 'you' who provides continuity and stability throughout your life . . . It is this 'you' who is at the very centre of your being, when all else is peeled away . . . It is this 'you' who is pure, permanent and unchanging . . . It is this 'you' who is connected directly to your God-Self . . . It is this 'you' who is your personal Self . . .

Now write down any feelings, thoughts or questions you wish to record.

_____

_____

_____

_____

_____

_____

_____

_____

Core Personality Identifications

As we have discovered, our partial identifications both serve us and limit us. They help us to define our world and to express ourself in it. They also hold us back from experiencing other ways of being, especially if we become rigidly identified with them or very attached to them. The following exercise helps us to experience that 'we are dominated by everything with which our Self becomes identified. We can dominate, direct and utilise everything from which we disidentify ourselves.'

First, turn back briefly again to Part 2 (p. 178) and review all of your responses to the question 'Who Am I?' Do it now before continuing.

Then consider the five responses you most strongly identified with at the time, the ones which seemed the nearest, the most accurate or the best descriptions of who you basically are. Make any changes you wish to make in your selections.

Rank all of them in order from 1 to 5, with 1 being the *least* significant, meaningful and important to you, and 5 being the *most* significant, meaningful and important. Write each of them on the appropriately-numbered line below.

Now address your identifications one by one. Ask yourself the following questions about each one, consider your experience and then write about it.

- What do I get from having this identification — how does it serve me?
- What do I have to pay to have this identification — how does it limit me?
- How would it be for me to let go of it permanently, to be without it for all time?
- Affirm to yourself: *'I HAVE THIS IDENTIFICATION, BUT I AM MORE THAN THIS IDENTIFICATION, AND SO I AM WILLING TO LET GO OF IT FOR NOW.'* If you are willing to do so, symbolically set aside the identification for the duration of this exercise. Then write down your feelings and thoughts about it.

1 _____
_____
_____
_____

2 _____
_____
_____
_____

3 _____
_____
_____
_____

4 _____
_____
_____
_____

5 _____
_____
_____
_____

If you did let go of any of your identifications, *who*, what place in you, did the letting go? If you were unable to let them go, *who*, what part of you, prevented you?

Affirm below, *'I AM I, A PERMANENT CENTRE OF PURE SELF-AWARENESS AND WILL.'* Then record any feelings or thoughts which writing your affirmation may prompt.

_____
_____
_____

Next in Part 5 we use the method of disidentification to address inner conflicts.

PART 5. DEVELOPING POTENTIAL

Functions of the Personal Self

Our personal Self has two primary functions. One is as an 'Observer' who objectively perceives and expresses *awareness*. But it is more than simply an impartial spectator. It also expresses the creative force of the *will*. Ideally, it uses these two functions to bring together all of our partial identifications into a unified, harmonious whole. Therefore it is the 'Conductor' of the orchestra of our subpersonalities in the performance of the score composed by our God-Self.

We can call upon our personal Self as an observer/conductor to help us to resolve the inner conflicts which prevent us from bringing more love into our life.

Inner Conflicts

When we experience ambivalence, indecision or conflict within ourself, we can say that two or more of our subpersonalities are in disagreement. For example, in deciding how to spend a free evening, we could say that one part of us might wish to go to the cinema, another part might prefer to spend time with a friend, another part might like to go for a long walk, while still other parts might like to stay home and read, watch television, have a hot bath or go to bed early.

When the issues are simple, inner conflict usually can be resolved relatively easily.

But what about the more complex ones? What happens when one part of ourself wants to be successful, while another lazy part does not want to have to work for it? Or when one part yearns to be true to ourself, while another part, afraid of rejection, tries to be all things to all people? Or when one part wants to bring more love into our life, and another fearful part tries to stop us?

Resolving Inner Conflicts

We present a helpful technique to address our inner conflicts. In the following exercise, we externalise them, that is, bring them out into the open where we can more easily deal with them. Our 'I' takes a central and facilitating position as the observer/conductor. You may wish to pre-record this exercise so that you may participate in it freely without interruption. Give yourself at least 20-30 minutes. Avoid rushing through it. Take your time.

First, take a few moments to identify within yourself a conflict of two different points of view relating to bringing more love into your life. Call each of them a subpersonality and create names for them which reflect their predominant attitude, behaviour or motivation, such as 'My Super Achiever' and 'My Lazy Bones', 'My Daredevil Risk-Taker' and 'My Frightened Child', or 'My Idealist' and 'My Judge'. Then describe the conflict and the difficulty it causes you.

_____

_____

_____

_____

NOTE. Throughout the following section, resist the temptation to go through the motions mechanically, so preventing yourself from participating in this exercise fully. Allow yourself to experience each step vividly.

Next find a position in the room where you have space around you to move, and stand comfortably erect . . . Close your eyes . . . Take a few deep breaths . . . Relax . . . Allow your body, emotions and thoughts to become still . . . Become like a calm, quiet lake . . .

Take a moment to enjoy the experience of standing comfortably on your own two feet . . . Then shift your weight gently from one foot to the other, rocking back and forth, and feel how balanced and stable you are in this position . . . This location — where you are standing in the room now — represents your own inner centre, your personal Self or 'I' . . . Affirm aloud, *'I AM I, A PERMANENT CENTRE OF PURE SELF-AWARENESS AND WILL'* . . . Experience the freedom which comes with this declaration . . .

When you are ready, open your eyes, look to your right and imagine the first subpersonality standing there . . . What is its typical posture? . . . How does it stand? . . . How does it place its head? . . . Its hands? . . . Its feet? (In other words, how do *you*, yourself, usually stand when you are taking the point of view represented by this subpersonality?) . . . Now choose to take an exaggerated giant step from where you are to the right, thereby stepping *into* this subpersonality . . .

In this new location, take on a whole new way of being . . . Using your imagination, portray, impersonate, assume the part of this subpersonality . . . Try it on like a coat . . . Become this subpersonality . . . Identify with this subpersonality . . . Be this subpersonality completely . . . First, adopt its physical posture . . . Hold your body in the position you have just now observed . . . Exaggerate it . . . How does it feel physically to be this subpersonality? . . . As this subpersonality, how do you stand? . . . How do you move? . . . Demonstrate it fully . . .

NOTE. As with other exercises involving your body and speaking aloud, it is natural to feel awkward and embarrassed at first. When you acknowledge your feelings, they will soon disappear.

Then what are the feelings, emotions and moods of this subpersonality? (How do *you*, yourself, usually feel when you are taking this point of view?) . . . Allow yourself to feel them and to express them — through movement or sound or words or preferably all three ways . . . Whatever you do, exaggerate it . . .

What are the thoughts, beliefs and attitudes of this subpersonality? . . . Allow yourself to experience them freely . . . What ideas do you have? . . . As this subpersonality, how do you use your mind? . . . (How do *you*, yourself, usually think when you are taking this point of view?) . . . Find your own ways to express it . . . Exaggerate it . . . As this subpersonality, say your name aloud, such as, 'I am the Victim' . . .

When you are ready, take an exaggerated giant step back to the left into the centre position again . . . As you do, experience leaving all of the subpersonality behind you . . .

Find yourself standing comfortably erect on your own two feet once again . . . Shift your weight gently from one foot to the other, rocking back and forth, and feel how balanced and stable you are in this position . . . Feel your centredness again . . . Feel the contrast between how you felt as the subpersonality a moment ago, and how you are feeling now in your centre, in your 'I', the detached observer/conductor . . .

Turn to the right, and say aloud to this first subpersonality, *'I HAVE YOU, BUT I AM NOT YOU. I AM I, A PERMANENT CENTRE OF PURE SELF-AWARENESS AND WILL'* . . . Experience the freedom which comes with this declaration . . .

When you are ready, look to your left and see the second subpersonality standing there . . . What is its typical posture? . . . How does it stand? . . . How does it place its head? . . . Its hands? . . . Its feet? . . .

Now choose to take an exaggerated giant step to the left, stepping *into* this subpersonality . . . Do it now . . .

In this new location, take on a whole new way of being . . . Using your imagination, portray, impersonate, assume the part of this other subpersonality . . . Try it on like a coat . . . Become this subpersonality . . . Identify with this subpersonality . . . Be this subpersonality completely . . . First, adopt its physical posture . . . Hold your body in the position you have just now observed . . . Exaggerate it . . . How does it feel physically to be this subpersonality? . . . How do you stand? . . . How do you move? . . . Demonstrate it fully . . .

Then what are the feelings, emotions and moods of this subpersonality? . . . Allow yourself to feel them and to express them — through movement or sound or words or preferably all three ways . . . Whatever you do, exaggerate it . . .

What are the thoughts, beliefs and attitudes of this subpersonality? . . . Allow yourself to experience them freely . . . What ideas do you have? . . . How do you use your mind? . . . Find your own ways to express it . . . Exaggerate it . . . As this subpersonality say your name aloud, such as, 'I am the Judge' . . .

When you are ready, take an exaggerated giant step back to the right and into the centre position again . . . As you do, experience leaving all of the subpersonality behind you . . .

Find yourself standing comfortably erect on your own two feet once again . . . Shift your weight gently from one foot to the other, rocking back and forth, and feel how balanced and stable you are in this position . . . Feel your centredness again . . . Feel the contrast between how you felt as the subpersonality a moment ago, and how you are feeling now in your centre, in your 'I', the detached observer/conductor . . .

Turn to the left, and say aloud to this second subpersonality, *'I HAVE YOU, BUT I AM NOT YOU. I AM I, A PERMANENT CENTRE OF PURE SELF-AWARENESS AND WILL'* . . . Experience the freedom which comes with this declaration . . .

Now choose to take an exaggerated giant step to the right, stepping back into the first subpersonality . . . Take a moment to re-identify with it, resuming its physical, emotional and intellectual ways of being . . .

As this subpersonality, begin to consider your needs . . . Then tell the other subpersonality what they are . . . Remember, you may or may not be particularly pleasant or agreeable . . . Be authentic and real . . . State your case . . .

When you are ready, take an exaggerated giant step back to the left and into the centre again . . . As you do, experience leaving the subpersonality behind you . . .

Find yourself standing comfortably erect on your own two feet once again . . . Shift your weight gently from one foot to the other, rocking back and forth, and feel how balanced and stable you are in this position . . . Feel your centredness again . . . Feel the contrast between how you felt as the subpersonality a moment ago, and how you feel now in your centre, in your 'I', the detached observer/conductor . . .

Turn to the right, and say aloud to this first subpersonality, *'I HAVE YOU, BUT I AM NOT YOU. I AM I, A PERMANENT CENTRE OF PURE SELF-AWARENESS AND WILL'* . . . Experience the freedom which comes with this declaration . . .

Now choose to take an exaggerated giant step to the left, stepping back into the second subpersonality . . . Take a moment to re-identify with it, resuming its physical, emotional and intellectual ways of being . . . Then how do you experience having to listen to the other subpersonality — the one you are in conflict with — telling you what it needs? . . . What is your reaction? . . . Express it now . . . Remember, you may or may not be particularly pleasant or agreeable . . . Be authentic and real . . .

Then consider your own needs . . . Tell the other subpersonality what they are . . .

When you are ready, take an exaggerated giant step back to the right and into the centre again . . . As you do, experience leaving all of the subpersonality behind you . . .

Find yourself standing comfortably erect on your own two feet once again . . . Shift your weight gently from one foot to the other, rocking back and forth, and feel how balanced and stable you are in this position . . . Feel your centredness again . . . Feel the contrast between how you felt as the subpersonality a moment ago and how you are feeling now in your centre, your 'I', the detached observer/conductor . . .

Turn to the left, and say aloud to this second subpersonality, *'I HAVE YOU, BUT I AM NOT YOU. I AM I, A PERMANENT CENTRE OF PURE SELF-AWARENESS AND WILL'* . . . Experience the freedom which comes with this declaration . . .

Now choose to take an exaggerated giant step to the right, stepping back into the first subpersonality . . . Take a moment to re-identify with it, resuming its physical, emotional and intellectual ways of being . . . Then how do you experience having to listen to the other subpersonality — the one you are in conflict with — telling you what it needs? . . . What is your reaction? . . . Express it now . . .

As this subpersonality, begin a direct dialogue with the other subpersonality about the conflict which exists between you . . . What do you have to say to each other? . . . How did it start? . . . What are the central issues? . . . Can you find any points of agreement? . . . Hold nothing back . . . Allow yourself to experience and express all of the feelings and thoughts, pleasant and unpleasant, which go with this conflict . . .

Continue to follow the sequence you have begun: (1) Disidentify from one subpersonality by stepping into the centre. (2) Feel your centredness contrasted with the previous subpersonality. (3) Make and experience the declaration, *'I HAVE YOU, BUT I AM NOT YOU. I AM I, A PERMANENT CENTRE OF PURE SELF-AWARENESS AND WILL.'* (4) Step into the other subpersonality and take a moment to re-identify with it. (5) Then continue the dialogue as this subpersonality.

Allow the dialogue to move back and forth freely between the two points of view. As you do, avoid making long monologues or speeches. Rather, let it be a give-and-take conversation or debate. Take all the time you need to allow these two subpersonalities to interact and explore their conflict. Give yourself at least ten minutes.

NOTE. In the dialogue, do not try to force or contrive a happy ending . . . It may come naturally; it may not. This conflict is legitimate and needs to be respected. Therefore, as you identify with each subpersonality, your task is simply to be as honest, open and real as you can be in representing its own position. If you persevere in this process long enough — perhaps over several sessions, depending upon the specific issues involved — the conflict *may* become resolved.

When the dialogue has come to an end for now, take an exaggerated giant step back into the centre one last time . . . Make and feel the declaration to both subpersonalities, *'I HAVE YOU, BUT I AM NOT YOU. I AM I, A PERMANENT CENTRE OF PURE SELF-AWARENESS AND WILL'* . . .

Now write down any feelings, thoughts and questions you wish to record. Note how you experienced being the observer/conductor and each of the subpersonalities.

_____

_____

_____

_____

_____

_____

_____

When we become aware of our avoidance, resistance, fear or other blocks, we can ask ourself what part of us, which subpersonality, is feeling it and why. Then, if we wish, we may choose to *identify with it*, stepping into it and exaggerating it so as to experience it more fully and more deliberately, until we can begin to recognise and accept it. Later we can choose to *disidentify from it*, stepping back from it to give us perspective to deal with it.

Thus we can choose to step into or out of our balanced, centred 'I', and *the act of choice becomes the point of power*, and not the avoidance, resistance or fear itself. Making this choice leads to increased inner freedom and self-mastery. There is great personal empowerment in disidentification, as it shows that *whatever we choose to step into, we can also choose to step out of*, and thus we need no longer be afraid or victim of our feelings, thoughts or any other parts of ourself. *The power and freedom to make this choice is always ours.*

'Right Proportions' Visualisation

Our inner conflicts can also often be dealt with effectively by putting them into a larger perspective in another way. We present the following visualisation exercise, created originally by Piero Ferrucci. You may wish to pre-record it so that you may participate in it freely without interruption. Give yourself at least 20 minutes to complete this exercise. Avoid rushing through it. Take your time.

First, take a few moments to identify a conflict within yourself. It may be the one you dealt with in the preceding exercise, or it may be a completely different one.

Then find a comfortable position . . . Close your eyes, sit up straight, take a few deep breaths and relax . . . Allow your body, emotions and thoughts to become still . . . Become like a calm, quiet lake . . .

Affirm silently to yourself: *'I HAVE A BODY, BUT I AM MORE THAN MY BODY . . . I HAVE EMOTIONS, BUT I AM MORE THAN MY EMOTIONS . . . I HAVE DESIRES, BUT I AM MORE THAN MY DESIRES . . . I HAVE A MIND, BUT I AM MORE THAN MY MIND . . . I HAVE ROLES, BUT I AM MORE THAN MY ROLES . . . I AM I, A PERMANENT CENTRE OF PURE SELF-AWARENESS AND WILL'* . . .

When you are ready, visualise yourself in the room where you are now . . . Picture in your mind's eye everything around you, exactly as it is . . . Now in your imagination, find yourself moving slowly upward, until you can look down and see the whole room in a single glance . . . Continue to move upward until you find yourself outside and above the building . . . Form a clear picture of the building, as you look down upon it . . .

As you rise higher and higher, see the building becoming smaller . . . From where you are now, the whole surrounding area lies below you, buildings, streets, trees . . . People are just barely visible in the streets . . . Consider for a moment how all people are at the centre of their own world, with their own feelings and thoughts, their own problems and projects, their own hopes and dreams . . . Watch them all moving around, living their own lives . . .

Continue your ascent . . . Your field of view expands, enabling you to see other outlying towns in the area, vast open fields, lakes and mountains . . . As you rise higher and higher, you can see the entire country now . . . You can glimpse other countries and oceans . . . Soon the whole continent is in sight . . . You see even more and more of the Earth, until you have the whole planet before you, blue and white, rotating slowly in empty space . . .

From this immense height, you can no longer see people, or even guess their existence . . . But you can be aware of them: billions of people, each one living on that same planet out there in front of you, breathing the same air . . . Billions of hearts, belonging to people of many different races, are beating down there . . .

Ask yourself: *Who* is it that is witnessing this spectacle now? . . . If you have a body, but you are more than your body; if you have emotions, but you are more than your emotions; if you have desires, but you are more than your desires; if you have a mind, but you are more than your mind; if you have roles, but you are more than your roles, then *who* is it that is experiencing this expansion of perspective now?

As you continue to move away from the Earth, see it becoming smaller and smaller . . . Other planets enter your field of view: bright Venus; red Mars; massive Jupiter . . . In fact, the whole solar system stretches out before you . . . Now become aware that the Earth has vanished from your view . . . Even the sun is but a tiny point of light among innumerable stars . . . And you lose all trace of it . . .

Billions of stars are all around you: below, above, on all sides . . . There is no more 'down', no more 'up' . . . All these billions of stars constitute but one galaxy in the universe . . . It is only one among unknown galaxies reaching out in every direction to infinity . . .

Slowly become aware of the infinity of time . . . Here there is no tomorrow and no yesterday . . . No haste . . . No pressure . . . Everything is scintillating peace and wonder . . . Ask yourself: *Who* is it that is experiencing all of this timeless splendour now? . . . *Who* are you?" . . . *Who* has a conflict? . . . From this perspective, what do you have to say to the personality which has the conflict?

(PAUSE HERE FOR AS LONG AS YOU WISH)

In your own time, allow everything to fade . . . Bring your attention back to the room where you are now . . . Open your eyes . . . Take a deep breath . . . And a gentle stretch . . . As you do, bring with you this sense of peace and wonder, this sense of expansion, this sense of disidentification from all that is, this sense of who you are, a permanent centre of pure Self-awareness and will.

Now write down any feelings, thoughts and questions you wish to record.

_____

_____

_____

_____

Next in Part 6 we present suggestions for using the method of disidentification.

PART 6. APPLYING IT

Using Disidentification

To summarise, disidentification helps us to (a) step back from whatever we are feeling, thinking and identifying with; (b) observe, use and harmonise all parts of ourself; (c) experience who we are, a permanent centre of pure Self-awareness and will; and (d) rest, nurture and heal ourself.

Its goal is to help us accept and express the gifts of *all* parts of ourself in ways which lead to self-mastery and wholeness.

Here are some suggestions for using disidentification. Practise each one of them daily for at least seven days and then report your experience with them on the following page *before you begin Session Eight*. In your report at the end of the week, note also when and how you may have experienced resistance to doing any or all of these exercises and techniques, and what you did about it.

1. **Affirmation**. Repeat the full Self-identification exercise presented in Part 4 (p. 184). In addition, use the shortened form of the exercise below at least five times throughout the day. As you do, feel each statement as an experienced fact.

> I have a body, but I am more than my body.

> I have emotions, but I am more than my emotions.

> I have desires, but I am more than my desires.

> I have a mind, but I am more than my mind.

> I have roles, but I am more than my roles.

> I am I, a permanent centre of pure Self-awareness and will.

2. **The Observer**. Immediately after making the affirmations above, take five minutes to observe yourself — such as your physical appearance, sensations and condition; your emotions and feelings and how you experience and express them; your wants and desires and how you satisfy them; your thoughts and ideas and what they mean to you; your subpersonalities and roles and how they influence you.

Say aloud over and over again, *'NOW I AM AWARE OF . . . ,'* and finish the sentence with whatever you are aware of about yourself in that moment. Avoid making judgemental or critical statements. Develop your ability to be more discerning, accurate and objective about yourself.

3. **Right Proportions.** Record the visualisation in Part 5 (p. 191). Listen to it to help you to reduce stress in your life, to relax, to step back from your physical sensations, feelings, desires, thoughts, identifications and roles, and to put your inner conflicts and outer problems into perspective.

NOTES AND DRAWINGS REPORTING RESULTS OF PART 6 EXERCISES

Suggested Reading

What We May Be, by Piero Ferrucci, is an excellent practical manual for psychological and spiritual growth. It introduces clearly and simply the visions and major techniques of Psychosynthesis. It is the book we recommend to read first if you want to learn more about Psychosynthesis and how to use it to resolve personal problems, improve relationships and explore life's meaning and purpose.

Personal Goal

Consider various simple, specific, observable actions you could take within the next few days which would be a step towards bringing more love into your life. Then choose one which seems important to you, one to take as a personal goal. Make a deliberate choice to achieve it. Write it down. Remember, making and implementing choices empowers and strengthens you.

_____

_____

_____

_____

Session Learnings

Turn back and review what you have done in this session. Then write down the three most important insights or learnings you have gained from it.

_____

_____

_____

_____

_____

_____

_____

Purpose

As stated at the beginning of Part 2, the purpose of Session Seven is to identify and experience your basic sense of self (and the freedom it brings), and to learn methods to resolve inner conflicts which prevent you from bringing more love into your life. To what degree has Session Seven achieved its general purpose for you?

_____

_____

_____

Congratulations! You have finished Session Seven. Please discuss your experience of this session with your support person *before you begin Session Eight.*

CHOOSING TO TAKE ACTION

PART 1. MAKING CONNECTIONS

Begin by reviewing Session Seven to reconnect with your process of development. Have you achieved the personal goal you set for yourself? How was it?

Next, if you have been doing the autogenic training presented in Session Two, Part 6 (p. 66), write about your progress with this method of stress reduction and relaxation. Have you noticed a decrease in muscular tension and headaches? Have you been sleeping better? Have your meditation times improved? If you have not been doing this exercise regularly, perhaps you may wish to start it now for a trial period.

Then, if you have chosen to take additional risks in bringing more love into your life since the beginning of the preceding session, write about your experience: what you did, how successful you were and what you learned.

Continue with these personal journal pages by *making connections with the theme, issues and exercises of this course*, recording whatever relevant memories, ideas, feelings, insights, dreams, 'unfinished business', interactions and other events in your inner and outer worlds have occurred since you completed Session Seven. Include related reading you may have done, questions on your mind and any other observations and connections with the course you wish to make.

_____
_____
_____
_____
_____
_____
_____
_____
_____
_____
_____
_____
_____
_____
_____
_____
_____
_____
_____
_____

Next in Part 2 we explore how you make decisions and choices

PART 2. TAKING STOCK

Purpose

The purpose of Session Eight is to experience that you have a great capacity for making and implementing decisions and choices, and that this capacity can be developed and strengthened to help you to bring more love into your life.

Every day we are faced with making choices. Some of them are relatively easy, perhaps because they have short-term effects, may involve only ourself and are already familiar to us. Examples of such choices might be which clothes we wear, what food we eat and when we go to bed. Other choices may be more difficult to make, perhaps because they have longer-term effects, involve others as well as ourself and are unfamiliar to us. They may relate to important aspects of our life, such as family, friends and other relationships, education, finances, health, housing, work, priorities and values.

This course states that bringing more love into our life is a deliberate action we can take. Like all personal actions, it requires us to make the choice to do it. Thus knowing more about how we make choices and how we put them into action may aid us in addressing our blocks to giving and receiving love more fully.

'Personal Limitations' Check-list

People give many different reasons for not being able to be or do certain things. Take a moment to consider each one of the following explanations. Mark the ones which you have said to yourself or to others at one time or another.

_____ **Age:** I am too young/too old/not the right age for it.

_____ **Culture:** I do not belong to the right __(class/nationality/race/religion)__.

_____ **Experience:** I am just a beginner/I have no/the wrong kind of experience.

_____ **Fears:** I am too afraid/I would rather be safe than sorry.

_____ **Finances:** I do not have the money/It is too costly/I cannot afford it.

_____ **Health:** I am not in good enough health/physical or emotional condition.

_____ **Obligations:** I am responsible for family/children/animals/property.

_____ **Qualifications:** I lack the proper ability/competence/education/skills/talent.

_____ **Support:** I do not have the proper help/I cannot do it all on my own.

_____ **Time:** I do not have the time.

_____ **Timing:** I feel it is too early/too late/not the right time for me.

_____ **Values and priorities:** I would rather be __(happy)__ than __(rich)__.

Take a moment to consider other limitations which have kept you from being or doing what you would like. Avoid judging them or yourself. Simply write them down.

_____

_____

_____

_____

'Authority and Power' Graph

Our attitude towards authority and power can influence how we make decisions. Some people respond to the issues of authority and power (and to the individuals and groups who exercise them) with genuine cooperation, obedience and support. They willingly follow the established rules and policies. Others react to authority with active or passive resistance, rebellion and other non-conforming behaviour. They habitually defy and oppose authority and power. They regularly challenge, ignore or subvert established rules and policies.

How about you? How do you deal generally with the issues of authority and power? Take a moment to consider your experience, and then write about it. Be honest, but avoid judging yourself. Your experience is your experience.

_____

_____

_____

_____

Mark an X on the graph below to indicate your general attitude towards these issues.

1 = I feel resistant and rebellious towards authority and power. I regularly feel compelled to challenge or subvert authorities and their rules.

5 = I feel cooperative and supportive towards authority and power. I regularly feel willing to follow and obey authorities and their rules.

1	2	3	4	5

Mark where your mother and father would have placed themselves. Be alert to the possibility that their beliefs and behaviour may have conditioned your own.

'Personal Empowerment' Graph

Our attitude towards authority and power in other people tends to be a reflection of how we experience our own authority and power. Thus, if we are accepting of these qualities in ourself, we are also usually accepting of them in others.

Some people feel fully empowered, that is, they experience their own personal authority, confidence, independence and ability to make choices and get things done. They are assertive, determined and initiating. Others feel fully disempowered, that is, they experience no personal authority, confidence or independence. Rather, they feel trapped by circumstance, with no real choice, and therefore feel helpless, powerless and victimised by others and by life.

How about you? How empowered or disempowered do you feel generally? Take a moment to consider your experience, and then write about it.

_____

_____

_____

_____

Mark an X on the graph below to indicate how empowered you feel generally.

> 1 = I am disempowered and trapped by circumstance. I often feel I have no other choice, and therefore I usually feel helpless, powerless and victimised by others and by life.

> 5 = I am empowered and experience my own personal authority, confidence, independence and power to make appropriate choices and get things done.

1	2	3	4	5

Mark where your mother and father would have placed themselves. Be alert to the possibility that their beliefs and behaviour may have conditioned your own.

'Making Decisions and Choices' Graph

Some people make decisions and choices quite easily. They have their own method or process which works well for them. Others have great difficulty. They are indecisive and cannot make up their mind. Or they are ambivalent and can appreciate all sides of an issue. Or they simply delay making a decision for as long as possible before committing themselves.

How about you? How are you with making decisions and choices? How easy or difficult is it? Take a moment to consider your experience, and then write about it.

_____

_____

_____

_____

Mark an X on the graph below to indicate how decisive you are generally.

> 1 = I have difficulty in making decisions, large or small. I am a very indecisive, ambivalent person, and never can make up my mind.

> 5 = I make decisions, large or small, quite easily. I never have any difficulty making them. I am a very decisive person.

1	2	3	4	5

Mark where your mother and father would have placed themselves. Be alert to the possibility that their beliefs and behaviour may have conditioned your own.

'Implementing Decisions and Choices' Graph

Some people implement or act upon their decisions and choices quite easily. They follow through from the original idea to its achievement with little difficulty. They breathe life into their decisions and then take the consequences. Others always have difficulty in carrying out their decisions and choices. They habitually encounter blocks and limitations which keep their decisions from being implemented. They either do not act at all, or fail to complete whatever they do begin or are unwilling to take responsibility for the consequences of their actions.

How about you? How are you with implementing your decisions and choices? Take a moment to consider your experience, and then write about it.

_____

_____

_____

_____

Mark an X on the graph below to indicate how you generally implement your decisions.

 1 = I have difficulty implementing my decisions, large or small. I find that something always seems to stop me from acting upon or completing them.

 5 = I implement my decisions, large or small, quite easily. I never have any difficulty in acting upon them and completing them.

1	2	3	4	5

Mark where your mother and father would have placed themselves. Be alert to the possibility that their beliefs and behaviour may have conditioned your own.

'Victim Subpersonalities' Check-list

Most people have a 'Victim' subpersonality, that is, when they feel like a victim of circumstances, when they feel helpless, powerless and victimised by others, or when they feel they have no choice, no options and nothing they can do about it. This part of themselves may be triggered off only occasionally by a certain person or situation, or it may be a more general, seemingly ever-present state.

How about you? When do you experience your 'Victim'? When do you feel helpless and disempowered? Mark below the people and situations which may occasionally cause you to feel powerless and victimised by others.

People
_____ My mother
_____ My father
_____ My family/relatives
_____ My lover/partner
_____ People of the same sex
_____ People of the opposite sex
_____ People in authority
_____ Friends
_____ Strangers

Situations
_____ When someone says 'no' to me
_____ When someone ignores me
_____ When someone rejects me
_____ When someone makes decisions affecting me
_____ When someone won't take 'no' for an answer
_____ When I encounter rigid laws and regulations
_____ When I feel I have no choice or alternative
_____ When I feel anxious, insecure or threatened
_____ With life, the universe and God

Take a moment to consider other people and situations which occasionally cause you to feel helpless, powerless, victimised or without choice. Then write about them.

_____

_____

_____

_____

PART 3. EXPLORING PERSPECTIVES

EILEEN

One can never know what is possible until one tries.
The most important part of any project is the decision to go ahead. — The Living Word

All through life we are making choices. Some choices are simple to make, whereas others seem so difficult. The difficult ones are a test for me: do I choose what is easy, comfortable and convenient, following the path of least resistance? Or do I use my will to summon the strength and courage I may need to move through my fears and deal directly with the person or situation? I find that it is rather like coming to a crossroads, having to make a decision about which road to take, carrying through with it and then living with the outcome.

A few years ago at the Findhorn Foundation David and I made several cassette tapes, one entitled *Loving Unconditionally*. We enjoyed our work together and soon we had the idea to give a week-long workshop on this theme. So we scheduled it twice one summer as part of the public education programme of the Foundation. However, the first workshop was a complete disaster as far as we were concerned. I did not understand David's approach. He seemed to concentrate on the blocks, the barriers, the fears. All of this negativity offended me. I very nearly walked out because I had always been told to see only the best in everyone and everything. I was unable to understand the process. Actually David was doing the basic 'personality work', preparing the ground first so that I could come along and plant the spiritual seeds of positive thinking, meditation and love in more receptive soil.

By the end of the workshop David and I were at loggerheads. He said he would never lead a group with me again until we had dealt with our own difficulties. My reaction was good riddance to him! But we were scheduled to give the same workshop again a few days later. What were we to do?

We met with the focaliser of the Education Branch who tried to help us settle our differences. I said I felt David had been too negative. David said he felt I had been very disruptive and temperamental. We were honest and open about our grievances with each other, but we came to no decision. We agreed to meet again in two days' time to decide what we would do about the second workshop. It was a very difficult situation for both of us. Neither of us had enjoyed working with the other. It would have been quite easy for us to call a halt at that point. The choice was ours. We were at a crossroads.

I spent much time in prayer and meditation about the whole situation. Here we were, giving a workshop on *Loving Unconditionally*, and we couldn't agree on anything, let alone love one another! Little did we realise that we were 'teaching' the most important lesson we needed to learn ourselves! Finally I received the inner guidance, 'Why are you trying to change David? Why can't you allow him to be himself?' This prompting got my hackles up, and then I realised that I could not change anyone except myself. I had to allow David to do what he needed to do, and myself to do what I needed to do. If we could complement each other, the group would benefit from our two different approaches. When the three of us met again, I shared my guidance and asked David if he would take a risk and be willing to try it again. He was very doubtful at first, but after some discussion we finally agreed to do the second workshop together.

By my choosing to allow David to be himself, and his choosing to allow me to be myself, we have worked together harmoniously for many years since that first workshop. We sometimes still have difficulties with each other, but when we do, we use our will to make the deliberate choice to work through the difficulty, and we grow in the process. We have come to experience that the choice is always ours.

DAVID

Dignity becomes possible only with choice. The choice is ours. — Ruth Nanda Anshen

Sometimes I am a very slow learner. Slowly, I have been learning that —

• Most, if not all, of my limitations are self-imposed, that is, they are brought about by choices I make either consciously or unconsciously, then kept firmly in place by my own behaviour patterns of fear, resistance and avoidance.

• When I say I *can't*, I usually mean I *won't*. So when I say I can't dance, draw or saw a straight line, I am actually saying I won't choose to make the effort to do so. Otherwise, even if I do these things poorly, I could practise doing them or find a friend, interest group or course to help me learn how to do them better.

• My beliefs about my limitations are like all beliefs, that is, they are only tinted sunglasses through which I perceive and create my experience, and which I can choose to change for other glasses which are more helpful. My not changing them (when I know I am able to do so) means that *I* am the one who builds and maintains all of the barriers in my life — the shields, the fences, the walls.

• All I need to do is to make the choice to *re-frame* whatever I believe is a limitation. 'I don't have the time for it' becomes '*How* do I find the time for it?' 'I don't have the money' becomes '*How* do I find the money?' 'I am too young or old for it' becomes '*How* to do it at my age?' In this way, I shift my focus from the problem to finding a solution to it.

• If I do not make a choice consciously, I end up making it unconsciously. In other words, my not deciding is deciding. I have 'not-decided' a lot of things in my life to avoid risks, responsibility and failure.

• Where there is a *will*, there is a way. How willing am I to look for another way? How willing am I to change, to grow, to fail, to succeed? How willing am I to make decisions and choices which empower and serve me?

• It sometimes takes honesty, openness and courage to make choices which support me — to say 'no' when it is easier for me to say 'yes'; to take a new and untried path; to live by my own values and priorities no matter what others may say.

• Life rewards action; it doesn't reward inaction. Therefore I gain nothing by sitting on the fence waiting for my ideal to manifest before I take action. I can make a choice and then await feedback from life about it. If it is an appropriate choice, then I can enjoy its benefits. If it is an inappropriate choice, I can learn my lessons from it, and then make another choice.

• It empowers me to make free and deliberate choices, no matter how large or small they may be. Making choices about how I live my life allows me, as the American Indians say, 'to stand firmly within my own circle of power', expressing my freedom and independence, and exercising my capacity to get things done.

• A completely centred, deliberate and willed choice is one where, with detachment, I am able to choose to do something, or equally choose *not* to do it. It is a choice which is not conditioned by fears, impulsive desires or 'shoulds'. It is one which leads to greater freedom and independence, rather than to limitation or dependence. It is a responsible choice, harmful neither to myself nor to others.

My ideal now is to make every choice I make a centred, deliberate and willed one.

PART 4. GAINING AWARENESS

'Empowerment' Experience Scan

In Part 2 you identified times when you feel disempowered and powerless or, as we can say, when you express your 'Victim' subpersonality. Now we invite you to explore the other side and identify times when you feel empowered and powerful.

In the following scan, allow to come to you obvious times when you feel powerful, such as 'when I drive a car, when I am in control, when I have influence or authority over people'. Also allow to come to you more subtle times, such as 'when I am sick, when I am in crisis, when I am helpless (because then I have the power to engage people's sympathy or sense of duty and to get a great deal of attention'.)

Now close your eyes . . . Sit up straight . . . Take a few deep breaths . . . Relax . . . Allow your body, emotions and thoughts to become still . . . Become like a calm, quiet lake . . .

When you are ready, say to yourself, *'I FEEL EMPOWERED AND POWERFUL WHEN . . .,'* and complete the sentence with a short phrase — whatever comes spontaneously to you. Do not *think* about it. Write down the first response which comes. Then do it again, this time allowing a new phrase to emerge. Write down the new response. If you blank out momentarily, simply begin again, knowing that something will soon come to you. Repeat the process again and again for at least ten minutes, or until you have filled the space below.

```
I FEEL EMPOWERED AND POWERFUL WHEN . . .




```

What is the overall quality, tone or impression of your responses? What similarities or patterns do you find? What other observations can you make?

_____

_____

_____

_____

Would you like to be more fully empowered? How do you imagine life would be for you if you were more fully empowered? What differences might there be, especially in your relationships?

_____

_____

_____

_____

The Act of Will

A Course In Miracles says that we need to find all of the barriers within ourself that we have built against love. One aim of this course is to help to do precisely that. However, even when we know some of our own barriers, we may have great difficulty in doing anything about them. What stops us from lessening or eliminating their influence upon us?

One answer may be that our blocks are stronger than our intention or will to overcome them. If so, then we need to develop our will as a step in bringing more love into our life.

What is the will? It is *not* what has been termed 'Victorian will', that is, strong will power, force, control, domination, manipulation or self-denial. It is *not* saying through clenched teeth, 'I *will* do this or that (if it kills me),' or, 'I *impose* my will upon you, whether you like it or not.' Nor is it an instinct, drive, urge or desire.

In *The Act of Will* Roberto Assagioli says: 'The true function of the will is not to act against the personality drives to *force* the accomplishment of one's purposes. The will has a *directive* and *regulatory* function; it balances and constructively utilises all the other activities and energies of the human being without repressing any of them.'

In its simplest form, then, *the act of will is the capacity to make a free and deliberate choice and then implement it effectively*. It is an act of volition designed to facilitate action.

The will is needed to mobilise all of our personal resources and to initiate and integrate change. Therefore we need the will to bring more love into our life.

'Will Pure Forms and Distortions' Assessment

The quality of will can be experienced and expressed in many ways. Some ways may be considered pure, while others are distorted through our needs, desires and experience. Listed below are examples of both forms. To get a sense of the will and how you relate to it, in the blanks provided put the number of the statement nearest to how you experience or express each quality of the will.

1. I never experience or express this quality.
2. I rarely experience or express this quality.
3. I sometimes experience or express this quality.
4. I often experience or express this quality.
5. I always experience or express this quality.

PURE FORMS OF THE WILL	DISTORTIONS OF THE WILL
_____Assertiveness/initiative	_____ Aggression/violence
_____Concentration/focus	_____ Ambivalence
_____Courage/daring	_____ Anger/resentment
_____Decisiveness	_____ Domination/imposition
_____Determination	_____ Fear of entrapment
_____Discipline	_____ Fear of losing control
_____Endurance/patience	_____ Helplessness/powerlessness
_____Energy/dynamic power	_____ Manipulation
_____Integration/synthesis	_____ Power-seeking
_____Mastery	_____ Rebellion
_____Order/organisation	_____ Resistance
_____Persistence/tenacity	_____ Rigidity/stubbornness

Now write down any feelings, thoughts or questions you wish to record.

_____

_____

_____

_____

'Will' Symbol and Drawing

Now we turn to your own inner experience of the will.

Find a comfortable position, sitting up straight . . . Close your eyes . . . Take several long, slow, deep breaths . . . Relax your body completely . . . Release all of the tension . . . Allow whatever emotions you may be feeling to fade away . . . Do the same with your thoughts . . . Become like a calm, quiet lake, which mirrors perfectly the blue sky, or the starry sky in the silence of the night . . . Be at peace and yet remain alert . . .

When you are ready, allow to come to you an image or sense which represents your will, your capacity to make and implement free and deliberate choices. . . . Take your time . . . Wait patiently in the silence, knowing that something will soon come to you . . . Be willing to accept whatever comes without judging, censoring or rejecting it . . . Simply be ready to observe and examine it, with the purpose of learning more about it . . .

As you begin to sense something, allow it to become more vivid . . . Note its size and shape . . . Its density and design . . . Its colour and texture . . . Explore it with as many of your senses as you can . . . Find the overall quality it suggests to you . . .

Then open your eyes, and express in a drawing below either the image itself, or its quality . . . If nothing has come to you, open your eyes, hold the question in mind and begin to draw freely and spontaneously, letting something come to you in that way . . .

MY WILL

Write down the overall *quality* of the symbol and any other words, feelings or thoughts which came to you during the exercise, or which you are aware of now. What new insight or awareness does this symbol and its quality give to you?

_____

_____

_____

_____

The Process of Choosing

Some people make choices *rationally*: they define their needs, gather information, identify viable options, analyse and evaluate each of them and then finally make a logical deduction, usually whichever one seems 'best' for them. Others make choices *intuitively*: they sense whatever 'wants to happen', or 'feels right' to them in the moment and they follow it without further consideration. These people may or may not then look for rational reasons to justify or support their intuitive choices.

Some people make choices rapidly, even spontaneously, while others delay making choices, keeping their options open for as long as they can.

How about you? Take a moment to consider your experience. What is your *primary* way of making decisions and choices? Does it follow closely any of these approaches? Or have you another way which works for you?

_____
_____
_____
_____

Now close your eyes . . . Sit up straight . . . Take a few deep breaths . . . Relax . . . Allow your body, emotions and thoughts to become still . . . Become like a calm, quiet lake . . . When you are ready, allow to come to you a recent time when you made an important free and deliberate choice . . . Allow the details of it to come back to you . . . When the whole experience becomes more clear, begin to focus upon the *process* you used to make your choice, rather than the *content* of the choice itself . . . How did you choose? . . . What was it like? . . . What qualities did the act of choosing have? . . . When was the moment of choice for you? . . . In your own time, open your eyes . . . Take a deep breath . . . And a gentle stretch . . . Then write about your process of choosing.

_____
_____
_____
_____

What prevents you from *making* decisions and choices more quickly and easily?

_____
_____
_____

What prevents you from *implementing* them more quickly and easily?

_____
_____
_____

What implications does your own choice-making process have for the basic principle of this course, that is, you can *choose* to bring more love into your life?

_____
_____
_____
_____

Have you actually made the choice yet to bring more love into your life?

_____
_____
_____
_____

We find that people typically respond to this question from either their head (that is, with a thought), or their heart (an aspiration). However the barriers and blocks to love usually reside within the solar plexus, or pit of the stomach, where gut-level feelings, such as fears, are often experienced. For many people — at least until they begin to strengthen their will — these gut-level feelings are so strong that they create powerful resistances which can weaken or render ineffective their own thoughts and other psychological functions. Put simply, fears can overpower thoughts and aspirations, just as one radio transmitter can jam another. We can use the will to stop this interference from happening.

'Personal Resistance and Avoidance' Check-list

Personal resistance is not the same as simple disagreement or difference of opinion. Rather, it is a conscious or unconscious act of defiance, opposition or rebellion, often fuelled by fear. As we have already indicated, resistance is a distortion of the will. We usually experience it within ourself when we want to avoid something — a person, a situation, a problem or ourself. It can help us delay, deflect or sabotage something, even those things we say we want. Such patterns usually start in childhood in response to a need to protect ourself, and we then carry them unconsciously with us into adulthood, long after we have outgrown the original need. They often become a habitual way of behaving.

In the short term, our resistance helps us to feel more safe and in control, and therefore more comfortable, or at least less uncomfortable. In the long term, however, it robs us of freedom of choice as well as a sense of fulfilment. Often pain builds up around the resistance as well. A loyal soldier defending us against 'the enemy', our resistance can be retired from active duty as we become aware that the 'war' is finally over.

Resistance takes many different forms. Listed below is a small sample. Mark the ones you experience as part of your own avoidance patterns.

_____**Boredom and impatience.** We resist by either deadening ourself through apathy and monotony, or becoming eternally restless.

_____**Confusion and indecision.** We never have to *do* anything as long as we remain in a constant state of upheaval, crisis or bewilderment.

_____**Intellectualisation.** We read books, attend lectures, take courses, keep journals, discuss, analyse and evaluate — but keeping it all safely on the mental level to avoid having to *do* anything about making changes in our life.

_____**Invisibility.** We withdraw quietly to the background, contribute little, may engage in silent sabotage or passive aggression or simply disconnect ourself from everyone.

_____**Judgement.** We find ways to make others or things 'wrong' or 'bad', and thus give ourself good reason to keep them at a safe, manageable distance.

_____**Lack of commitment.** By withholding commitment, we seek to avoid the possibility of risk, responsibility and both failure and success.

_____**Procrastination.** We create circumstances to delay our having to confront a person, situation or problem.

_____**Rationalisation.** We find good 'reasons' (such as those listed at the beginning of Part 2) for doing whatever we want to do and avoiding everything else.

_____**Rebellion.** We are quick to express our righteous indignation and act in defiance of whatever we wish to avoid. 'Nobody is going to tell *me* what to do!'

____**Self-indulgence.** We resist by allowing ourself to be dominated and controlled by our own self-ishness, laziness or other self-serving desires.

____**Victimisation.** As long as we can feel we are a victim of circumstances, and have someone or something else to blame for our own situation, we can avoid being accountable for who we are and how we live our life.

____**Work and activity.** We obligate ourself with other responsibilities and so stay busy, occupied, distracted and unavailable.

How else do you avoid things? Take a moment to consider your experience, and then write about it. Be honest, but avoid judging yourself.

_____

_____

_____

_____

How do these ways of resisting serve you — what basic human needs do they fulfil? How might you meet these needs in more constructive and effective ways?

_____

_____

_____

_____

Now we pose our question again, and ask you to pay close attention to your *gut-level* feelings this time before you answer: Have you actually made the choice yet to bring more love into your life? Which part of you responds to the question?

_____

_____

_____

_____

'The Hero's Journey' Visualisation

Where is the will — the capacity to make a free and deliberate choice and then implement it effectively — in all of this resistance? Obviously, it is missing.

How do you block yourself from experiencing and expressing your will? This exercise helps you to find your blocks and forms of will to overcome them. Avoid rushing through it. Take your time. Give yourself at least 20-30 minutes for it.

In your imagination you are going to take a journey in search of a spiritual treasure hidden in a cave. In the end you do find the treasure, but first along the way you encounter several obstacles, distractions and difficulties which appear to you spontaneously. Be aware of what they are and how you deal with each one of them, finding inner resources to overcome them. Continue exploring throughout the visualisation; avoid getting stuck in any one part of the journey. Allow various episodes or scenes to unfold as part of your exploration until you finally find the treasure.

The value of this exercise is in whatever it tells you about your obstacles, how you use the will in life, how you deal with obstacles and how you seek your treasures.

Either take notes as you go along, or speak aloud, giving a firsthand account of whatever you are experiencing in each moment of the visualisation. For example 'Now I find myself in this setting . . . Now I see this . . . Now I am doing that . . . Now I encounter this . . . Now I come to that . . .' Record the exercise as you do it, for later re-play and study.

Now find a comfortable position, sitting up straight . . . Close your eyes . . . Take several long, slow, deep breaths . . . Relax your body completely . . . Release all of the tension . . . Allow whatever emotions you may be feeling to fade away . . . Do the same with your thoughts . . . Become like a calm, quiet lake, which mirrors perfectly the blue sky, or the starry sky in the silence of the night . . . Be at peace and yet remain alert . . .

When you are ready, allow to come to you an image or sense of your being embarked upon an extended journey in search of a hidden spiritual treasure which is to be found in a cave . . . Wait patiently in the silence, knowing that an opening scene will soon come to you . . . Be willing to accept whatever comes without judging, censoring or rejecting it . . . Simply be ready to participate in it, with the purpose of learning more about yourself . . .

When you begin to sense something, allow it to become more vivid . . . Explore it with as many of your senses as you can . . . When the scene is very clear to you, begin to look around you . . . Where do you find yourself? . . . What time of day is it? . . . What is the weather? . . . How are you dressed? . . . Are there others around you? . . . What do you seem to be doing? . . . Allow your adventures along the way to finding the treasure to begin now . . .

Continue your journeying and exploring until you find the treasure in a cave . . . After 20 to 30 minutes, and only after the treasure has been found, in your own time allow everything to fade . . . Bring your attention back to the room where you are now . . . Open your eyes . . . Take a deep breath . . . And a gentle stretch . . .

Now write down any feelings, thoughts and questions you wish to record. Note especially the nature of whatever distractions and obstacles you encountered, the qualities they represent to you (for example, confusion, judgement, procrastination, rebellion or victimisation) and especially how you overcame each one of them.

_____

_____

_____

_____

_____

_____

_____

_____

_____

_____

_____

PART 5. DEVELOPING POTENTIAL

Stages in the Act of Will

Now we invite you to test the act of will itself by applying it to the issue of bringing more love into your life.

The act of will may be divided into six successive stages:

- Exploring a purpose to be achieved
- Deliberating upon it
- Choosing to do it
- Affirming your intention to do it
- Planning how to do it
- Executing or implementing it

Obviously we do not move deliberately through all of these stages for everyday choices we make, nor is there a need to do so. *We do recommend using them all, however, when considering an important issue or change in your life.*

The value of this method is that it empowers us, strengthens our will and helps us to achieve our purpose systematically. We are usually more effective with some of these stages than with others. By exploring and experiencing one stage at a time now, you may discover weaknesses in your own decision-making and decision-implementing process, and can then strengthen them.

NOTE. PLEASE READ THROUGH THE WHOLE OF PART 5 TO GAIN AN OVERVIEW OF THE ENTIRE PROCESS BEFORE YOU BEGIN TO RESPOND TO ANY OF THE EXERCISES BELOW.

Stage One — Exploring a Purpose to Be Achieved

The first stage in the act of will is to identify a specific purpose which you wish to achieve. For this exercise, find a purpose which would help you to deal with your *blocks* to bringing more love into your life, for example, 'To increase my self-esteem,' 'To demonstrate more faith and trust,' 'To reach out and make new friends,' or 'To take risks with honesty and openness.' As you explore, make certain you find a purpose you feel enthusiastic about, one you feel is worthwhile and important, something you definitely intend to achieve. State it clearly and precisely, beginning with, *'I USE MY WILL TO . . .'*

_____

_____

_____

_____

Next, what are your motives or reasons for wishing to achieve this particular purpose? What will it give you — what are its benefits, values, advantages to you? Knowing its potential rewards serves to motivate you and keep your interest high.

_____

_____

_____

_____

Stage Two — Deliberating Upon Your Purpose

The second stage in the act of will is to consider the various ways you may achieve your purpose — actions, activities and projects — together with their likely outcomes and consequences, so that you may choose deliberately the best available option from a wide range of possibilities.

One method of deliberation is to brainstorm ways to achieve your purpose. Remember, in brainstorming the point is to allow many ideas to come to you as quickly as possible. Now is *not* the time to evaluate, judge or reject any idea. (You will do so later.) Rather, include and write down everything as it occurs spontaneously to you. Enjoy your creativity and originality. Allow yourself to be inspired. Avoid rushing through the exercise. Take your time. Give yourself at least ten minutes.

WAYS TO ACHIEVE MY PURPOSE

Examine your responses. Mark all of the ideas which are worth considering for implementation. For this exercise, limit your consideration to those options which you are willing and able to achieve within the next week or two. Explore their likely consequences, both favourable and unfavourable, and consider how willing you are to accept full responsibility for them.

Next, as a part of your deliberation, turn within to your own inner source of wisdom to seek information, guidance and support concerning the purpose you have chosen and the various options you have identified for achieving it. To facilitate this process, use the Attunement Exercise from Session Three, Part 5 (p. 91). In addition, you may also wish to use the Receptive and Reflective Meditations, also found in Session Four, Part 5 (pp. 109-112).

Now find a comfortable position, sitting up straight . . . Close your eyes . . . Take several long, slow, deep breaths . . . Relax your body completely . . . Release all of the tension . . . Allow whatever emotions you may be feeling to fade away . . . Do the same with your thoughts . . . Become like a calm, quiet lake, which mirrors perfectly the blue sky, or the starry sky in the silence of the night . . . Be at peace and yet remain alert . . .

This time allow yourself to relax even more deeply . . . Count backwards slowly from ten to one, and on each succeeding number feel yourself moving step by step further into the very centre of your being . . . Experience yourself making a connection with your own inner source of wisdom, that pure permanent centre deep within you which has the answer to any question you could possibly ask about yourself . . .

When you are ready, ask your inner source of wisdom for the information, guidance and support you need regarding the purpose you are considering, and the options for achieving it . . . Take your time . . . Wait patiently in the silence, knowing that something will soon come to you, knowing the help you seek is already on its way . . .

In your own time, allow everything to fade . . . Count slowly from one to ten, and on each succeeding number feel yourself coming outward to your normal level of alert wakefulness again . . . Bring your attention back to the room where you are now . . . Open your eyes, take a deep breath . . . And a gentle stretch . . .

Now write down your feelings, thoughts and whatever else you wish to remember from this exercise, noting any inner response you may have received regarding your purpose and the options for achieving it.

_____

_____

_____

_____

_____

_____

_____

Next contact your support person and state your purpose clearly, giving several options you are considering and their likely consequences, along with the results of your attunement. Encourage your support person to ask you questions and give you feedback. Write down the main points.

_____

_____

_____

_____

If you are a member of a supportive affinity group, such as a meditation, prayer or study group, you may also wish to take your deliberation into the group for review. It is our experience at the Findhorn Foundation that involving a sympathetic group can be very helpful in all stages of the act of will.

Stage Three — Choosing an Option

Sooner or later, the deliberation stage must be brought to an end, and therefore the third stage in the act of will is to make a choice among the options. It means deciding upon one of them and discarding the others.

Now choose the one option for achieving your purpose that you prefer, one that has realistic possibilities of success, one you are willing and able to achieve within the next week or two. Write it down clearly and precisely, beginning with, *'I USE MY WILL TO . . .'* together with any feelings or thoughts you have about the option and your process of choosing it.

_____

_____

_____

_____

Stage Four — Affirming Your Intention

The fourth stage in the act of will is to affirm your intention and commitment to achieving your purpose. You may feel this stage is unnecessary, and yet by now you are aware that resistance can sabotage or defeat your own best efforts.

Create an affirmation which reflects your willingness to achieve your purpose. Write it down, beginning with, *'I,   (NAME) , . . .'* Use your affirmation regularly until you achieve your purpose. Remember that visualising the successful outcome of your purpose as you write and say your affirmation also helps you to manifest it.

_____

_____

_____

_____

Stage Five — Planning How to Achieve Your Purpose

The fifth stage in the act of will is to prepare a detailed plan for achieving your purpose. Like Stage Two, this stage involves deliberation, but in very specific terms, and directed towards only one option.

Now formulate a plan for achieving your purpose. Consider such factors as:

- *What* specific steps you will take and in what sequence
- *When* you will take them, their timing and their duration
- *Where* you will take them
- *Who* else will be involved or will need to be considered
- *Which* resources you will require: equipment, materials, money, space, time
- *How* you will evaluate your efforts: criteria to use to measure your success

MY PLAN FOR ACHIEVING MY PURPOSE

Consider how you could sabotage or defeat your own efforts towards achieving your purpose. How might your resistance show itself? If it does, how will you deal with it? Will you allow it to stop you? Or will you make a deliberate choice (an act of will) to acknowledge the resistance, and then to proceed in spite of it?

_____

_____

_____

_____

Finally, regularly visualise in graphic detail the successful achievement of your purpose. Vividly imagine its ideal resolution. As you do so, allow feelings of enthusiasm, determination and expectancy to grow within you. Remember always to feel and think positively about your purpose and its successful outcome.

Stage Six — Implementing Your Plan

The final stage in the act of will is to direct the execution of your plan, skilfully calling upon all of your inner resources in support of your purpose: sensory perceptions, emotions and feelings, desires and drives, intellect, imagination and intuition. Avoid manipulating, imposing or forcing anything to happen. Rather, maintain a clear, positive intention, remain flexible and facilitate the achievement of your purpose within the next week or two. Then report the final results below.

Assessing the Outcome

How successful were you in achieving your purpose, as measured by your own criteria? What did you learn from the action you took? Which of the stages in the act of will were you most comfortable with, and which ones triggered resistance or other problems? Which stages may account for your difficulties in addressing your blocks to bringing more love into your life? Write down any other observations you wish to make about your experience of making a considered, free and deliberate act of will.

_____

_____

_____

_____

_____

_____

_____

_____

_____

This six-stage process is an empowering one, as it strengthens and trains our capacity to make free and deliberate choices and to put them into action effectively. As the ladder of Session One, Part 4 (p. 30) suggests, using the will to make choices brings greater freedom.

PART 6. APPLYING IT

Training the Will

Roberto Assagioli observes that 'every act of the will trains the will, and each bit of training allows for further acts of will'. Piero Ferrucci calls this interaction a 'virtuous circle'.

Here are a few suggestions for training your will, your capacity for making and implementing free and deliberate choices. Give each one of them five minutes a day for at least seven days, and then report your experience with them on the following page *before you begin Session Eight.*

1. Verbal Affirmation. Choose one of the pure forms of the will listed in Part 4 (p. 210), that you wish to awaken or strengthen within yourself. Create an affirmation which affirms your complete embodiment and expression of the quality. Use the affirmation in the various ways outlined in Session Five, Part 6 (pp. 145-146).

2. Daily Record. Keep a record of a few of the choices you make. Record relevant details, such as how you make the choice, who (what part of you — which subpersonality) makes the choice and who implements it, the nature of any resistance you may experience to making or implementing it, how the choice (and the process you use to make it) empowers and serves you or disempowers and limits you.

3. Deliberate Choices. Make and implement a series of deliberate choices, and voice them aloud. For example, 'Now I choose to put my pen on the table. Now I choose to close this book. Now I choose to stand up. Now I choose to make myself a cup of tea. Now I choose to walk into the kitchen. Now I choose to open the cupboard. Now I choose to take out a cup.' Make your every act the result of a totally willed, deliberate, explicit choice. One value of this exercise is that it helps you to experience how automatic, habitual and unconscious your actions usually are.

4. Creative Meditation. Adapt this exercise presented in Session Four, Part 5 (pp. 112-113) by using your imagination to visualise how life would be for you if you were more fully empowered, expressing your will. Move slowly scene by scene throughout a full day's activities, beginning with awakening and your morning routine, and ending with your retiring for the night. Include various interactions with others at work, leisure and home. Allow yourself to experience all the feelings and thoughts which go with this ideal model of yourself.

5. Action Affirmation. Then follow the above exercise by behaving 'as if' you already fully possessed the desired personal empowerment and its qualities of authority, confidence, independence and will. How do you sit, stand, walk, speak? What other external, physical gestures, postures and actions are there? Take a few minutes each day to create and express all of the outer signs of personal empowerment. Then notice if maintaining the outward physical signs results in corresponding inner feelings. Refer to the original instructions for this technique in Session Five, Part 6 (p. 147).

In your report, note also when and how you may have experienced resistance to doing any or all of these exercises and techniques, and what you did about it.

NOTES AND DRAWINGS REPORTING RESULTS OF PART 6 EXERCISES

Optional Techniques

As interest, time and energy permit, you may wish to experiment with other ways of developing and strengthening the will. These exercises also illustrate how you may adapt familiar techniques to a specific issue in your life.

1. Act of Will. Practise regularly applying all six stages of the act of will in Part 5. Give special attention to the stages which are challenging or troublesome for you.

2. Re-framing. Turn back to Part 2 (p. 202) and choose one of the limitations which blocks you. Accept that it is simply a pair of glasses which you will change for another pair. Then re-frame it by putting the words *how to* in front of it, for example 'I lack the proper ability, competence, education, skills, talents' becomes '*How to* develop the proper ability, competence, education, skills, talents?' Then adopt this 'how-to' statement as a purpose, and brainstorm ways to achieve it. Choose one of your responses and implement it.

3. Subpersonality. Choose one of the distortions of the will listed in Part 4 (perhaps your favourite form of resistance) which you often experience and express in life. Treat it as a subpersonality. Visualise going to the house in the meadow and dialoguing with this part of you, as you did in Session Six, Part 5 (pp. 165-171). How does it serve you? How does it limit you? What does it need? Take it to meet the wise and loving guide for advice as to how to deal with it.

4. Evocation. Choose one of the pure forms of the will listed in Part 4 (p. 210) you wish to awaken or strengthen within yourself. As with the quality of openness in Session Four, Part 5 (pp. 117-118), first observe yourself in a mirror and feel its opposite quality in your body, later expressing its positive presence within you through movement, affirmation and visualisation.

5. Creative Writing. Write an imaginary dialogue between your personality and your will. How do they relate to each other? What do they have to say to each other? Choose the format you would like the dialogue to take: perhaps a telephone conversation, a magazine interview or a one-act radio or television play. Alternatively, conduct a Chair Exercise between these two parts of yourself.

Remember, making choices strengthens the will, which in turn makes it easier to make choices. So keep making choices, as often and as freely and deliberately as you can!

Suggested Reading

The Act of Will, by Roberto Assagioli M.D., serves as the inspiration for this session. He examines aspects of the will (strong will, skilful will, good will, Transpersonal Will, Universal Will); the many qualities or pure forms of the will; and the stages of willing. He concludes: 'Since the outcome of successful willing is the satisfaction of one's needs, we can see that the act of will is essentially joyous. And the realisation of the self, or more exactly of *being a self,* gives a sense of freedom, of power, of mastery which is profoundly joyous.'

Relevant to the theme and approach of this course, he says: 'To cultivate human love that is satisfying, enduring and creative is truly an art. Human love is not simply a matter of feeling, an affective condition or disposition. To love *well* calls for all that is demanded by the practice of any art, indeed of any human activity, namely an adequate measure of discipline, patience and persistence. All these we have seen to be qualities of the will.'

Thus choosing to bring more love into our life is essentially an act of will.

Personal Goal

Consider various simple, specific, observable actions you could take within the next few days which would be a step towards bringing more love into your life. Then choose one which seems important to you, one to take as a personal goal. Make a deliberate choice to achieve it. Write it down. Remember, making and implementing choices empowers and strengthens you.

_____

_____

_____

_____

Session Learnings

Turn back and review what you have done in this session. Then write down the three most important insights or learnings you have gained from it.

_____

_____

_____

_____

_____

_____

_____

_____

Purpose

As stated at the beginning of Part 2, the purpose of Session Eight is to experience that you have a great capacity for making and implementing decisions and choices and that this capacity can be developed and strengthened to help you to bring more love into your life. To what degree has Session Eight achieved its general purpose for you?

_____

_____

_____

_____

Congratulations! You have finished Session Eight.

Please discuss your experience of this session with your support person _before you begin Session Nine_.

CHOOSING TO CHANGE

PART 1. MAKING CONNECTIONS

Begin by reviewing Session Eight to reconnect with your process of development. Have you achieved the personal goal you set for yourself? How was it?

Then if you have chosen to take additional risks in bringing more love into your life since the beginning of the preceding session, write about your experience: what you did, how successful you were and what you learned.

Continue with these personal journal pages by *making connections with the theme, issues and exercises of this course,* recording whatever relevant memories, ideas, feelings, insights, dreams, 'unfinished business', interactions and other events in your inner and outer worlds have occurred since you completed Session Eight. Include related reading you may have done, questions on your mind and any other observations and connections with the course you wish to make.

_____

_____

_____

_____

_____

_____

_____

_____

_____

_____

_____

_____

_____

_____

_____

_____

_____

_____

_____

_____

_____

Next in Part 2 we explore how you make decisions and choices.

PART 2. TAKING STOCK

Purpose

The purpose of Session Nine is to explore how you relate to change and maintenance, and to present principles and methods to help you to identify and make the specific changes needed to bring more love into your life.

The effective use of change — and its polar opposite, maintenance — is needed if we are to open ourself to giving and receiving love more freely and fully. One change is to find and remove all of the barriers and blocks which we have built against love within ourself. Another change is to re-frame or let go of whatever fears and beliefs have kept our blocks firmly in place. A third change is to take more risks. The task is clear and simple, but not necessarily easy!

Change

What is change? It is simply a difference of some kind, a movement or shift from one thing to another. Change can be gradual or instantaneous, subtle or intense, minor or major in its impact. Change brings challenge, disorder, instability and the unknown. Change also allows for newness, growth, progress and evolution. How do you feel about change? What does change mean to you?

_____

_____

_____

_____

What is your greatest difficulty or challenge with change?

_____

_____

_____

_____

Maintenance

Most people are more aware of change than they are of maintenance, and yet, in its own way, maintenance also affects our bringing more love into our life.

What is maintenance? It is the opposite of change. We talk of maintenance of the status quo, or keeping everything the same as it is now. Thus maintenance is simply a conservation, a continuation or a preservation. It respects, embraces and carries on with the present moment as it is, without making any changes. How do you feel about maintenance? What does maintenance mean to you?

_____

_____

_____

_____

What is your greatest difficulty or challenge with maintenance?

_____

_____

_____

_____

'Change — Maintenance' Graph

Change and maintenance are at opposite ends of the same spectrum, and we generally feel more at ease with one of these qualities than with the other.

Some people are quite comfortable with change and may even find it very attractive. They are usually impatient or restless with the status quo, and seek the freedom and stimulation which change offers them. They find it easy and enlivening to take risks. They often pursue change for the sake of change, and they feel a need to keep moving on to experience whatever is new and different to them.

Others are quite comfortable with maintenance, and may even find it very attractive. They are usually doubtful or fearful of change, and seek the order, stability and security which the status quo offers them. They find it difficult and challenging to take risks. They often resist change simply because it is a change, and they feel a need to continue and preserve whatever is known and familiar to them.

Mark an X on the graph below to indicate how you relate generally to these issues.

　　　1 = I feel very comfortable with keeping things as they are. I find change difficult and resist it. I always prefer to maintain the status quo, embracing the known, and all I am familiar with.

　　　5 = I feel very comfortable with changing things. I find change attractive and pursue it. I always prefer to let go of the status quo, and move into something new and different, move into the unknown.

1	2	3	4	5

Mark where your mother and father would have placed themselves. Be alert to the possibility that their beliefs and behaviour may have conditioned your own.

As with most personal characteristics, we usually express a mixture of both of these polarities. We may pursue change in one part of our life, such as employment, while we pursue maintenance in another part, such as relationships.

When do you pursue change? When do you resist maintenance?

_____

_____

_____

_____

When do you pursue maintenance? When do you resist change?

_____

_____

_____

_____

Take a few moments to review some of the major changes in your life.

Do you usually choose and initiate the change? Do you respond only after the change comes into your life? Or do you wait until you are absolutely forced by circumstances before you begin to do something about it? Consider your experience, and then write about it.

_____

_____

_____

_____

Forgiveness

One change we usually need to make before we can bring more love into our life involves forgiveness. We hold on to past hurt, close down and shut off to protect ourself and become unavailable emotionally both to give and to receive love.

How do you feel about forgiveness? What does forgiveness mean to you? How easy or difficult is it for you to forgive — yourself as well as others?

_____

_____

_____

_____

What hurt in your own life are you hanging on to — and whom do you need to forgive?

_____

_____

_____

_____

For what do you need to forgive yourself — what real or imagined hurt have you caused yourself or others?

_____

_____

_____

_____

Next in Part 3 we relate our experience with the topics of change and maintenance.

PART 3. EXPLORING PERSPECTIVES

EILEEN

It is amazing how soon you can get used to change as long as you have the courage and conviction that the changes which are taking place are all for the very best. — Opening Doors Within

Change is what life is all about for me. I am always thankful when I see changes going on all around me and within me. It means there is movement and life. I would be concerned if changes were not taking place. It would mean death.

There have been times when it has been easy to change, and I have simply flowed with the changes. But there also have been painful times when I have resisted making necessary changes, and I have gone along reluctantly, kicking and screaming all of the way.

Over the years I have learned that it is not the nature of the change but my resistance to it which causes the pain. I know now that a change is a problem only if *I* make it one. I am learning more and more to go along with the changes, without fear or resistance, and as I do, life becomes so much easier.

As I have said earlier, sometimes the old must die for the new to come forth. The chrysalis must give way for the butterfly to emerge. I know with me the old ideas I was taught as a child had to go to allow new ones to take their place. I had to empty out the bucket before I could refill it with pure, clear water.

I feel the secret is never to be afraid of change, never to be afraid of expansion. Look at nature! There is no stress or strain in nature. A seed goes through its full cycle. In a sense, it does not have to *do* anything. It only has to allow it all to happen. How naturally a flower unfolds without any resistance! An animal lives its whole lifetime adapting moment by moment from one change to the next. So nature does not remain static. It is ever-changing. I know I cannot remain in the same state all the time either. I have learned that a perfect pattern runs through my life, and that each change which comes is a part of my God-Self's plan for me. I find I get used to change much more easily when I remember to accept change as a *gift* from God, offering me lessons, insights and growth.

So the challenge of change is not for me to look for ways to deal with the difficulties I may associate with change, but rather to be open to accept the *gifts* which change brings. The question is, can I accept each change in my life as a stepping-stone to something new and more wonderful, and not as a stumbling-block to trip me up? Can I accept each change as a blessing?

When I look back at the changes which have taken place in my life and the valuable lessons I have learned and how they have expanded my outlook, I realise that benefits have come from *everything* which has happened to me, although I have not always seen them at the time.

I know that I can bring powerful changes into my life and open the door to blessings by practising forgiveness. I bless and release others, and I am blessed in return. As I practise forgiveness, I am at peace with anyone who has offended me or with anyone I have offended. I put love in charge of my mind. Love heals my thoughts and sets me free from unforgiving thoughts. I forgive myself. I forgive others. I put love in charge of my heart. Love fills my heart with peace and keeps me emotionally balanced and poised. Love forgives and forgets.

In life there is no going back, only forward, and that is what makes it so exciting and rewarding, because there is always something new around the corner. There is always another step to take, always another change waiting for us.

DAVID

To live is to think and act, and to think and act is to change. — As A Man Thinketh — James Allen.

'Change is the law of life,' I once heard an Eastern philosopher say. It is certainly the one thing in life we all can count on (besides death and taxes), and so I agree with everything Eileen says about change.

An added challenge for me is how to honour and keep in my life whatever is necessary and desirable *while* making changes. Not all change is a sign of progress. Making a change only for the sake of change can be a sign of restlessness or impatience, and can bring instability, confusion and even chaos. The challenge for me is how to be open to change, how even to invoke change, while also knowing what to *maintain* in my life, and how to do it within the midst of change.

So I feel an ever-present need not only to change, to grow and to expand, but also to find ways for change and maintenance to coexist, to blend and hopefully even to dance together.

Another challenge I have is my resistance to change. Of the major jobs I have held in my life, I feel I would have benefited from leaving every one of them at least a year before I actually did. I could make the same statement about the primary relationships I have had. For much of my life, I often failed to 'read the writing on the wall'. I ignored all of the warning signs, and change burst forth upon me with painful consequences. Now I am learning how to 'collaborate with the inevitable' in order to avoid my own resistance and the pain and suffering it causes. I am reminded of philosopher Ivan Illich's observation, 'Pain is an experience. Suffering is a performance.' I am finally giving up the need for the performance.

One reason I have resisted change is because of my fear of the unknown. I am afraid that I am going to lose something I value as a result of the change, such as comfort, self-esteem or security. Change becomes an adversary that I try to hold off. I need to remind myself regularly of the teaching from *A Course In Miracles*: 'It takes great learning to understand that all things, events, encounters and circumstances are helpful.'

My attitude towards change has been especially strong when I have come to the end of a major chapter in my life, such as the completion of a job, a relationship or my time of living in a given place. These changes have always been very unsettling and have caused me much stress and worry. I dread all that I have to go through to readjust to the changes so that I can settle back down again.

A useful image at such times is picturing myself as a reporter on a big-city newspaper working in a gigantic room with hundreds of desks and everyone scurrying around to meet daily deadlines. I imagine myself having just completed one story and handing it in to the editor. He quickly reads it, acknowledges my effort and then hands me another assignment which he promises to be even more exciting and important than the last one. I thank him for his trust and encouragement, and dash out expectantly to begin the new assignment.

Then I transfer this scenario to my present situation: when I acknowledge that my God-Self is the editor, and that the situation I am completing and the unknown situation I am facing are important assignments from my God-Self, I put everything into a larger context and I am able to accept the change more readily. I find that my fears diminish and my trust increases.

When I experience a change I am going through as a crisis, I try to remember a helpful image from Psychosynthesis. It suggests that a personal crisis is simply my God-Self knocking on the door of my personality, trying to get my attention and saying, 'Come on, it's time for you to take another step. It's time for you to grow. It's time for you to be more of who you really are. I am here. I will help you.'

PART 4. GAINING AWARENESS

Nothing Remains the Same

Opening Doors Within makes this observation about change:

'There are times when the new unfolds so gradually that you are not aware of the changes which are taking place until you suddenly realise it has all happened without your being aware of it. At other times you can see the changes taking place in front of your eyes as they unfold step by step. Then there are times when things happen overnight — rather as in winter, when you go to bed at night and the world outside is normal, and when you wake up in the morning, everything is covered with snow. You have not had to do a thing about it; it has all happened in the most miraculous way.

'There are many different ways in which the new will be revealed. All you have to do is go along with it and not resist it. Change need not be painful. It is inevitable because nothing can remain the same; and if you look into your heart, you would not want it to do so.'

What is your reaction to this statement? What are your feelings and thoughts about it?

_____

_____

_____

_____

What new insight or awareness does this observation — and your response to it — give you regarding the need to make changes within yourself in order to bring more love into your life?

_____

_____

_____

_____

'Change — Maintenance Pure Forms and Distortions' Assessment

As with all transpersonal qualities, change and maintenance can be experienced and expressed in many ways. Some ways may be considered pure, while others are distorted through our experience, needs and desires. Listed below are selected examples of both forms. To get a sense of them and how you relate to each of them, in the blanks provided put the number of the statement nearest to how you experience or express each quality.

> 1. I never experience or express this quality.
> 2. I rarely experience or express this quality.
> 3. I sometimes experience or express this quality.
> 4. I often experience or express this quality.
> 5. I always experience or express this quality.

233

PURE FORMS OF CHANGE	DISTORTIONS OF CHANGE
_____ Creativity	_____ Dissipation of energy
_____ Enthusiasm	_____ Fear of entrapment
_____ Freedom	_____ Fear of limitation
_____ Growth	_____ Impatience/restlessness
_____ Spontaneity	_____ Inconsistency
_____ Vitality	_____ Scatteredness/Ungroundedness

PURE FORMS OF MAINTENANCE	DISTORTIONS OF MAINTENANCE
_____ Containment	_____ Attachments
_____ Duty/loyalty	_____ Boredom
_____ Grounding	_____ Closed-mindedness
_____ Honouring of tradition/roots	_____ Fear of letting go
_____ Order	_____ Fear of the unknown
_____ Peace	_____ Inertia/laziness
_____ Stability/strength	_____ Rigidity/resistance to change

How we relate to change and maintenance affects the way we relate to our own specific blocks to love and our willingness to overcome them.

'Change' Symbol and Drawing

Next we turn to your own inner experience of change, and gain insight into how you feel about it, what it means to you and the essential quality it suggests to you. This increased awareness may be a helpful step in making the changes necessary to bring more love into your life.

Now find a comfortable position, sitting up straight . . . Close your eyes . . . Take several long, slow, deep breaths . . . Relax your body completely . . . Release all of the tension . . . Allow whatever emotions you may be feeling to fade away . . . Do the same with your thoughts . . . Become like a calm, quiet lake, which mirrors perfectly the blue sky, or the starry sky in the silence of the night . . . Be at peace and yet remain alert . . .

When you are ready, allow to come to you an image or sense which represents the topic of change . . . Take your time . . . Wait patiently in the silence, knowing that something will soon come to you . . . Be willing to accept whatever comes without judging, censoring or rejecting it . . . Simply be ready to observe and examine it, with the purpose of learning more about it . . .

As you begin to sense something, allow it to become more vivid . . . Note its size and shape . . . Its density and design . . . Its colour and texture . . . Explore it with as many of your senses as you can . . . Find the overall quality it suggests to you . . .

Then open your eyes, and express in a drawing below either the image itself or its quality . . . If nothing has come to you, open your eyes, hold the topic in mind and begin to draw freely and spontaneously, letting something come to you in that way . . .

CHANGE

Write down the overall *quality* of the symbol and any other words, feelings or thoughts which came to you during the exercise, or which you are aware of now. What new insight or awareness does this symbol and its quality give to you?

_____

_____

_____

_____

'Maintenance' Symbol and Drawing

Now we explore your inner experience of maintenance.

Close your eyes again . . . Sit up straight . . . Take a few deep breaths . . . Relax . . . Allow your body, emotions and thoughts to become still . . . Become like a calm, quiet lake . . .

When you are ready, allow to come to you an image or sense which represents the topic of maintenance . . . Take your time . . . Wait patiently in the silence, knowing that something will soon come to you . . . Be willing to accept whatever comes without judging, censoring or rejecting it . . . Simply be ready to observe and examine it, with the purpose of learning more about it . . .

As you begin to sense something, allow it to become more vivid . . . Note its size and shape . . . Its density and design . . . Its colour and texture . . . Explore it with as many of your senses as you can . . . Find the overall quality it suggests to you . . .

Then open your eyes, and express in a drawing below either the image itself or its quality . . . If nothing has come to you, open your eyes, hold the topic in mind and begin to draw freely and spontaneously, letting something come to you in that way . . .

MAINTENANCE

Write down the overall *quality* of the symbol and any other words, feelings or thoughts which came to you during the exercise, or which you are aware of now. What new insight or awareness does this symbol and its quality give to you?

_____

_____

_____

_____

Where Change Is Needed

Now we focus on exactly where change needs to come in your life for you to love and be loved more freely and fully. First, list three specific barriers or blocks within yourself which you have built against love.

_____

_____

_____

_____

Then write down the personal assumption, attitude or belief which underlies and keeps firmly in place each one of these blocks.

_____

_____

_____

_____

How willing are you to re-frame or let go of these limiting assumptions, attitudes or beliefs?

_____

_____

_____

_____

What specific changes *within yourself* do you need to make before you can bring more love into your life?

_____

_____

_____

_____

Finally, how willing are you to make these changes so that you actually are able to bring more love into your life?

_____

_____

_____

_____

'Change Is Normal, Natural and Necessary' Exercise

Here is a method designed to help you feel more comfortable with change and the gifts it brings. It provides you with helpful insights about any change in your life and guides you through it step by step. You may use this exercise to address one of the changes which you identified in the preceding section, or a change which is already in your life, or a change which seems to be on its way to you or a change which you would like to have come into your life.

As with all of the exercises in this course, you may use this one over and over again as often as you wish, using the same or other changes. We suggest that you pre-record this exercise to gain maximum benefit from it. Pause on the tape 10-30 seconds, or whatever time seems comfortable and appropriate, at every . . . to allow you to experience each step fully. Avoid rushing through it. Take your time.

Now close your eyes . . . Sit up straight . . . Take a few deep breaths . . . Relax . . . Allow your body, emotions and thoughts to become still . . . Become like a calm, quiet lake . . . Release as much as possible whatever feelings and thoughts you may have about change . . . Let them go . . . For now, give yourself permission simply to accept change as something normal, natural and necessary . . .

Take a few moments to experience change as it occurs in the life cycles of nature . . . First, in the plant kingdom . . . Visualise a flower seed in your hand . . . Then see the seed being planted . . . Now see the first green shoot bursting through the soil . . . Next see it slowly becoming a young plant . . . See it becoming fully mature . . . Notice that the plant does not resist growth or change; it adapts and flows with it . . . See it creating blossoms and seeds with which to reproduce itself . . . See it ageing . . . dying . . . and returning to the source of all creation . . . See and feel that all of these changes are normal, natural and necessary, and that they are made under God's direction . . .

Next experience the animal kingdom . . . Visualise a small wild animal . . . See it as only a few days old, completely dependent upon others . . . Then see it eating . . . playing . . . and sleeping . . . Now see it gaining in size and weight . . . See it becoming fully mature . . . Notice that the animal does not resist growth or change; it adapts and flows with it . . . See it having young of its own . . . See it ageing . . . dying . . . and returning to the source of all creation . . . See and feel that all of these changes are normal, natural and necessary, and are made under God's direction . . .

Now experience the human kingdom . . . Visualise an unknown baby . . . See it as only a few days old, completely dependent upon others . . . Then see it becoming an infant and beginning to walk and talk . . . Next see it becoming a child, playing with its friends . . . Notice that the child does not resist growth or change; it adapts and flows with it . . . See it becoming an adolescent, learning more about life . . . See it becoming an adult, moving into the wider world, perhaps starting a career or family . . . See it ageing . . . dying . . . and returning to the source of all creation . . . See and feel that all of these changes are normal, natural and necessary, and are made under God's direction . . . Allow to come to you a memory of a major change you once went through, and how you experienced it. Recall the good which has come to you from it. Write down the main points of the change and your experience of it.

_____

_____

_____

_____

Choose one of the changes *within yourself* you identified in the preceding section which you need to make before you can bring more love into your life. Focus your attention upon the exact nature of the change. What precisely is happening, or what do you want to happen?

_____

_____

_____

What is this change asking of you?

_____

_____

_____

Allow to come to you two or three benefits this change could bring into your life.

_____

_____

_____

_____

What are your feelings and thoughts about this change?

_____

_____

_____

_____

Are you aware of any fear, resistance or any other negative feeling within you concerning this change? If so, what is its source — where does it originate?

_____

_____

_____

_____

Recognise that this negativity limits you and your relationships. Choose to take action *despite* its influence upon you. Affirm below your willingness to move beyond it.

_____

_____

_____

_____

Then affirm below your openness and willingness to make this change.

_____

_____

_____

_____

What is the ideal resolution of this change — how would you like it to turn out?

_____

_____

_____

_____

Take a few moments now to visualise this ideal resolution unfolding successfully step by step, and so help to bring it about . . . Picture it in great detail . . . What is a practical step you can take concerning this change?

_____

_____

_____

_____

Are you willing to commit yourself to take this step? If so, visualise yourself taking this specific step successfully . . .

Then imagine yourself having moved through the entire change. What has the change done for you — what is its gift to you? How are you and your life different, especially your relationships?

_____

_____

_____

_____

If this change were a stepping stone to something greater in your life, what might that be?

_____

_____

_____

_____

Next turn within and attune to your own inner source of wisdom to seek information, guidance and support concerning this change . . .

Allow yourself to relax more deeply . . . Count backwards slowly from ten to one, and on each succeeding number feel yourself moving step by step further into the very centre of your being . . . Experience yourself making a connection with your own inner source of wisdom, that pure permanent centre deep within you which has the answer to any question you could possibly ask about yourself . . .

When you are ready, ask your inner source of wisdom for the information, guidance and support you need regarding the change you are considering . . . Take your time . . . Wait patiently in the silence, knowing that something will soon come to you, knowing the help you seek is already on its way . . .

In your own time, allow everything to fade . . . Count slowly from one to ten, and on each succeeding number, feel yourself coming back to your normal level of alert wakefulness again . . . Bring your attention back to the room where you are now . . . Open your eyes . . . Take a deep breath . . . And a gentle stretch . . .

Now write down whatever you wish to remember from your attunement, noting any inner response you may have received regarding your change.

_____

_____

_____

_____

_____

_____

_____

Next in Part 5 we explore the nature of forgiveness and its contribution to bringing more love into our life.

PART 5. DEVELOPING POTENTIAL

Forgiveness

In Session Two, Part 5 (p. 60), we say that fear is a primary factor which keeps us from bringing more love into our life. Now we focus upon forgiveness as another basic factor. Many people in our workshops find forgiveness is the most powerful topic we present. Why? They discover that forgiveness helps them to change.

What is forgiveness? *A Course in Miracles* says, 'Forgiveness is letting go the past. Forgiveness is letting go of whatever we think people, the world or God has done to us, as well as whatever we think we have done to them.' Forgiveness, then, is an act of release. Therefore a change of heart and mind is the first step in forgiveness, whether we are directing it towards ourself or others.

The greatest act of healing is the act of forgiveness. It is also the most difficult. Forgiveness helps us to empty out the old to make room for the new. It empties out the old anger, blame, fear, guilt and pain, and makes room for the new freedom, vitality, joy, love and peace.

Forgiveness is an act of self-kindness, a gift to ourself. It may also heal the other person, but *ultimately forgiveness is done for ourself, to heal ourself, to free ourself.* Forgiveness does not imply, 'I will forgive you if or when you . . . ,' but 'I will forgive you because I must, if I ever hope to continue to live freely and fully again.'

All forgiveness starts with self-forgiveness. Only then can we forgive others.

We need to accept the past. Then we need to let it all go so that we can accept who and where we are today, *now*. Why cling to pain? Why cling to the past? Why hold on to the very thing which keeps us from love! We need to have mercy on ourself and others. We need to allow ourself back into our own heart. Allow ourself to be healed. Allow ourself to be free. Allow ourself to love and be loved.

A word of caution is necessary. If we believe we have forgiven someone, but are indifferent towards that person, it is not true forgiveness. If we believe we have forgiven someone and now we avoid seeing that person, it is not true forgiveness.

True forgiveness is to release our hurt, to release the past, and to feel towards that person now as we felt before the situation occurred. True forgiveness allows others to be themselves. As Mother Teresa of Calcutta has said, 'To forgive takes love; to forget takes humility.'

Most of the techniques you have already experienced in this course may be adapted to the topic of forgiveness. We present several suggestions for you in Part 6.

Remember to use prayer. We can pray to our God-Self, asking for help. Here is a short, simple prayer we find helpful.

Today I ask the divinity within to help me to forgive completely.
Here is my heart. Cleanse it.
Renew my spirit so that I may be loving to everyone.
I no longer want to hold anyone in judgement and condemnation.
I let your love move in and through me
so that I may willingly forgive and forget all offences completely.
I am grateful for your help. Thank you.

Forgiveness and Release Exercise

This exercise is another way to bring the healing effects of forgiveness into our life. It helps us to begin to empty out the old, and to make room for the new. It has seven steps, all of which should be done in one sitting, when you have a room to yourself without interruption for 45-60 minutes.

Now close your eyes . . . Sit up straight . . . Take a few deep breaths . . . Relax. Allow your body, emotions and thoughts to become still . . . Become like a calm, quiet lake . . .

Step 1. When you are ready, allow to come to you the name of someone in your life who has hurt you, or caused you great pain and suffering. It may have been a parent, relation, lover, partner, friend, co-worker or someone else. The situation may have taken place recently, or it may have been years ago when you were quite young.

Write down the name of the person, what happened and your reaction at the time.

Even now it may cause you great pain to recall this person and situation. Allow it all to come back to you. Be with it. Feel deeply into the whole situation.

Allow the pain, anger, resentment, jealousy or whatever emotions are connected with this person and situation to come up within you now. Allow yourself to feel it. Realise that it is all still there inside you.

You may find yourself struggling with this exercise, or struggling with the whole situation. You may find tears of sadness, anger or resentment welling up within you. If so, allow them all to flow. Go deeper and deeper. Allow yourself to take part fully in the healing and freeing process of forgiveness and release.

Step 2. When you are ready, staying in touch with the person, the situation, your feelings and thoughts, say aloud, as if you were talking directly to this person, *'I RESENT . . . ,'* and complete the sentence with a few words — whatever comes spontaneously to you. Do not *think* about it. Write down the response. Then do it again, this time allowing different words to emerge. Write down that response. If you blank out momentarily, simply begin again, knowing that something will soon come to you. Repeat the process for at least ten minutes, even if you find that certain responses keep returning to you, or that you have filled the space below before then.

Express whatever resentments come to you (for example, 'I resent you for what you did to me. I resent you for hurting me. I resent you for being so insensitive. I resent you for being so selfish.'). Do not be concerned about whether your resentments are rational, justifiable, consistent or fair. The point is to allow *whatever and all* you are feeling and thinking to come out. You are addressing your own subjective experience of the person and situation (which you carry inside you), so you can 'say it all'. Remember, this is a healing and a freeing process for you.

Use this opportunity to say all you need to say to this person. Express the feelings and thoughts which are inside you. Hold nothing back. Let it all come out now: the hurt, the pain, the suffering, the anguish. Stay in touch with your feelings and express them freely.

I RESENT . . .

Step 3. When you are ready, staying in touch with the person, the situation, your feelings and thoughts, say aloud, as if you were talking directly to this person, *'I DEMAND . . . ,'* and complete the sentence with a few words. Carry on with the exercise as before for at least ten minutes, even if you find that certain responses keep returning to you, or that you have filled the space below before then.

Express whatever demands come to you (for example, 'I demand you apologise to me. I demand you accept me as I am. I demand you treat me as an adult. I demand you stop judging me.'). Do not be concerned about whether the demands are rational, justifiable, consistent or fair. The point is to allow *whatever and all* you are feeling and thinking to come out. Remember, this is a healing and a freeing process for you.

Use this opportunity to say all you need to say to this person. Express the feelings and thoughts which are inside you. Hold nothing back. Let it all come out now, the anger, the fury, the rage, the power. Stay in touch with your feelings and express them freely.

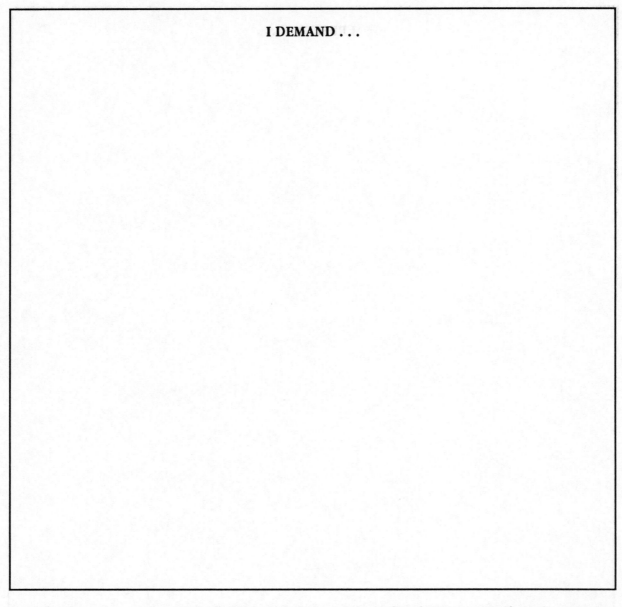

I DEMAND . . .

Step 4. You will never be able to forgive anyone else until you first forgive yourself. So the next step is to forgive yourself for feeling this way about the person or situation. Say to yourself, *'I STOP JUDGING MYSELF. I STOP BLAMING MYSELF. I STOP CONDEMNING MYSELF. I FORGIVE MYSELF. MY HOLDING ON TO THESE EMOTIONS AND THOUGHTS ONLY SERVES TO BLOCK ME, AND I DO NOT WANT TO BE BLOCKED ANY MORE. I CHOOSE TO BE FREE. I CHOOSE TO MOVE ON. I CHOOSE TO BE AT PEACE.'* Say a little prayer and ask for forgiveness. Make sure you are open and willing to accept it.

Step 5. Few people are totally without positive qualities or deeds. All situations have gifts or lessons for us. So when you are ready, staying in touch with the person, the situation, your feelings and thoughts, say aloud, as if you were talking directly to this person, *'I APPRECIATE . . . ,'* and complete the sentence with a few words, finding things which you can sincerely appreciate about this person. Carry on with the exercise as before for at least ten minutes, even if you find that certain responses keep returning to you, or that you have filled the space below before then.

Express whatever appreciation, clarity and understanding comes to you. Keep it all positive. Remember, this is a healing and a freeing process for you.

I APPRECIATE . . .

Step 6. The next step, whenever you are freely willing to take it, is to forgive this person and the situation. Release all of it. The distress. The pain. The anguish. Let it all go. Put it behind you so that you may be free to move on in your life, to be healed, to love and be loved.

NOTE. If you are presently unwilling to forgive this person, do not force yourself to try to do so, and do not judge yourself for being unready to forgive. Repeat Steps 1-5 regularly until such time as you are ready to forgive this person. If you feel you have already done all you can do to forgive this person, and yet remain troubled or dissatisfied, do the Altar Exercise presented in Part 6.

When you are ready to forgive this person, staying in touch with the person, the situation, your feelings and thoughts, say aloud, as if you were talking directly to this person, *'I FORGIVE . . . ,'* and complete the sentence with a few words. Carry on with the exercise as before for ten minutes, even if you find that certain responses keep returning to you, or that you have filled the space below before then.

Express whatever is in your heart: the compassion, the mercy, the love. Let it all come out. Remember, this is a healing and a freeing process for you.

I FORGIVE . . .

Step 7. Visualise a radiant beam of sunlight shining down upon you and this person. See the light completely enfold and fill you. Imagine it healing you.

Give thanks for all that has taken place, even if you feel a completion has not yet been fully achieved. Simply know deep within you that a healing is taking place. Picture it happening. Feel it happening. Have faith that it is happening.

Then affirm to this person, *'I SEE THE DIVINITY IN YOU, I BLESS YOU AND I RELEASE YOU.'* Continue using this affirmation in the days ahead until you see the divine spark in this person, and you feel that a change has occurred within you towards this person.

To be sure, the process of forgiveness and release takes time, patience, grace and a deep inner knowing, but it definitely does work.

Forgiveness is the key which unlocks the door to bringing more love into our life. It is a powerful method we can *choose* to use whenever we are willing to let go of the past, and move freely and expectantly into a more whole, more fulfilling future.

Review your responses to each one of the seven steps. Write down any feelings, thoughts and questions you wish to record.

_____

_____

_____

_____

_____

_____

_____

_____

_____

_____

Next in Part 6 we present suggestions for applying the topics of change, maintenance and forgiveness in your everyday life.

PART 6. APPLYING IT

Change, Maintenance and Forgiveness

Here are a few suggestions for dealing with change, maintenance and forgiveness. Practise at least three of the first five of them daily for at least seven days, and then report your experience with them on the following page *before you begin Session Ten*.

1. Attunement. Contact your source of inner wisdom for information, guidance and support to help you to identify and make the specific changes needed to bring more love into your life.

2. Act of Will. (a) Make a deliberate act of will to *change* something in your life, for example a habit, pattern or routine, such as how you bathe and dress yourself, how and what you eat, the route you take when you go out or whatever you do in your spare time. Then notice how you feel about making the change.

(b) Also make a deliberate act of will to *maintain* something in your life, for example to do something for a longer period of time than you would prefer, to delay something you would prefer to do now, to honour a tradition or to perform an act of duty or loyalty. Then notice how you feel about the act of maintenance.

3. Visualisation. (a) Imagine yourself as a bucket, emptying out the old and stagnant, and filling up with the new and fresh. Draw pictures to ground the images, staying aware of your feelings and thoughts as you do so. (b) Then imagine how it would be in everyday terms to let go of all your fear, insecurity, distrust and pain, and open up to a life filled with safety, joy, love and peace.

4. Daily Risks. At least once an hour (set a kitchen timer) ask yourself, 'What risk do I need to be taking right now?' Then take at least one risk each day.

5. Forgiveness Inventory. (a) List everyone and everything you can possibly think of that has ever caused you deep hurt and pain. Go back as far as you can remember and write down every hurt, every insult, every physical, emotional and mental injury you have received. When you are finished, if you do not have any of the following people on your list, add them: your father and mother, your children, God and yourself!

(b) When your list is as complete as you can make it, begin at the top of it and take each item at a time. Bring an image of the person or situation to mind and say, *'I FORGIVE YOU COMPLETELY. I HOLD NO UNFORGIVENESS BACK. I FORGIVE YOU FOR WHATEVER YOU MAY HAVE DONE, INTENTIONALLY OR UNINTENTIONALLY, WHICH CAUSED ME PAIN. I FORGIVE YOU. MY FORGIVENESS FOR YOU IS TOTAL. I AM FREE AND YOU ARE FREE.'* Allow this person or situation to be touched by your forgiveness. For just an instant move beyond the past and let your hearts touch in compassion and mercy. When you have finished, say goodbye, release the person or situation, let go of the past and move on to the next one on your list. Stay fresh, focused and authentic.

(c) Once you have forgiven everyone and everything on your list, continue to focus upon forgiveness by making it a habit to spend a few minutes every evening at bedtime to forgive those people from the past who still cause you some problem because you have not released them, in addition to anyone from that particular day who may have upset you. Do not go to sleep with any unforgiveness in your heart.

In your report, note also when and how you may have experienced resistance to doing any or all of these exercises and techniques, and what you did about it.

NOTES AND DRAWINGS REPORTING RESULTS OF PART 6 EXERCISES

Optional Techniques

Here are a few more suggestions for dealing with these topics.

1. Experience Scan. Learn more about your behaviour patterns by scanning your own attitudes, beliefs, feelings, thoughts and experience on each of these topics: *CHANGE IS . . . , MAINTENANCE IS . . . , FORGIVENESS IS . . .*

2. Messages and 'Shoulds' Scan. (a) Find out what messages and 'shoulds' about change you received as a child from your mother, father, close relatives, religious leaders or teachers and the mass media, and write them down. (Refer to Session Two, Part 4, p. 56 for detailed instructions.) Note how each message and 'should' makes you feel now. (b) Then cross out any of your messages and 'shoulds' which no longer have value to you. (c) Finally visualise yourself handing back and letting go of each of the unwanted messages and 'shoulds' to the person from whom you received them. Repeat the procedure for maintenance and forgiveness.

3. Models of Behaviour. Find models for inspiration and emulation from among people you know who (a) deal responsibly and creatively with change and maintenance, (b) deal bravely and positively with fear and (c) deal lovingly and effectively with forgiveness.

4. Brainstorming. Consider the various changes (large and small) you can make in your own life now which would bring more love into your life by: (a) lowering your barriers and blocks to love; (b) re-framing your limiting beliefs about yourself and others; and (c) taking more risks in your life.

5. Chair Exercise. To bring your inner process out into the open, carry on a dialogue between either (a) the part of you which wants to change and the part of you which wants to maintain the status quo, or (b) the part of you which is ready and willing to forgive and the part of you which clings resolutely to injustice and hurt. How do they each limit you? How do they each serve you? What does each one need? How can they live together more harmoniously?

6. Altar Exercise. Use this visualisation exercise *only after you have done all you can do* to resolve and heal a challenge with another person or situation in your life. Visualise a large altar standing before you. Experience yourself taking the person or situation which is troubling you to the altar and place the person or situation upon the altar. Then as you move away from the altar, say, *'GOD, I CANNOT DO ANYTHING MORE WITH THIS SITUATION. I HAND IT OVER TO YOU AND RELEASE IT. PLEASE TAKE IT.'* Say it with your whole heart. As you do so, open yourself to something happening between you and the divinity within you. Open to the feeling that a heavy burden is being lifted from you and you are free of it. Then give thanks.

Suggested Reading

1. *A Course in Miracles* says there are only two emotions: love and fear. Aggression, resentment, separation and guilt are all guises adopted by fear. Joy, forgiveness and peace of mind are all aspects of love. The miracles which it teaches are the shifts in perception which enable us to view the world through the eyes of love, rather than through the eyes of fear. The *Course* focuses upon forgiveness as a central theme, and it includes 365 daily lessons providing practical application of its teachings.

2. *The Human Side Of Human Beings,* by Harvey Jackins, presents an introduction to Re-Evaluation Counselling, a method to help us become free of rigid patterns of behaviour caused by experiences of being hurt in the past. The approach is directed primarily towards the discharge of repressed emotion as the key to healing, freedom and the re-emergence of full rationality.

Personal Goal

Consider various simple, specific, observable actions you could take within the next few days which would be a step towards bringing more love into your life. Then choose one which seems important to you, one to take as a personal goal. Make a deliberate choice to achieve it. Write it down. Remember, making and implementing choices empowers and strengthens you.

_____

_____

_____

Session Learnings

Turn back and review what you have done in this session. Then write down the three most important insights or learnings you have gained from it.

_____

_____

_____

_____

_____

_____

_____

_____

Purpose

As stated at the beginning of Part 2, the purpose of Session Nine is to explore how you relate to change and maintenance, and to present principles and methods to help you to identify and make the specific changes needed to bring more love into your life. To what degree has Session Nine achieved its general purpose for you?

_____

_____

_____

_____

Congratulations! You have finished Session Nine.

Please discuss your experience of this session with your support person _before you begin Session Ten_.

CHOOSING TO LOVE UNCONDITIONALLY

PART 1. MAKING CONNECTIONS

Begin by reviewing Session Nine to reconnect with your process of development. Have you achieved the personal goal you set for yourself? How was it?

Then, if you have chosen to take additional risks in bringing more love into your life since the beginning of the preceding session, write about your experience: what you did, how successful you were and what you learned.

Continue with these personal journal pages by *making connections with the theme, issues and exercises of this course*, recording whatever relevant memories, ideas, feelings, insights, dreams, 'unfinished business', interactions and other events in your inner and outer worlds have occurred since you completed Session Nine. Include related reading you may have done, questions on your mind and any other observations and connections with the course you wish to make.

_____

_____

_____

_____

_____

_____

_____

_____

_____

_____

_____

_____

_____

_____

_____

_____

_____

_____

_____

_____

_____

_____

_____

_____

_____

_____

_____

_____

_____

_____

_____

_____

_____

_____

_____

_____

_____

_____

_____

_____

_____

_____

_____

_____

_____

_____

_____

_____

_____

_____

_____

_____

_____

_____

_____

Next in Part 2 we explore how you relate to the topic of unconditional love.

PART 2. TAKING STOCK

Purpose

The purpose of Session Ten is to present principles and techniques that will help you to love more unconditionally.

Definitions

Conditional love refers to our placing restrictions on who or when we are willing to love. It is loving people only when they meet certain conditions that we impose upon them, and withdrawing our love when our conditions are not met. Unconditional love is loving people freely, fully and openly, with no expectations, demands or restrictions. It gives total acceptance and respect, and does not criticise or judge. Unconditional love is constant, and not turned on and off as in conditional love.

How do you feel about unconditional love? What does it mean to you?

_____

_____

_____

_____

Recall a moment in your life when you have either loved or been loved unconditionally — with complete acceptance and no expectations. How was it? What qualities did the experience have for you?

_____

_____

_____

_____

Next complete this sentence spontaneously: *'WHAT PREVENTS ME FROM LOVING MORE UNCON-DITIONALLY IS . . . '*

_____

_____

_____

_____

'Expectations and Demands' Check-list

As we love – a partner, family member, friend or another — most of us have unmet needs which result in our making certain demands of others. The less we are able to get our own needs met in healthy, appropriate ways, the more demanding we are. We may express our demands quite clearly and directly, or we may hold onto them silently within ourself. We consider our demands valid, reasonable and necessary before we open ourself to love.

How about you? How do you love? Mark all of the expectations, conditions or demands below which you have now, or have had about loving yourself and others. Be honest, but avoid judging yourself.

I WILL LOVE YOU ONLY IF YOU . . .

_____ Accept and respect me just as I am.

_____ Acknowledge, encourage and understand me.

_____ Adore me, consider me attractive, capable, intelligent, responsible, wonderful.

_____ Agree with me and let me have my own way.

_____ Amuse me, entertain me and keep me from being bored.

_____ Are faithful to me, good to me, loyal and true to me.

_____ Are absolutely perfect and live up to all of my expectations.

_____ Communicate honestly and openly with me.

_____ Do things for me (errands/favours/chores).

_____ Give me what I want from you (attention/babies/money/security/sex/trinkets).

_____ Have things in common with me, share my beliefs, interests and values.

_____ Listen to me, follow my advice and do what I tell you to do.

_____ Love me in return.

_____ Make me feel good, happy, needed, secure and special.

_____ Prove to me that you deserve my love and trust.

_____ Provide me with companionship and keep me from being lonely.

_____ Put me first in your life.

_____ Satisfy me and fulfil all of my needs.

_____ Take care of me and protect me.

_____ Treat me as an adult and as an equal.

_____ Do not annoy or irritate me.

_____ Do not ask me to make commitments.

_____ Do not expect me to take unwanted responsibility.

_____ Do not cause me problems or trouble.

_____ Do not condemn, criticise, demean or judge me.

_____ Do not hurt me or cause me pain.

_____ Do not lie to me.

_____ Do not question or challenge me.

_____ Do not reject me or walk out on me.

_____ Do not take me for granted.

_____ Do not try to change me or ask me to change.

_____ Do not use or abuse me.

_____ Do not make any demands on ME!

Write down other expectations, conditions or demands you have for giving out your love.

_____

_____

_____

_____

'Conditional and Unconditional Love' Graph

Some people give their love to others only when certain conditions are met, as illustrated in the expectations and demands listed above. They withdraw their love when these conditions are unmet or violated. They choose very carefully whom they love. Their love is conditional.

Others give their love freely, fully and openly without such conditions, expectations or demands. They do not withdraw their love because of who others may be, or what they may do. They do not choose whom to love, but keep their love flowing out to everyone equally. Their love is unconditional.

How do you give your love? With conditions or without them? First, take time to consider your experience, and then write about it. Be honest, but avoid judging yourself.

_____

_____

_____

_____

Mark an X on the graph below to indicate the way you give love out to others.

 1 = I give my love only under certain conditions. I withdraw my love if these conditions are unmet or violated. I choose very carefully to whom I give my love. My love is totally conditional.

 5 = I give my love freely, fully and openly without expectations, conditions or demands. I keep my love flowing out equally to others, regardless of what they may be or do. My love is totally unconditional.

_____

| 1 | 2 | 3 | 4 | 5 |

Mark where your mother and father would have placed themselves. Be alert to the possibility that their beliefs and behaviour may have conditioned your own.

What would it take for you to begin to let go of some of your demands and express your love more unconditionally? What would you need to be, to do or to have?

_____

_____

_____

_____

If you were willing to let go of one particular condition or demand as a first step in this process, which one would you choose?

_____

_____

_____

_____

'Unconditional Love' Assessment

Listed below are statements which reflect the essence of unconditional love. To take stock of how you relate to unconditional love in *all* of your relationships, in the blanks provided put the number of the statement nearest to your own experience.

1. I never have this experience in my relationships.
2. I rarely have this experience in my relationships.
3. I sometimes have this experience in my relationships.
4. I often have this experience in my relationships.
5. I always have this experience in my relationships.

———— I can be myself at all times.

———— I allow others to be themselves without criticising, judging or condemning them.

———— I can love and love and go on loving someone, asking nothing in return.

———— I can love someone with the same depth, and to the same degree, regardless of whether we are together or apart.

———— I can still love someone when I do not like or approve of something that person has said or done.

———— I can love someone enough that I can cease helping that person because I know if I go on helping, I will hold up that person's growth and evolution.

———— I can love someone enough that I can let that person go to grow and mature.

———— I can love someone enough that I can accept that person leaving me for someone else and hold no bitterness, resentment or jealousy.

———— I can love everyone equally, acknowledging our interconnectedness and unity.

What are your feelings and thoughts about these statements — and about how you assess yourself with regard to them?

_____

_____

_____

_____

If you were to choose one of these statements as a personal goal to achieve, which one would it be?

_____

_____

_____

_____

How open and willing are you to bring more *unconditional* love into your life?

_____

_____

_____

_____

The choice is yours.

PART 3. EXPLORING PERSPECTIVES

EILEEN

Let the divine love within you flow freely. Never be afraid to show your love.
Express that unconditional love to all you come into contact with. — The Living Word

For some time now, I have felt the primary lesson to learn in life is to love. It has been my experience that we have basically only two choices in how we love: we can love conditionally or unconditionally.

A few years ago I was sitting in a bus when I found myself having an inner dialogue with myself. I felt I needed to write it down, so I found an envelope and a pencil in my handbag, and wrote:

Can you say to me and I say to you, 'I love you,' without either of us feeling uncomfortable, threatened or that something is expected of either of us? Can we love each other, regardless of our age, sex or origin, with pure, understanding love? With unconditional love? The world needs this sort of love. All humanity needs this sort of love. Can we love this way? I feel we can, but it is not something simply to be talked about. It is something to be acted upon, to be experimented with.

That dialogue was the start of a quest for wholeness in my life, and I am still learning how to put this unconditional love into practice. I have read about it, and I have received inspiration in meditation on the subject. I have come to learn that unconditional love is an expression of the divinity within each one of us. It is an all-embracing love. It gives acceptance, if not always approval, to everyone and everything. It is unique and universal, within reach of all of us. It is vitalising. It is nurturing. It expects or demands absolutely nothing in return. It is its own reason for being.

I feel we all have a tremendous job to do. It is the silent work of creating more and more unconditional love in the world. It is like the yeast in a lump of bread dough which does its work very quietly and silently without any fuss. Yet without it the bread would be a solid lump. As we begin to love unconditionally, so will the heaviness in our own life be lightened.

I have learned that if we love solely from the emotional level, then we consciously or unconsciously are expecting something in return. Our love is then conditional, and is often possessive, indulgent, needy or sentimental. As long as we function principally from the emotional level, we are a slave to our own emotions, a puppet on the strings of our own emotions, in one emotional melodrama or soap opera after another.

When we function from the level of unconditional love, recognising and giving thanks to the God-Self within as the source of this divine love, we begin to know the meaning of freedom, and we are no longer tied up in knots emotionally.

How few of us function from this level! When we do, how often we are misunderstood by those people who function principally from the emotional level! How complicated relationships become when they can be so simple and straightforward! All the more reason for us to change our outlook, our whole way of thinking, if necessary, and so help those around us to change their way of thinking.

I have learned that unconditional love does not come all at once. It starts in small ways and then grows one step at a time. Its benefits are enormous.

Life is more abundant and fulfilling when we choose unconditional love as the primary principle which guides us. It is a deliberate choice we can make, one which serves us, everyone around us and the very planet itself. We transform the world as we transform ourself with the power of unconditional love.

DAVID

'I don't know what your destiny will be, but one thing I know: the only ones among you who will be really happy are those who have sought and found how to serve.' — Albert Schweitzer

My first experience of unconditional love was with family pets. I remember many times as a child pouring my heart out to Gillie, our Boston bull terrier, who seemed to be the only one around who accepted me on my bad days as well as good.

As I grew a bit older, (but still young enough to need my mother's permission to cross the street) my world also grew, and with it my experience of unconditional love. We lived in a small town, very close to the main street shops. On my own, I started visiting shopkeepers, all of whom soon became part of my extended family. There was Eva who had the flower shop, where I would sit by the hour in the backroom while she made up wedding and funeral bouquets . . . Jim, a white-haired Italian greengrocer, who on hot summer days would cut open a cool watermelon and share it with me . . . Kuly, a Hungarian cobbler, who would shut down all of his noisy machinery, take out his fiddle and play tunes from the old country . . . Tom, who ran the popcorn wagon in front of our only department store, always found time to talk.

I believe the love these people showed me was completely unconditional, as I had nothing to give in return beyond my own innocence and curiosity. They asked nothing of me. They only gave. I felt acknowledged by them all. I felt recognised, seen, heard. I felt accepted, included, embraced, special. The best part was that I didn't have to do anything for it. I could just be myself.

As I grew up, I discovered how relatively easy it is for me to give unconditional love to children and animals, and how difficult it is to love adults unconditionally. Why? Why can't I freely acknowledge, accept and respect adults as readily as children and animals, asking nothing in return?

The answer is that I can. I have learned that I can choose to do it — to step beyond my fears and to open my heart. I believe the secret to loving unconditionally is to love from a position of strength, independence and wholeness, all qualities that I know I can develop and strengthen within myself.

When I first began to work with Eileen, I remember thinking, what is the point of unconditional love when I have challenge enough with the 'regular' kind of love! Slowly I began to learn that we don't love for love's sake. Rather, we love unconditionally as an act of *service*, a way of giving freely of ourself, a way of serving one another, humanity and the world. I have observed that a time comes in our personal development when we realise that we are not isolated, independent individuals, but rather that we are all interdependent. We experience genuine care and concern for others, become more aware of the larger whole and feel a deep desire to share our riches with others.

I feel that true service is being who we are at all times and expressing as best we can our inherent transpersonal qualities, including unconditional love. The process of evolution engages us all to be conscious cooperators, and so we need to be willing to see the needs of the whole and direct our resources to meet these needs.

The key to service is doing what we *want* to do, not *have* to do, in an effortless way. A Psychosynthesis trainer we know suggests two guiding principles for deciding whatever we wish to do in our life: 1) Make a contribution. 2) Do it wholeheartedly one hundred per cent.

Sometimes I ask myself *how* can I best serve, *what* is the greatest need, *where* can I give one hundred per cent? Sooner or later my questions bring to mind a saying which provides the answer: 'Ask not what the world needs; ask rather what makes your heart sing, and go do that. For what the world needs is people with hearts that sing.'

PART 4. GAINING AWARENESS

Letter from Your God-Self

In Session Three, Part 4 (pp. 84-85) you wrote a personal letter expressing all that you needed to say to God — your feelings and thoughts, doubts and fears, joys and appreciations. Now we invite you to receive a reply to your letter.

What do you imagine your God-Self, the divinity within the very core of your being, has to say to you about you and your relationship to unconditional love? You have the opportunity now to find out. Have a pen nearby for this exercise.

Now find a comfortable position, sitting up straight . . . Close your eyes . . . Take several long, slow, deep breaths . . . Relax your body completely . . . Release all of the tension . . . Allow whatever emotions you may be feeling to fade away . . . Do the same with your thoughts . . . Become like a calm, quiet lake, which mirrors perfectly the blue sky, or the starry sky in the silence of the night . . . Be at peace and yet remain alert . . .

When you are ready, allow to come to you an image or sense of your being in the room where you are now . . . In your imagination see yourself sitting just the way you are . . . Begin to notice a very strong, very pure point of light glowing within you . . . Let it become very clear, very definite and yet very soft, too . . .

This shining light is a symbol of your God-Self, the highest level of your being which loves you very much indeed . . . It is your God-Self, this radiant light within you, which fashions your life by creating all of your lessons, your opportunities, your many blessings . . . It loves you . . . It protects you . . . It supports you . . . It guides you . . . It wants only the very best for you in every way . . .

Allow your attention to move closer and closer towards this point of light . . . Now choose to move *into* the light . . . Relax into it completely . . . Become the light . . . Identify with the light . . . Be the light . . . As you do, begin to feel the radiance . . . the purity . . . the love which you have for this special person sitting here . . .

Being the God-Self, the divinity within this person, you have watched a journey unfold, a journey which you, yourself, have planned and created . . . Over the years you have watched this special person move along this journey, step by step . . . You have witnessed the highs and lows . . . The challenges and changes. . . The opportunities, lessons and blessings . . . Every single day for thousands of days now you have given this person your unceasing love, protection, support and guidance . . . Feel the depth of that compassion and devotion within you now . . .

During all of this time, you have also seen the way this person relates to love . . . You have seen the hesitation, the struggle . . . You have seen the release and the movement forward . . . You also see farther along the journey to what lies ahead . . . What do you have to say to this person now? . . . What would be helpful? . . . What would be reassuring? . . . What does this person need to hear from you today? . . . Begin with whatever you are inspired to say about unconditional love . . .

When you are ready, write it all down in a loving letter to this special person . . . Hold nothing back . . . Express it all now . . . Let it flow . . .

Today's date _____

Dear _____

_____

_____

_____

_____

_____

_____

_____

_____

_____

_____

_____

_____

_____

_____

_____

_____

_____

_____

_____

_____

_____

_____

_____

_____

_____

_____

_____

_____

_____

_____

_____

_____

_____

_____

_____

_____

_____

_____

_____

_____

_____

_____

_____

_____

_____

_____

_____

'Loving Unconditionally' Visualisation

Some participants in our workshops say that unconditional love is far too idealistic for them and that they would only be inviting failure if they ever were to try to achieve it. They feel it is a concept which is so far above and beyond them that they would not know even how to begin to develop it within themselves.

The place to begin is here. The time to begin is now. The way to begin is to choose to give unconditional love a high priority in your life. Start with this exercise to gain your own inner experience of unconditional love.

This visualisation was produced originally as the audio cassette *Loving Unconditionally*. If you do not have it, we suggest that you pre-record this exercise to gain maximum benefit from it. Pause 10-30 seconds, or whatever time seems comfortable and appropriate, at every . . . to allow you to experience each step fully. Give yourself at least 20 minutes to complete it. Avoid rushing through the exercise. Take your time.

Now find a comfortable position, sitting up straight . . . Close your eyes . . . Take several slow, deep breaths . . . Continue to breathe slowly and deeply . . . Observe your body . . . Do whatever is necessary to be completely free and relaxed physically . . .

Observe your emotions . . . Whatever feelings you may be experiencing, pleasant or unpleasant, simply release them for the moment . . . They are your reactions to whatever is happening in your life and you will not need them for this visualisation . . . Do whatever is necessary to be completely free and relaxed emotionally . . .

Observe your mind . . . Do the same with any thoughts you may be having . . . Release them as well . . . You do not need your intellect and its analytical and judgemental nature to distract you . . . Do whatever is necessary to be completely free and relaxed mentally . . . Release, relax and let go . . .

When you are ready, focus your attention inside your body to where your heart is . . . For a moment put your hand over your heart and feel it beating . . . Within your heart is the seed of divine love, of unconditional love . . . Experience it now for yourself by imagining what unconditional love is like . . . Perhaps for you it is a colour . . . A feeling . . . A radiance . . . A vibration . . . A warmth . . . A wave . . .

At first, experience it on its own, unrelated to anyone or anything . . . Allow pure love to be with you now . . . Sense it as love . . . Trust it as love . . . Accept it as love . . . Take it as your own inner experience of love . . . Use it for now as your personal reference of what unconditional love is for you . . .

Accept it for what it truly is: divine love, all-embracing love, universal, vitalising, nurturing love . . . Love which expects nothing in return . . . Love which gives compassionate acceptance and respect to everyone and everything . . .

Let this unconditional love within you slowly radiate throughout your whole being . . . Feel it filling you . . . Feel it enfolding you . . . Feel loving yourself unconditionally . . . Accepting yourself . . . Trusting yourself . . . Forgiving yourself . . . Appreciating yourself . . . Feel this unconditional love healing . . . Balancing . . . And making whole every part of your being . . .

Sense this unconditional love gradually expanding outward beyond your own self, until it fills the entire room you are in now . . . As you do, expand your awareness with it . . . Move with it . . . Grow with it . . . Feel being part of it . . . Experience this unconditional love overflowing into the entire building, then beyond the building . . .

Love is given to us so that we may share it with others, so begin to sense this unconditional love forming into a stream and radiating into your own community . . . Sense it filling and enfolding all of those you love: your family . . . your friends . . . Sense it filling and enfolding anyone you may dislike or are having problems with at this time . . . Allow unconditional love to come back to you from each person as well . . . Feel the healing power of unconditional love bring you together in oneness with everyone and everything . . .

Sense all of these separate streams coming together into a single flow of love . . . As you do, experience unconditional love being both unique and universal . . .

Sense this unconditional love expanding and radiating out to your whole country . . . As you do, feel connected with it . . .

Sense this unconditional love expanding and radiating out to the whole planet . . . As you do, feel and accept your oneness with it . . .

Sense this unconditional love expanding and radiating out to the whole universe . . . As you do, feel and accept your own wholeness . . .

Sense this unconditional love expanding and radiating out to the whole cosmic creation . . . As you do, feel and accept your own perfection . . .

Sense this unconditional love expanding and radiating out to embrace the whole heart and mind of God . . . As you do, feel and accept your own divine essence . . .

Slowly bring your attention back to your own presence . . . As you do, experience the unconditional love you have been feeling as being entirely within your own heart, where, in fact, it has always been centred and will always be . . . Know that, wherever you may be, or whatever is happening to you, this love remains here within your heart, ready to bring you the peace you are feeling right now . . .

Be aware also that you may draw upon its limitless supply any time you want, simply by choosing to do so . . . Trust that you may repeat as often as you like this experience of using unconditional love to connect on the inner planes of Spirit with everyone and everything . . .

In your own time, open your eyes, and as you do, bring the unconditional love you are feeling now with you . . . Bring it out . . . Externalise it . . . Continue to experience it fully . . . Accept it as an expression of who you are at the very core of your being, and of who everyone else is as well . . .

As you feel this unconditional love within you now, know also that you are feeling the God-Self within you, for God is love . . .

Now write down any feelings, thoughts and questions you wish to record.

_____

_____

_____

_____

_____

_____

_____

PART 5. DEVELOPING POTENTIAL

'Unconditional Love' Creative Meditation and Drawing

As parents and teachers we learn to separate the child from its behaviour. We don't stop loving a child simply because it does something we don't like. Most of us have much more difficulty applying this principle in our adult relationships.

In *The Power of Unconditional Love*, Key Keyes Jr. says, 'The only way I can love unconditionally is to distinguish between a *person* and their *programming*, which causes the person's behaviour . . . People are like the tape recorder. They are, in their essence, OK just as they are. But they can run off tapes in their minds that make them do things that are unacceptable, unskilful and harmful to themselves or others. *I can totally reject and even actively oppose what a person is saying or doing.* And at the same time, I can continue to *love that person* no matter what their behaviour is. My ego just has to let me remember that the person is *not* the mental tapes (conditioning, habits of mind or *programming*) they have learned.'

How about you? Are you able to separate people from their behaviour? Are you able to love people *despite* what they may do or say?

How would you like to express your love? It is to your advantage to decide precisely whatever you want in relation to love and to hold it clearly in mind as a realistic and attainable picture of how you would like your life to be. We may call it an *ideal model*. Holding such an image in your awareness helps to achieve whatever you want, in this case unconditional love.

In Session One, Part 5 (p. 38) you were given a symbolic glimpse into the future *('IN RELATION TO LOVE, WHERE AM I GOING?')*. That exercise may have suggested a specific next step for you to take, or it may have given you a more general context, hinting at the potential the future holds for you.

We build upon that impulse now with a visualisation and drawing exercise, so have your materials ready. We suggest that you pre-record this exercise to gain maximum benefit from it. Pause on the tape 10-30 seconds, or whatever time seems comfortable and appropriate, at every . . . to allow you to experience each step fully. Give yourself at least 20 minutes to complete this exercise. Avoid rushing through it. Take your time.

Now close your eyes . . . Sit up straight . . . Take a few deep breaths . . . Relax . . . Allow your body, emotions and thoughts to become still . . . Become like a calm, quiet lake . . .

From our Session Six focus upon subpersonalities, you are aware that we carry within ourself various images of who we are at certain times or in certain situations. They are only partial images, exaggerations and distortions and they often conflict with one another. It helps to become aware of them, for with awareness comes the freedom and power of choice.

First, it is human nature for us occasionally to feel and think poorly of ourself, to judge or criticise ourself as being not loving and lovable enough, or as being a failure in some way. Such an inner image is always far worse than we actually are; it is an exaggeration or distortion, yet one we accept as absolutely true of ourself at certain times . . .

Take a moment to consider how you sometimes feel and think poorly about yourself in relation to love, and the way in which you may judge, criticise or *underestimate* yourself . . .

When you are ready, allow to come to you an image or sense which represents this one-sided view of yourself . . . Take your time . . . Wait patiently in the silence, knowing that something will soon come to you . . . Be willing to accept whatever comes without judging, censoring or rejecting it . . . Simply be ready to observe it, with the purpose of learning more about it . . .

As you begin to sense something, allow it to become more vivid . . . Note its size and shape . . . Its density and design . . . Its colour and texture . . . Explore it with as many of your senses as you can . . . Find the overall quality it suggests to you . . .

Then open your eyes and express in a drawing below either the image itself or its quality . . . If nothing has come to you, hold the topic in mind and begin to draw freely and spontaneously, letting something come to you in that way . . .

MY UNDERESTIMATED IMAGE OF MYSELF IN RELATION TO LOVE

Write down the overall *quality* of the symbol and any other words, feelings or thoughts which came to you during the exercise, or which you are aware of now. What new insight or awareness does this symbol and its quality give to you?

_____

_____

_____

_____

Now close your eyes again . . . Take a few deep breaths . . . Relax . . .

We also carry an inner image of ourself as being *far better* than we actually are. It is an opposite exaggeration or distortion, yet one we accept as absolutely true of ourself at certain times . . .

Take a moment to consider how you *overestimate* yourself in relation to love and the way in which you may exaggerate how you are . . .

When you are ready, allow to come to you an image or sense which represents this one-sided view of yourself . . . Take your time . . . Wait patiently in the silence, knowing that something will soon come to you . . . Be willing to accept whatever comes without judging, censoring or rejecting it . . . Simply be ready to observe it, with the purpose of learning more about it . . .

As you begin to sense something, allow it to become more vivid . . . Note its size and shape . . . Its density and design . . . Its colour and texture . . . Explore it with as many of your senses as you can . . . Find the overall quality it suggests to you . . .

Then open your eyes and express in a drawing below either the image itself, or its quality . . . If nothing has come to you, hold the topic in mind and begin to draw freely and spontaneously, letting something come to you in that way . . .

```
+----------------------------------------------------------------------+
|          MY OVERESTIMATED IMAGE OF MYSELF IN RELATION TO LOVE         |
|                                                                      |
|                                                                      |
|                                                                      |
|                                                                      |
|                                                                      |
|                                                                      |
|                                                                      |
|                                                                      |
|                                                                      |
|                                                                      |
|                                                                      |
|                                                                      |
+----------------------------------------------------------------------+
```

Write down the overall *quality* of the symbol and any other words, feelings or thoughts which came to you during the exercise, or which you are aware of now. What new insight or awareness does this symbol and its quality give to you?

_____

_____

_____

_____

Now close your eyes again . . . Take a few deep breaths . . . Relax . . .

We also carry an inner image of ourself *as we would like to appear to others*, in contrast to how we actually are. It, too, is an exaggeration or distortion, yet one we accept as absolutely true of ourself at certain times . . .

Take a moment to consider how you would like to appear to others in relation to love . . .

When you are ready, allow to come to you an image or sense which represents this one-sided view of yourself . . . Take your time . . . Wait patiently in the silence, knowing that something will soon come to you . . . Be willing to accept whatever comes without judging, censoring or rejecting it . . . Simply be ready to observe it, with the purpose of learning more about it . . .

As you begin to sense something, allow it to become more vivid . . . Note its size and shape . . . Its density and design . . . Its colour and texture . . . Explore it with as many of your senses as you can . . . Find the overall quality it suggests to you . . .

Then open your eyes and express in a drawing below either the image itself or its quality . . . If nothing has come to you, hold the topic in mind and begin to draw freely and spontaneously, letting something come to you in that way . . .

MY IMAGE OF HOW I WOULD LIKE TO APPEAR TO OTHERS IN RELATION TO LOVE

Write down the overall *quality* of the symbol and any other words, feelings or thoughts which came to you during the exercise, or which you are aware of now. What new insight or awareness does this symbol and its quality give to you?

_____

_____

_____

_____

Now close your eyes again . . . Take a few deep breaths . . . Relax . . .

Finally, we carry an inner image of _how we feel other people would like us to be or expect us to be_ in relation to love. It, too, is an exaggeration or distortion, yet one we accept as absolutely true of ourself at certain times . . .

Take a moment to consider the expectations you believe others have of you in relation to love, and how you feel they would like you to be . . .

When you are ready, allow to come to you an image or sense which represents this one-sided view of yourself . . . Take your time . . . Wait patiently in the silence, knowing that something will soon come to you . . . Be willing to accept whatever comes without judging, censoring or rejecting it . . . Simply be ready to observe it, with the purpose of learning more about it . . .

As you begin to sense something, allow it to become more vivid . . . Note its size and shape . . . Its density and design . . . Its colour and texture . . . Explore it with as many of your senses as you can . . . Find the overall quality it suggests to you . . .

Then open your eyes and express in a drawing below either the image itself or its quality . . . If nothing has come to you, hold the topic in mind and begin to draw freely and spontaneously, letting something come to you in that way . . .

MY IMAGE OF HOW OTHER PEOPLE EXPECT ME TO BE IN RELATION TO LOVE

Write down the overall *quality* of the symbol and any other words, feelings or thoughts which came to you during the exercise, or which you are aware of now. What new insight or awareness does this symbol and its quality give to you?

_____

_____

_____

_____

Now review each one of these four drawings and how you feel about them.

Then stand up . . . Close your eyes . . . Using your imagination, feel the weight of these images upon your body . . . Feel how they limit you . . . Feel how they hold you back . . . Feel how they restrict you . . .

As you remain standing, let your body begin to move to shake these images off and away from you . . . Shake your arms and hands, as though shaking off water . . . Then allow your legs to shake as well . . . Finally, shake your whole body . . . Shake off the symbolic weight of all of these images . . . Allow all of these exaggerated and distorted images of yourself to drop off . . . *Choose* to be free of them all . . . Continue to shake them off until you feel completely free of them . . .

Then be still for a moment and experience how you feel . . . What differences are there? . . . In your own time, open your eyes and sit down again . . .

What did you feel as you were doing the exercise? What are you feeling and thinking now?

_____

_____

_____

_____

Now close your eyes again . . . Take a few deep breaths . . . Relax . . .

Take a few moments to imagine how you would like to be, ideally, in relation to *unconditional* love . . . How loving and lovable you would like to be . . . How you would like to love more fully . . . Freely . . . Fearlessly . . . Unconditionally . . . Make certain you avoid all 'shoulds' . . . Let whatever you imagine be your free choice . . . Not a model of perfection . . . But a realistic and attainable ideal . . . Something which would be possible to achieve in your life . . . Something you are willing to be . . .

Then, when you are ready, allow to come to you an image or sense which represents this ideal model of yourself . . . Take your time . . . Wait patiently in the silence, knowing that something will soon come to you . . . Be willing to accept whatever comes without judging, censoring or rejecting it . . . Simply be ready to observe it, with the purpose of learning more about it . . .

As you begin to sense something, allow it to become more vivid . . . Note its size and shape . . . Its density and design . . . Its colour and texture . . . Explore it with as many of your senses as you can . . . Find the overall quality it suggests to you . . .

Now open your eyes and express in a drawing below either the image itself or its quality . . . If nothing has come to you, hold the topic in mind and begin to draw freely and spontaneously, letting something come to you in that way . . .

MY IDEAL IMAGE OF MYSELF IN RELATION TO UNCONDITIONAL LOVE

Write down the overall *quality* of the symbol and any other words, feelings or thoughts which came to you during the exercise, or which you are aware of now. What new insight or awareness does this symbol and its quality give to you?

_____

_____

_____

Imagine how it would be if you had more of this quality in your life. How would your life be different? How would it be the same?

_____

_____

_____

Specifically how would your relationships with people around you change? With parents, partners, family, friends, co-workers and others?

_____

_____

_____

You have one more important step to take — to build a clear model of your ideal image of yourself and then to fix it in specific detail in your mind. In this way you harness the great power of positive thinking and creative visualisation. Remember, an image held in our imagination serves as a blueprint which eventually may manifest in our life.

Now close your eyes one last time . . . Take a few deep breaths . . . Relax . . .

Visualise yourself as being this ideal model of yourself in relation to unconditional love . . . How do you appear physically? . . . How does your face appear? . . . Your eyes? . . . Your stance? . . . The rest of you? . . .

Then in your imagination try on this quality like a coat . . . Merge with it . . . Become it . . . Be it . . . Feel what it is like to be this ideal model completely . . .

Take a few minutes to visualise yourself in a number of everyday situations, possessing and acting out satisfactorily the quality of your ideal model . . . Bring your feelings fully into it as well . . .

Include scenes in which you interact successfully in the various personal and professional roles you play, involving perhaps your parents . . . Partners . . . Family . . . Friends . . . Co-workers . . . Other people in your life . . . Avoid rushing through this exercise . . . Take your time . . . Make it as real and as vivid as possible . . . Remember, you are creating a blueprint, a plan to unfold . . .

In your own time, allow everything to fade . . . Bring your attention back to the room where you are now . . . Open your eyes . . . Take a deep breath . . . And a gentle stretch . . .

Now write down any feelings, thoughts and questions you wish to record.

_____

_____

_____

_____

_____

_____

_____

Repeat regularly this last stage of the ideal model creative meditation to breathe life into your blueprint.

After a time, you may wish to repeat the entire process, finding a new image or symbol, with a new quality and a new ideal model visualisation as a new blueprint to manifest in your life. When you do, avoid all 'shoulds'. Keep your ideal model a realistic and attainable one.

'Transforming Power of Unconditional Love' Visualisation

More and more we are shown that our planet is one vast interconnected whole. The farthest person on earth from us is only a telephone call away, a computer link away, a satellite television transmission away. The billions of us who inhabit planet Earth are now inextricably interconnected by advanced technology. But we have always been interconnected by other 'inner technology' as well: the farthest person is also only a meditation away, a prayer away, a creative visualisation away.

We all are parts of this whole; we all are subpersonalities constituting the whole of humanity. Each of us is here to serve the whole for the benefit of the whole. Being part of the whole, each of us is served as well.

We present the following exercise as one means to express and radiate unconditional love in service to humanity and to the planet. In this visualisation we apply the power of unconditional love to transform situations in your life and in the wider world. We suggest that you pre-record this exercise to gain maximum benefit from it. Give yourself at least 20 minutes to complete it. Avoid rushing through the exercise. Take your time. Repeat it as often as you like.

Now close your eyes . . . Sit up straight . . . Take a few deep breaths . . . Relax . . . Allow your body, emotions and thoughts to become still . . . Become like a calm, quiet lake . . .

When you are ready, allow to come to you a memory of a time when your love transformed a situation, perhaps another person's life, even for a brief moment . . . Take your time . . . Wait patiently in the silence, knowing that something will soon come to you . . . Be willing to accept whatever comes without judging, censoring or rejecting it . . . Simply be ready to observe it . . .

When you begin to sense something, allow specific details to come to you . . . Begin to re-create and re-experience it . . . Observe and explore the experience with as many of your senses as you can . . . Feel the feelings in your body . . . Notice where your love came from . . . Was it spontaneous — did it just happen? . . . Or was it a conscious, deliberate act upon your part? . . .

Now allow to come to you a current challenging person or situation in your life . . . Take your time . . . Wait patiently in the silence, knowing that something will soon come to you . . .

When you begin to sense something, allow specific details to come to you . . . Feel the feelings in your body, the need, the conflict or distress . . . Let it be very real but avoid becoming lost in it . . .

Return to the place within you where you felt the power of love a moment ago . . . Re-experience that power in you . . . Feel the love . . . Now direct that love, that power, to fill and enfold the person or situation you are having difficulty with at present . . .

Imagine how that person or situation would be different if transformed . . . How would it be? . . . How would it feel? . . . Create it for yourself now . . . Feel the power of your love flowing through your heart, your body, your whole being . . . Feel the atmosphere lighten . . . Experience the transforming power of unconditional love . . .

Next visualise some aspect in the world which is in need, in conflict, in distress . . . Take your time . . . Be willing to accept whatever comes without judging, censoring or rejecting it . . . Simply be ready to observe it . . .

When you begin to sense something, allow specific details to come to you . . . Picture it in your mind . . . See the people . . . See the Earth . . . Feel in your body the feelings they feel . . . Feel what the Earth feels . . .

Now deliberately draw upon the reservoir of divine love, of unconditional love, within you . . . Direct your love to the aspect of the world you have chosen . . . Feel your heart open . . . Visualise a stream of unconditional love pouring from your heart, radiating outwards and enfolding the Earth . . . See it enfolding the people . . . See it transforming the whole situation . . . Feel the power of your unconditional love uplifting and bringing joy and peace to everyone and everything . . .

How does it appear now? . . . Allow your imagination to re-create the situation as being totally transformed . . . Imagine the people's faces . . . Imagine how they feel . . . How does the Earth appear? . . . How does the Earth feel? . . .

Affirm to yourself, 'I HAVE THE DIVINE POWER WITHIN ME TO TRANSFORM THE WORLD WITH UNCONDITIONAL LOVE . . . I SEE IT TRANSFORMED NOW' . . .

In your own time, allow everything to fade . . . Bring your attention back to the room where you are now . . . Open your eyes . . . Take a deep breath . . . And a gentle stretch . . .

Now write down any feelings, thoughts or questions you wish to record.

_____

_____

_____

_____

_____

_____

You Are!

We always conclude our workshops with the poem *You Are!* by William Arthur Ward, from the Unity publication *You Are A Remarkable Person*. Don't be put off by the masculine pronouns; allow yourself to resonate with what lies beyond the words.

> *If God is . . . and He is!*
> *If God is Love . . . and He is!*
> *If you are made in His image . . . and you are!*
> *Then you are Love.*
> *You are a child of Love.*
> *You are an expression of Love.*
> *You are a channel of Love.*
>
> *If God is . . . and He is!*
> *If God is Truth . . . and He is!*
> *If God lives in you . . . and He does!*
> *Then you are Truth.*
> *You are a child of Truth.*
> *You are an expression of Truth.*
> *You are a channel of Truth.*
>
> *If God is . . . and He is!*
> *If God is Wholeness . . . and He is!*
> *If you are wholly of God . . . and you are!*
> *Then you are Whole.*
> *You are a child of Wholeness.*
> *You are an expression of Wholeness.*
> *You are a channel of Wholeness.*

Once we experience for ourself the many benefits of bringing more *unconditional* love into our life, we celebrate the true freedom and joy of the Spirit.

PART 6. APPLYING IT

Expressing Unconditional Love

Here are a few suggestions for bringing more unconditional love into your life. Practise each one of them daily for at least seven days, and then report your experience with them on the following page *before you begin the final Completion and Feedback section* which finishes the course for you.

1. **Affirmation.** To avoid judging, criticising and condemning others (another loyal soldier enlisted to help you to feel safe and secure), affirm silently to yourself whenever you meet another person, or whenever you are tempted to think unkindly towards someone, *'I SEE THE DIVINITY WITHIN YOU, I LOVE YOU UNCONDITIONALLY AND I BLESS YOU.'* Remind yourself to look beyond all outer appearance and behaviour. Recognise and appreciate people for who they are — a permanent centre of pure Self-consciousness and will.

2. **Creative Meditation.** Repeat the final stage of this ideal model exercise from Part 5. Relive it vividly in your imagination to enhance its effectiveness. Then find ways to enact it in your everyday life.

3. **Angels and Mortals.** Each year in early December, Findhorn Foundation members play a game called 'Angels and Mortals'. They write their own names upon slips of paper and put them into a hat. When everyone has done so, they then draw out a name and they become instant 'angels' for their 'mortals' so chosen. Thus everyone is both an angel and a mortal.

From then until Christmas the angels' task is to love, appreciate and bless their mortals in as many different ways as they can imagine, anonymously — mortals never know who their angels are until Christmas morning. Angels find creative ways, as well as willing helpers, to let their mortals know they are being watched over by caring guardian angels.

Whatever form these ways take, they are all acts of unconditional love because all participants must trust that, as mortals, they will receive the full and loving attention of their own angel, *independent* of however much they may do for their own mortal. Thus their attention can be more focused upon giving than receiving. In this game when everyone gives, everyone receives.

To practise unconditional love, we invite you to become an 'angel' for someone! Do not wait until Christmas. Do it now. Choose a 'mortal', perhaps someone in your family, church or meditation group, a co-worker, a neighbour or your postman, and begin to find ways to acknowledge, appreciate and do simple little things for the person — all anonymously, of course.

If you feel shy, awkward or embarrassed about following this suggestion, remember, you are doing it for the other person, not for yourself. It need not take a great expenditure of time, money or effort — only love. Do not hold yourself back. Open your heart and focus upon the love, the caring, the joy of giving. Then report your experience on the following page.

Continue to appreciate and bless the same person for as long as you want to do so. Or adopt a new mortal every week! Never reveal your identity. Then you can be assured that all the wonderful things you do for your adopted mortals are acts of pure unconditional love.

In your report note also when and how you may have experienced resistance to doing any or all of these exercises and techniques, and what you did about it.

NOTES AND DRAWINGS REPORTING RESULTS OF PART 6 EXERCISES

SUMMARY OF COURSE TECHNIQUES AND RESOURCES

For reference, we list the principal techniques and resources presented during the course. Use your intuition and imagination to apply them in different ways to bring more unconditional love into your life.

Acting 'As If', to manifest a desired inner state by enacting outer behaviour.

Acts of Will, to make and implement choices which serve rather than limit you.

Affirmations, to create a positive blueprint and then bring about a desired outcome.

Assessments, to take stock of your experience with a given topic.

Attunements, to contact your source of inner wisdom for inspiration and help.

Autobiography, to explore, connect and express various parts of your past.

Autogenic Training, to relax and to be more receptive to other techniques.

Brainstorming, to identify alternative solutions to problems.

Chair Exercises, to bring your inner process out into the open.

Creative Meditations, to manifest the ideal model of how your life can be.

Dialogues with Your God-Self, to communicate directly with your inner centre.

Disidentifications, to step back from partial images to gain greater Self-awareness.

Drawings, to explore and express a topic creatively and graphically.

Evening Reviews, to become aware of attitudes and behaviour patterns.

Evocation Exercises, to establish and strengthen desired qualities within yourself.

Experience Scans, to survey your attitudes, beliefs, feelings and thoughts.

Forgiveness Exercises, to free yourself by letting go of past hurt and pain.

Identifications, to step into and take on partial images to gain greater awareness.

'If I Had the Courage' Scans, to identify fears and the risks to take to ease them.

Imageries, to use your imagination to evoke a desired symbolic image of a subject.

Inner Conflict Resolution, to reconcile differing desires, needs and wants.

Letter-Writing (to God, a parent, yourself), to express the unexpressed within you.

Messages And 'Shoulds' Scans, to identify and let go of past conditioning.

Mirror Techniques, to make a direct connection with your inner being.

Models of People, to use as inspiration and for emulation.

Morning Previews, to plan how to express useful subpersonalities during the day.

Personal Goals, to choose, implement and achieve desired outcomes.

Prayers, to ask your God-Self for information and support.

Reading, to gain new direction, inspiration and perspective.

Receptive Meditations, to evoke images and symbols, and to deepen awareness.

Reflective Meditations, to foster understanding and evaluation of a topic.

Self-Appreciations, to identify, acknowledge and reinforce your personal assets.

Subpersonalities, to deal with identifications, images, desires, needs and blocks.

Support Person or Group, to give and receive encouragement, insight and help.

Visualisations, to access, explore, enrich and ground your inner life.

Word Cards, to evoke and develop desired personal qualities.

Suggested Reading

1. *The Power of Unconditional Love: 21 Guidelines for Beginning, Improving, and Changing Your Most Meaningful Relationships,* by Ken Keyes Jr., presents a strategy to love unconditionally which includes separating the person from the problem. 'Love the person; work with the problem.'

2. *Unconditional Love,* by John Powell, S.J., says, 'Either I attach conditions to my love for you or I do not. To the extent that I do attach such conditions, I do not really love you. I am only offering an exchange, not a gift. And true love is and must always be a free gift.'

Personal Goal

Consider various simple, specific, observable actions you could take within the next few days which would be a step towards bringing more love into your life. Then choose one which feels important to you, one to take as a personal goal. Make a deliberate choice to achieve it. Write it down. Remember, making and implementing choices empowers and strengthens you.

_____

_____

_____

_____

Session Learnings

Turn back and review what you have done in this session. Then write down the three most important insights or learnings you have gained from it.

_____

_____

_____

_____

_____

_____

_____

Purpose

As stated at the beginning of Part 2, the purpose of Session Ten is to present principles and techniques that will help you to love more unconditionally. To what degree has Session Ten achieved its general purpose for you?

_____

_____

_____

_____

Congratulations! You have finished Session Ten. Please discuss your experience of this session with your support person *before you begin the following section to finish this course.*

COMPLETION & FEEDBACK

Purpose

We say that this course consists of three stages. The first one began when something inside you said 'Yes' to doing the course. The second began when you addressed the sessions. The third stage begins when you carry all you have learned into your daily life.

The purpose of this final session is to help you to conclude the second stage and to enter fully into the integration stage of the course.

'Next Steps' Brainstorming

We are always standing at a crossroads where we have the choice of bringing more love into our life. It is a choice which has to be made over and over again, day by day, moment by moment. For our entire lifetime, we have an infinite succession of 'next steps' which we can choose to take — or not — to bring more love into our life.

What are some of the 'next steps' you might take?

One method to learn about possible steps is to brainstorm them. Remember, in brainstorming the point is to allow many ideas to come to you as quickly as possible. Avoid evaluating, judging or rejecting any idea for the moment. Simply write down *everything* as it occurs spontaneously to you.

Find out how many different 'next steps' you can imagine, without stopping to consider how comfortable, costly, effective or practical they may be. Include absurd, fantastic, zany ideas as well, for they often hold the seeds of creative possibilities. Make sketches to help you remember images which come. Enjoy your creativity.

Now close your eyes . . . Sit up straight . . . Take a few deep breaths and relax . . . Allow your body, emotions and thoughts to become still . . . Become like a calm, quiet lake . . .

When you are ready, say to yourself, *'MY NEXT STEP IN BRINGING MORE LOVE INTO MY LIFE IS TO . . . ,'* and complete the sentence with a few words — whatever comes spontaneously to you. Do not *think* about it. Write down the first response which comes. Then do it again, this time allowing different words to emerge. Write down the new response. If you blank out momentarily, simply begin again, knowing that something will soon come to you. Repeat the process again and again for at least ten minutes, or until you have filled the space provided.

MY NEXT STEP IN BRINGING MORE LOVE INTO MY LIFE IS TO . . .

Examine your responses. Mark all of the ideas worth considering for implementation.

Choose one of them as a goal or purpose to achieve, and write about it.

_____
_____
_____
_____

Next create a plan to bring it about. Be specific about what, when, where and how you plan to do it, and what the challenges or risks might be.

_____
_____
_____
_____

Then put your plan into action.

When you have achieved this 'next step', return to your brainstorming list — or if necessary create a new list — to choose your subsequent 'next step'. Maintain the momentum of your progress. Be aware that you will never exhaust your supply of 'next steps'. *No matter what your past experience or present state of mind and heart, there is always a 'next step' you can take to bring more love into your life.*

Writing a Letter to Yourself

To help you to complete the course in a systematic manner and to begin to digest and integrate your learning, we invite you to write down a summary of your experience.

We are often told in our workshop that this exercise is one of the most helpful ones we present. Perhaps you will agree. Here are the instructions:

1. Write a detailed, thorough letter to yourself in which you summarise your whole experience with this course. You may do it in one sitting or you may wish to take several days. It is important to take all the time you need so that you feel quite satisfied and complete when you are finished. The contents are up to you. No one else will see the letter, so you may be perfectly honest and open about what you write. Here are some suggestions:

- Review your status at the beginning of the course on each of the major session topics listed. Then take stock of your present status on each of them. Assess whatever progress you have made. Include one or more insights you have gained about each of the topics.

    a. Your experience of love: how you feel about it; what it means to you.
    b. Your fears, blocks and barriers to bringing more love into your life.
    c. Your security, trust and faith; your relationship to your God-Self.
    d. Your honesty and openness with yourself and others.
    e. Your attitudes and beliefs about yourself, others and how life works.
    f. Your partial images you hold of yourself and how they influence you.
    g. Your capacity to step back from yourself to find clarity and choice.
    h. Your will: making and implementing choices deliberately and effectively.
    i. Your experience of change, maintenance, resistance and forgiveness.
    j. Your willingness to love everyone equally and unconditionally.
    k. Your willingness to identify and take 'next steps' in a lifelong process.

- Give examples of risks, personal goals and other actions you have taken to bring more love into your life since you began the course: what you did, how successful you were and what you learned.

- Promise yourself (if you are willing to do so) to return at a specific time — say, after one or two years — to do the entire course over again to increase your awareness, to go deeper and farther with it, to assess your ongoing personal development and to keep the topic 'alive' and vital for you.

- Remind yourself to thank your support person and all the others around you who give you encouragement, inspiration and love.

2. When your letter is as complete as you can make it, write your own name and address on an envelope, put the letter inside and seal it. Put a stamp on it.

3. Give the letter to your support person to hold for three months and then post back to you.

4. When your letter arrives, read through it carefully and then celebrate the progress you have made since you wrote it. Use it as a reminder to take another 'next step' to bring more love into your life.

BRINGING MORE LOVE INTO YOUR LIFE: THE CHOICE IS YOURS

To complete this course, answer the following questions. First take a moment to consider your experience and then write about it.

Which principles or ideas in this course have you found to be the most helpful?

_____
_____
_____

Which exercises and techniques have been the most helpful?

_____
_____
_____

What helpful insights or learnings about yourself have you gained?

_____
_____
_____

How do you assess your progress in bringing more love into your life? Have you re-framed or otherwise modified your attitudes, beliefs or behaviour? In what ways?

_____
_____
_____

To what degree have you achieved your original Session One purpose and objectives for doing this course? What 'next steps' do you intend to take?

_____
_____
_____
_____

Use the space below to write anything else to help you gain a sense of completion with this course. Then, if you are willing, photocopy the preceding page together with this page when you are finished with it and send them to the authors care of Findhorn Press, The Park, Findhorn, Forres IV36 0TZ, Scotland. We welcome your comments about your experience with the course. Sign your name if you wish, or remain anonymous. Thank you for your feedback!

_____

_____

_____

_____

_____

_____

_____

_____

_____

_____

_____

_____

_____

_____

_____

_____

_____

_____

_____

_____

_____

_____

_____

_____

_____

_____

_____

_____

_____

SUGGESTIONS FOR USING THE COURSE
WITH SMALL GROUPS

This course is designed for you to do all of the questions and exercises completely by yourself. However, for increased benefit, you may wish to form a small group to meet regularly to share your experience of the course materials, learn from each other and give and receive encouragement and support.

We have presented this course many times as an intensive seven-day residential workshop at the Findhorn Foundation, and as a one-evening-a-week course in London. In addition, one or both of us have presented portions of the course as weekend workshops in such places as Berlin, Brussels, Copenhagen, Munich and Paris. From our experience we offer the following suggestions for using the course with small groups.

1. Purpose. First, decide upon the primary purpose of the group. For example do you want a *study* group which investigates and discusses the various topics presented; or a *support* group which encourages participants to talk honestly and openly about their own personal experience? As the organiser you may make this decision in advance and then attract participants who resonate with your chosen purpose, or you may gather a few friends together and let the group itself decide what it wants. The purpose and direction of the group need to be clearly understood by everyone from the very beginning to avoid unrealistic or conflicting expectations.

2. Scheduling. To provide continuity, we suggest that the group meets regularly at the same time and place. If you intend to follow our format and cover all of the materials in the course, resist the temptation to offer the course as a ten-week or twelve-week package. Time pressures can defeat your original purpose and can incite group frustration and resistance (too much, too fast, not enough time to digest). Our recommendation is to have an ongoing, open-ended group which can move through the course at its own comfortable rate, taking as much time as it needs. Who knows, you may enjoy the experience so much that you decide to continue meeting as a group after you have completed the course itself.

3. Pacing and Size. One challenge you may have is how to give people enough time to talk about their experience with the course materials as openly and deeply as they are prepared to do, while maintaining a comfortable momentum. The size of the group will influence the pace at which you move through the course. We suggest a minimum of four and a maximum of eight people so that everyone feels involved and contributes freely to discussions without detriment to the general pace you wish to set.

4. Introductions. The first meeting of the group needs to create a welcoming atmosphere of safety and trust. All participants should have the opportunity to introduce themselves, telling what attracted them to the group, what they would like to get from it, what challenges they have with love and what qualities or skills they bring to the group.

5. Agreements. Also during the first meeting we suggest that the group establishes by consensus whatever agreements it wants in order to foster safety and efficiency, for example starting and stopping sessions on time, maintaining confidentiality (not repeating to others outside the group whatever is said within the group) or encouraging participants to express their feelings as well as their thoughts. It is helpful to make all such agreements quite clear and explicit from the beginning.

6. Leadership. The Findhorn Foundation experience is for the leader to be a fully participating member of the group — not an outsider apart from it — and for the responsibility for the group and its progress to be shared equally by all of the participants. In this way, everyone is a student and everyone is a teacher, regardless of age or experience, and everyone learns from everyone else. You may also wish to experiment with rotating the leadership role among the participants so that everyone feels more actively involved and responsible for the group.

7. Homework. We suggest that participants do the course materials on their own at home and then use the group to relate whatever their experience has been and to offer and receive support with their current challenges in bringing more love into their life.

8. Group Exercises. The effects of meditations, visualisations and other exercises are often magnified and enhanced when they are experienced in groups, so we suggest repeating some of them within the group. Participants often undergo a deepening of their original experience with exercises and learn the value in repeating them. Pre-record the instructions so that everyone may participate freely.

9. Balance. Mark Twain said, 'It is a terrible death to be talked to death,' so ensure that each meeting of the group has a proper balance between discussion and exercises repeated from the course. As needs can change, regularly invite feedback from the group concerning this balance.

10. Circles. We suggest that participants sit in a circle as it allows everyone to make eye contact with each other and encourages communication and participation.

11. Completion. The final meeting of the group needs to give all participants the opportunity to say or do whatever they want in order to feel complete with the course and the group. Participants may wish to read out their responses to the five questions on page 282 to begin their completion process. You may also include an Appreciation Circle, giving all participants time to offer constructive observations to each person in turn, such as how they have seen the person develop during the course, admirable qualities and traits they have noticed in the person and other sincere appreciations intended to provide positive reinforcement.

12. Friendly Disclaimer. This course is an educational one intended to foster self-knowledge, self-understanding and self-acceptance. It is not meant as a therapy of any kind. While the topics, methods, exercises and techniques of the course can be quite revealing, powerful and healing for people, the authors accept no responsibility for individual reactions to the course and its materials.

Finally, we welcome comments about your experience with this course within a group setting. Address all correspondence to the authors care of Findhorn Press, The Park, Findhorn, Forres IV36 0TZ, Scotland.

REFERENCES & RECOMMENDED READING

A COURSE READING LIST

The following works are listed in the course as suggested reading. Many are available in both British and American editions and several in languages other than English.

Assagioli, M.D., Roberto. *The Act of Will: A Guide to Self-Actualization and Self-Realization.* Wellingborough NN8 2RQ, England: Crucible, 1990. ISBN 1 852740 82 5.

Caddy, Eileen, and Platts, David Earl, Ph.D. (ed.) *Opening Doors Within.* Forres IV36 0TZ, Scotland: Findhorn Press, 1987. ISBN 0 905249 66 6.

Daily Guideposts. Carmel, New York 10512: Guideposts Associates, Inc. **NOTE.** This book is sold by mail order direct from the publisher only, with an all-new edition published annually for each calendar year.

Emery, Stuart. *Actualizations: You Don't Have to Rehearse to Be Yourself.* Garden City, New York: Dolphin Books, 1978. ISBN 0 385131 22 4.

Ferrucci, Piero. *Inevitable Grace. Breakthroughs in the Lives of Great Men and Women: Guides to Your Self-Realization.* Wellingborough NN8 2RQ, England: Crucible, 1990. ISBN 1 852740 64 7.

Ferrucci, Piero. *What We May Be. The Vision and Techniques of Psychosynthesis.* Wellingborough NN8 2RQ, England: Crucible, 1989. ISBN 1 852740 53 1.

Foundation For Inner Peace. *A Course in Miracles.* London EC4P 4EE, England: Arkana, 1985. ISBN 1 850630 16 X.

Gendlin, Ph.D., Eugene. *Focusing.* New York, New York 10036: Everest House, 1978. ISBN 0 896960 10 2.

Jackins, Harvey. *The Human Side of Human Beings: The Theory of Re-Evaluation Counselling.* Seattle, Washington 98111: Rational Island Publishers, 1978. ISBN 0 911214 03 8.

Jampolsky, M.D., Gerald G. *Love is Letting Go of Fear.* Berkeley, California 94707: Celestial Arts, 1979. ISBN 0 890872 46 5.

Jeffers, Susan. *Feel the Fear and Do It Anyway.* London SW1V 2SA, England: Arrow Books Limited, 1991. ISBN 0 099741 00 8.

Keyes, Jr., Ken. *The Power of Unconditional Love: 21 Guidelines for Beginning, Improving and Changing Your Most Meaningful Relationships.* Coos Bay, Oregon 97420: Love Line Books, 1990. ISBN 0 915972 19 0.

Leonard, Jim, and Laut, Phil. *Vivation: The Science of Enjoying All of Your Life.* Cincinnati, Ohio 45208: Vivation Publishing Company, 1990. ISBN 0 961013 24 9.

Powell, S.J. John. *Unconditional Love.* Niles, Illinois 60648: Argus Communications, 1978. ISBN 0 895050 29 3.

Ray, Sondra. *I Deserve Love: How Affirmations Can Guide You to Personal Fulfillment.* Millbrae, California 94030: Les Femmes Publishing, 1976. ISBN 0 890879 09 5.

Rowan, John. *Subpersonalities: The People Inside Us*. London EC4P 4EE, England: Routledge, 1990. ISBN 0 415043 29 8.

Viscott, M.D., David. *Risking*. New York, New York 10020: Pocket Books, 1977. ISBN 0 671626 90 6.

Wakefield, Dan. *The Story of Your Life: Writing a Spiritual Autobiography*. Boston, Massachusetts 02108: Beacon Press, 1990. ISBN 0 807027 09 X.

Zuck, Colleen, (ed.) *Daily Word* Monthly Magazine. Unity Village, Missouri 64065: Unity.

A FINDHORN FOUNDATION READING LIST

Caddy, Eileen, and McVicar, Roy (ed.). *The Dawn of Change: Selections From Daily Guidance on Human Problems*. Forres, Scotland IV36 0TZ: Findhorn Press, 1979. ISBN 0 905249 39 9.

Caddy, Eileen, and Hollingshead, Liza. *Flight into Freedom: The Autobiography of the Co-Founder of the Findhorn Community*. Shaftesbury, England: Element Books, 1988. ISBN 1 852300 21 3.

Caddy, Eileen, and McVicar, Roy (ed.). *Footprints on the Path*. Forres IV36 0TZ, Scotland: Findhorn Press, new edition 1992. ISBN 0 905249 80 1.

Caddy, Eileen, and McVicar, Roy (ed.). *Foundations of a Spiritual Community*. Forres IV36 0TZ, Scotland: Findhorn Press, new edition 1991. ISBN 0 905249 78 X.

Caddy, Eileen, and McVicar, Roy (ed.). *God Spoke to Me*. Forres IV36 0TZ, Scotland: Findhorn Press, new edition 1992. ISBN 0 90 5249 81 X.

Caddy, Eileen, and McVicar, Roy (ed.). *The Living Word*. Forres IV36 0TZ, Scotland: Findhorn Press, 1977. ISBN 0 905249 69 0.

Caddy, Eileen, and Platts, David Earl, Ph.D. (ed.). *Opening Doors Within*. Forres IV36 0TZ, Scotland: Findhorn Press, 1987. ISBN 0 905249 66 6.

Findhorn Community and Maynard, Edwin (ed.). *Faces of Findhorn*. Forres IV36 0TZ, Scotland: Findhorn Press, 1980. ISBN 0 905249 48 8. (Now out of print)

Findhorn Community. *The Findhorn Garden: Pioneering a New Vision of Humanity and Nature in Cooperation*. Forres, Scotland IV36 0TZ: Findhorn Press, 1988. ISBN 0 905249 70 4. (US edition published by HarperCollins.)

Findhorn Community. *One Earth* quarterly magazine. Forres IV36 0TZ, Scotland.

Hawken, Paul. *The Magic of Findhorn*. London, England: Fontana, 1976. ISBN 0 006341 78 0. (US edition published by Harper & Row.)

Riddell, Carol. *The Findhorn Community: Creating a Human Identity for the 21st Century*. Forres IV36 0TZ, Scotland: Findhorn Press, 1991. ISBN 0 905249 77 1.

A PSYCHOSYNTHESIS READING LIST

Assagioli, M.D., Roberto. *The Act of Will: A Guide to Self-Actualization and Self-Realization.* Wellingborough NN8 2RQ, England: Crucible, 1990. ISBN 1 852740 82 5.

Assagioli, M.D., Roberto. *Psychosynthesis: A Manual of Principles and Techniques.* Wellingborough NN8 2RQ, England: Crucible, 1990. ISBN 1 852740 72 8.

Assagioli, M.D., Roberto. *Transpersonal Development: The Dimension Beyond Psychosynthesis.* London W6 8JB, England: Crucible, 1991. ISBN 1 852740 62 0.

Brown, Molly Young. *The Unfolding Self: Psychosynthesis and Counselling.* Los Angeles, California 94901: Psychosynthesis Press, 1983. ISBN 0 961144 40 8.

Ferrucci, Piero. *Inevitable Grace. Breakthroughs in the Lives of Great Men and Women: Guides to Your Self-Realization.* Wellingborough NN8 2RQ, England: Crucible, 1990. ISBN 1 852740 64 7.

Ferrucci, Piero. *What We May Be: The Vision and Techniques of Psychosynthesis.* Wellingborough NN8 2RQ, England: Crucible, 1989. ISBN 1 852740 53 1.

Fugitt, Eva D. *"He Hit Me Back First!" Creative Visualization Activities for Parenting and Teaching. Self-Esteem Through Self-Discipline.* Rolling Hills Estates, California 90274: Jalmar Press, 1983. ISBN 0 915190 36 2.

Hardy, Jean. *A Psychology With a Soul: Psychosynthesis in Evolutionary Context.* London W8 5TZ, England: Arkana, 1987. ISBN 0 140192 18 2.

Parfitt, Will. *The Elements of Psychosynthesis.* Shaftesbury, England: Element Books, 1990. ISBN 1 852301 56 2.

Rowan, John. *Subpersonalities: The People Inside Us.* London EC4P 4EE, England: Routledge, 1990. ISBN 0 415043 29 8.

Whitmore, Diana. *The Joy of Learning: A Guide to Psychosynthesis in Education.* Wellingborough NN8 2RQ, England: Crucible, 1990. ISBN 1 852740 18 17.

Whitmore, Diana. *Psychosynthesis Counselling in Action.* London EC2A 4PU, England: Sage Publications, 1991. ISBN 0 803982 79 8.

NOTE. To obtain the international *Psychosynthesis Directory* which lists professional centres, group trainers and individual counsellors and psychotherapists around the world, send US $8.00 to:

> Psychosynthesis Distribution
> 2561 Tioga Way
> San Jose
> California 95124, USA

Or:

> Sacramento Psychosynthesis Center
> PO Box 161572
> Sacramento
> California 95816, USA